CH00690215

# Jack

# Jack

## *The Sailor with the Navy Blue Eyes*

JOHN W. DAVIES

The Pentland Press
Edinburgh–Cambridge–Durham–USA

© J. W. Davies, 1995

First published in 1995
by The Pentland Press Ltd
1 Hutton Close
South Church
Bishop Auckland
Durham

All rights reserved.
Unauthorised duplication
contravenes existing laws.

British Library
Cataloguing in Publication Data

A catalogue record for this book
is available from the British Library

ISBN 1–85821-254-5

Typeset by Carnegie Publishing Ltd., 18 Maynard St., Preston
Printed and bound by Antony Rowe Ltd., Chippenham

I would like to dedicate this book to all my friends, past and present, of which I am pleased to have many. Each one will know exactly how much I appreciated them, and nobody will be forgotten.

To Biel, of the
Plough, Harrow
Catford,
the pub that helped make this
book possible.
Best Wishes
from
Jack        16.7.97

# *Jack*

This is not meant to be an autobiography; it is merely the true story of events that occurred during the first four years of the Second World War.

They happened to an ordinary young man with no idea of what the future would hold for him. He had no desire for heroics, the Royal Navy simply became a 'way of life', but it is hoped that in some small way he managed to contribute to the war effort.

If a fondness for alcohol is apparent, no excuses are made; he was no worse than many, and no better than most. Someone once said that 'Life is for living'. In Coastal Forces this was very relevant, and everybody did their best to enjoy life to the full, 'one day at a time'.

Someone suggested that this story be called 'The Life and Loves of a Sailor', but as no two men are identical in either themselves or their way of living, such a title would not be considered appropriate. It is realised that in reality we all fought for our country in our own different ways.

# Contents

# Preface

MANY BOOKS have been written about the 'little ships' of His Majesty's Coastal Forces, but each one is different, as seen by its author, who, almost without exception, would have served in this elite force as an officer.

Although serving aboard the same boat, an officer views things in an entirely different light to that of a rating, so their stories are told differently. They also have access to confidential signals, detail and information denied to men of the lower deck. This meant that in many instances ratings were left to guess or imagine what went on, so in this book stories, although true, lack a certain amount of detail.

War is not being condoned when I emphasise that it is not only to do with killing an enemy. It is also to do with learning to live with one's fellow beings, and with making new and lasting friendships. It is to do with having a different way of life forced upon you, and having to make the best of it.

In Coastal Forces there existed a certain camaraderie between the officers and men, based upon the mutual respect that can only be gained by sharing the same dangers, and in countless instances by forfeiting their lives.

# Foreword

## by T.W. Gould, VC, RN (Ret.)

I am extremely honoured to be asked to write a foreword to this book even though I wasn't privileged to have served with the author, as we were each in the branch of the Royal Navy to which we were respectively suited and qualified.

I have often said of the Motor Torpedo Boats and their crews, that they compared very favourably with the 'Wooden Ships and Iron Men' of Nelson's day and, jokingly, have described them as 'Cardboard Cartons packed with the Navy's Toughest'.

We met a short time after the cessation of hostilities, as members of the Royal Naval Association in Bromley, Kent, and have remained friends ever since. Although we have never discussed our personal wartime experiences, I was very much aware of the hazardous duties these small frail craft had to contend with, and believed that the crews should have collected more decorations and awards than they did.

This book will read well, and I trust be well read!

Tommy Gould

# CHAPTER I

# *The Beginning*

ANOTHER Sunday morning, just like any other at that time of
the year. The open air swimming pool's season was nearing
its end. The usual regular swimmers were there and, as the weather
was quite good, there were a number of casual visitors too, making
a total of around thirty people using the pool at Bellingham,
south-east London, on the morning of September 3rd 1939.

Everything was normal, nobody acted as though this day was
going to be different to any other. There may have been a few of
the swimmers who knew that their country had given an ultimatum to Nazi Germany to get out of Poland; probably even fewer
realised that the ultimatum was due to expire that morning. We
were all young, in our 'teens', enjoying life to the full, possibly
selfishly, as is often the case with youth, but devoid of hatred
towards anyone right then.

The country had already experienced an emergency, a war
scare, months earlier. In fact, along with some other lads I had
reported to the Territorial Army Drill Hall at Grove Park, south-
east London, and had tried to join the Army. Fortunately, for me
in particular, the friendly officer in charge of the Drill Hall could
see that we were all under age, so he sent us packing, with the
advice that if hostilities were to break out, we would get the
chance to join if old enough then.

Looking back, it would have been a terrible mistake. I have
never been soldier material, despite the love of rifle drill etc. that
was to develop later in my life. We were simply headstrong

youngsters, feeling somewhat elated and patriotic, and without thinking of possible consequences we might easily have made fools of ourselves.

Those lads that were with me then, however, were not my friends of the swimming pool; these were lads that had grown up with me, sons of my immediate neighbours, all of a similar age. We had known each other since our first days at school, the same school that was to be featured, sadly, later on during the war. Not one, when the war did break out, considered joining the Navy, most of them waited to be conscripted into the Army instead. That would never have suited me.

A friendship had developed between several of the young men who met at the pool every week, in all weathers, every Saturday and Sunday morning. Sometimes they remained there the whole day, until the pool closed. Their ages were between sixteen and seventeen, and their only thoughts for the future centred upon their family life, their weekly wage packet, and to meet there at the pool. In fact they were, at that time, only very casually interested in the company of girls. Perhaps I was the exception, but I hid it from my friends, mainly I suppose because I was unable to make contact with the one girl that mattered to me.

The usual good-natured horseplay was going on in and around the swimming pool when suddenly the unusual sound of air-raid sirens filled the air. The time was eleven o'clock, and it was Sunday September 3rd 1939. Realisation struck home to us all; we remembered, and then knew that war had actually broken out, it had officially been declared. Our country, Great Britain, was now at war with Nazi Germany. Even then the real seriousness and all it implied had yet to penetrate our minds. We never thought of it as being funny, we were grown up enough for that, but we were experiencing something entirely new to us, and we really did not know what might happen.

The pool attendants called everybody out of the water. They

were not too sure of what was happening themselves, but in a funny way they considered it to be safer if we were out of the pool. Later a message was received from a local Council Officer, instructing them to close the swimming pool and give out the instruction that it would remain closed indefinitely, for the duration of the war at least. We were then told to get dressed and to leave the premises immediately.

Everybody obeyed the instructions, except me. I decided that I must have one last swim, and be the very last person to do so, so in I dived, and leisurely swam the length of the pool before getting out, despite angry shouts from the attendants. Frankly, I could not see that I was doing any harm, it would not alter anything, and that was to be the very last time that I would ever swim in that pool.

We had all arrived upon bicycles, just as we normally did, so before leaving for our homes, arrangements were made for us all to meet that evening, with the vague idea of keeping in touch with each other, if nothing else. Up to a point we did. Most of us were employed in the City of London, in offices or warehouses, but none of us knew what to expect next, or even if we still had jobs to go to, war was something new to us. We had all listened to stories told by uncles, aunts and others who had lived through the Great War of 1914–1918, but had never known that it was going to happen to us. Times and living conditions had altered so much since that war that we most certainly had no idea as to how this one would be going to affect us.

Two of the lads, Noel Sumner and Ernie Searle, eventually joined the Army along with several other local lads. Laurie Scotchbrook and I would join the Royal Navy, followed later by Len Appleby, although it would not be until after the war had ended that I was to know this, and thought it a pity that our paths never crossed while we were serving, for he was always a very likeable fellow. Those joining the Army did not have long to wait before they were called to the colours; some never even had to wait until they reached eighteen before going. But Laurie and I did wait, and continued to enjoy our friendship together, despite the dreaded Blitz on London that was soon to follow.

For several years before the outbreak of hostilities my feelings towards one girl in particular had been far from casual or platonic, but a spotty complexion and an inferiority complex prevented me from making any direct overtures. The inferiority complex was only obvious where making conversation with girls was concerned; although I had an elder sister, the gap between our ages was too great for me to benefit from the relationship. She had been a teenager when I was still not much more than a baby and I never saw much of her at all, until a few years before she married. That complex had no effect on my other ways, as my schoolmasters in later years were to find out. Now that war had begun I probably would not be able to see this girl again and in fact I was not to see her until 1945 when when war had ended in Europe.

Laurie however was different. He had every confidence in his ability to charm and any approaches to girls were made with every confidence and without hesitation, usually with considerable success. This usually meant that if someone interested me, and she had a friend, all I had to do was to point Laurie in the direction of the friend and a foursome was guaranteed. It was never left to Laurie to do the choosing, his preference was towards older women, with whom I always felt out of my depth. So on occasions when he did pair up with someone older I would leave him to it.

Despite the many air attacks that London endured during the Blitz, Laurie and I were out enjoying ourselves every night. We were reasonably good as dart players and never lacked competition. We also danced a great deal, frequenting a small dancing school situated above a garage in Lewisham. It was affectionately known as 'The Barn', and it was not much more than that, not a very large barn either. The dancing lessons were taught by an elderly couple, whom everybody simply called Ma and Pa, and they were an extremely nice pair. We never took instruction, but after lessons finished a general dance took place, and non-pupils were allowed to join in. For this privilege we were charged the princely sum of sixpence each, and although the dancing was to music from a gramophone, it was very good value.

It was here that I found myself attracted to someone very much indeed. Her name was Hilda. She was not very tall, was slim, dark and sultry looking in the nicest possible way, and she was very, very shy. Despite my feelings towards that someone else, I felt that something more than just a casual friendship could develop between Hilda and myself; but although at that time I did not know, it just was not to be.

The bombing helped to bring us together quite closely; she used to be terrified immediately the sirens sounded, as indeed many people were, so it was not unusual for me to feel very protective towards her, and she was grateful for my company upon those occasions. As she always came dancing with a friend, it was not difficult to make up a foursome as Laurie found the friend attractive. Hilda and I remained good friends until after I had joined the Navy, when we drifted apart. She may even have left London by then – many did because of the severity of the Blitz. Anyway, my feelings eventually cooled and faded away, not completely however, as she was a very attractive girl. At least I thought so. Looking back I realise that Fate never intended that anything would develop, yet strangely kept alive my interest in someone else.

Eventually July 20th 1940 arrived. It was my birthday and I was at last eighteen years old. Laurie would be eighteen upon the following day. Both of us looked older than our years, which was why publicans never doubted that we were old enough to purchase alcohol in their pubs. Laurie was now living with my mother and myself, his family having split because of the London Blitz. The

*Bellingham Open Air Baths, 1939.*

two of us had now become inseparable. The friendship that had begun at the swimming pool had become a lasting one, and one that I valued very much. Every member of my family liked Laurie, and any arrangements they made always included him.

The war was now well under way, and although we knew we would be called 'to the Colours' eventually, we were impatient to go. In any case we did not want to be conscripted into any old service. Our minds were made up; we intended to join the Royal Navy, and nothing else would do. We were influenced by the fact that my brother Alan was already serving in the Navy, aboard HMS *Warspite*, one of the greatest battleships afloat at that time.

It was at Laurie's suggestion that we walked to nearby Kidbrook, to the Yorkshire Grey public house, where they had recruiting offices for all the services.

On arrival we made straight for the Royal Navy section, where we were greeted by an ageing Chief Petty Officer, possibly, although he would never have admitted it, too old for sea-time.

The Chief listened with a smile to our request. We explained to him that we were more than just keen to do our bit. We wanted to join for twenty-two years, to finish with a pension, and to make the Royal Navy our career.

'Sorry, lads, we are not taking anyone for that length of time now,' the Chief replied.

'OK, then, we will join for twelve years,' we cried.

'No, lads, we are not taking anyone for twelve years either,' came the Chief's answer.

Still we were not put off. At our age we thought that we knew it all, such was the impetuousness of youth. 'We will join for seven and five years then,' we said.

Again came the rejection, but this time with a smile, and the Chief added that we could join for 'hostilities only', and if the war ended in England's favour, we could then sign on for longer if it was allowed, and – the Chief emphasised this bit – 'if we were still keen'. Of course we had no doubts in our minds as to how the war was going to end; it could only end in England's favour, we never doubted that for one moment. So we signed as fast as we could write our names.

We expected to be called to go within a few days, but nothing was further from the truth; obviously the Navy could manage without us at this stage of events. The wait to be called seemed endless and frustrating, but there was nothing that we could do that might speed things up, nothing but to wait for the great day to come.

It must be made clear that my mother was not pleased at all with what we had done. The only redeeming feature was that Laurie and I would be together. I think that she had the idea that by being together, I would be protected by him in some way. It turned out that nothing was going to be further from the truth.

The great day arrived: letters and travelling warrants for February 26th 1941. We had to report to the Naval Patrol Office at Paddington railway station. There we met eight other lads, who were also *en route* to HMS *Raleigh*, the new entry's training base at Torpoint, Cornwall. In Naval terms, it was classed as a ship, but in reality it was nothing more than a collection of Nissen huts, wooden shacks that served as dormitories, and large hangar-like sheds that were used for dining halls and lecture rooms, and rifle drill and marching if the weather was very bad.

Our journey from Paddington seemed to go on for ever, partly because, as we were about to leave London, an air attack was just beginning. The enemy aircraft were still to the east of London, so our train was allowed to leave the station with all the speed it could muster. Once we were well away from London it slowed down almost to a crawl, perhaps because if moving slowly there was a possibility that it would not be noticed by enemy aircraft. From then on it was 'slow, slow, stop, slow'. We could have walked to Plymouth more quickly.

It was my first long train journey, previously I had only caught trains at Catford to go to the City of London, some ten or eleven miles only. I never knew if Laurie had made long journeys by train before, or if the other eight lads had.

Eventually we arrived at Plymouth, where a lorry was waiting to transport us to Torpoint, our new home for the next three months. We learnt that the driver had been waiting at the station for several hours. He was not at all concerned, being used to trains from London being late, and it gave him the opportunity to have a few drinks and enjoy the absence of red tape and discipline for a while.

Our actual time of arrival at HMS *Raleigh* was 2300 hrs Naval time, when we had our first taste of Naval cooking. It was – unforgettable, it really was. The meal waiting for us consisted of cold cod, cold greasy chips and luke-warm greasy cocoa. Not one bit like home cooking, and the cold atmosphere of the huge dining hall did nothing to cheer us.

Life at the training ship was far from exciting. We learnt to march correctly and with pride; we learnt seamanship, to row a whaler, which to us was simply a big rowing-boat, and to fire a rifle. The Chief Petty Officer who had been put in charge of us had retired from the Service prior to war breaking out, but had been recalled. It was probably the best thing that could have happened to him, as he had lost his entire family during the Blitz upon Plymouth.

When the weather was too wet for comfort (the instructor's comfort, not ours) we did our marching inside one of the drill sheds, but it was when we were marching around the parade ground (the holiest of holy places), that we did get some amusement. In our class there were four lads from Stornaway. They were, of course, first class seamen, but they just could not distinguish their left from their right. Consequently, when we were marching with them in our ranks, we used to finish up in some peculiar situations, chaotic can be the only word to describe what happened, and often it was beyond the instructor's comprehension to know exactly how these situations even began. I believe that eventually the Admiralty gave in and sent them back to their island homes, where they would contribute far more to the war effort by manning their fishing boats than they ever could have done wearing the uniform of the Royal Navy.

Another episode could have been disastrous for our entire class, and it was sheer luck that it was not. Our class was detailed to fire watch in Plymouth. Some nights we were lucky and nothing fell near us; on those occasions we used to slip out into the nearest pub for a few drinks. However, on one particular night we were expected to fire-watch and guard against theft, a building that contained the belongings of men who had died or who were lost at sea. This building was completely detached and stood alone in an area just north of Union Street. It consisted of two stories above the ground floor, and was built entirely of wood.

Half of our class would be on duty from 2000 hrs until midnight, and the other half, including Laurie and myself, were to take over until 0400 hrs. After that we were expected to tidy up, make ourselves presentable, and be ready to be transported back to *Raleigh*. All very simple, so it seemed, except that our Chief gave us restricted leave, which merely meant that we were not to go beyond certain boundaries that he laid down.

The Chief would be going home. He appointed one of us to be in charge, not that anyone took any notice of him, but it helped to ease the Chief's conscience. Unfortunately we all drank too much and although we returned to the building in good time, we all then went to sleep. The lads who were on duty came off as they were scheduled to, and also went to sleep without waking us, leaving nobody guarding the building, and all the time one of the worst air attacks on Plymouth was taking place.

When we woke in the morning, the air-raid had finished, but all the surrounding buildings had been flattened by bombs. Our timber shack was untouched, although many other buildings nearby were still burning. We had slept through one of Plymouth's worst ever air-raids, in what was potentially the most dangerous building in the city. Not only was that lucky for us, but we were also lucky that nobody else knew what had happened.

After the Chief had given us our instructions he had gone home having complete faith in us. He never knew or even dreamt that we might let him down. In fact, not knowing was perhaps fortunate for him as well as us. When he returned in the morning, we reported that all was well, we had no casualties, and that there was no damage to the building or its contents. We were being quite truthful, and by keeping quiet we probably saved him from having a heart attack, or at least an abnormal increase in his blood pressure.

The daily drills and lessons went on as usual. They were never halted during air attacks; the training ship had its own anti-aircraft guns and defences should they become necessary, and they did open fire on numerous occasions. Mostly the attacks were upon the city itself, but on one occasion a bomb did hit the Petty Officers' mess in HMS *Drake*, the Navy's main barracks for its Western Command, and approximately three miles from *Raleigh* as the crow flies.

As in all three services, and probably the Fire Brigade and Police as well, the older and more experienced men were never slow in giving advice to new entries, 'rookies' as the Army called them. One piece of advice was always: 'never volunteer for anything', but at the same time, the 'Powers that be' always drummed into us that 'one volunteer is worth ten pressed men', and when they spoke we never really had much choice at all.

When my brother Alan and I had been together last, before Laurie and I donned uniforms, he advised me to seize the chance if it came along to train as an anti-aircraft gunner. He was aboard HMS *Warspite* when it took part in the Battle of Narvik. Alan's reasoning was that in any action against the enemy, an anti-aircraft gunner was in the best position to see what was going on. It did not necessarily mean that you stood any better chance of survival, in fact it would be less if enemy aircraft came within machine-gunning distance, but he was adamant about this, and at that time I accepted what he told me as being gospel. So with this firmly planted in my mind, I kept a watchful eye upon the Training notice board for information that might offer such an opportunity.

One fine day it appeared, a notice asking for volunteers to take a course to be trained as anti-aircraft gunners (LC), in short AA3(LC). What the LC stood for, nobody knew at this stage; our instructors definitely did not, and they said that the Gunnery officer was equally ignorant. It was many months before I learnt that they stood for 'light craft'. I was not worried, the AA3 was enough for me, so, full of enthusiasm, I reported to the Regulating Office and volunteered for the course.

Laurie, however, was not of the same mind; he was going to volunteer for the Fleet Air Arm, so it was now obvious that we were going to part company. Experience in later years proved that the chances of friends staying together throughout their service career were not only slim, but damn near impossible. Laurie did not get his wish though, I don't know why, and he went into what was usually known as 'General Service', a Naval expression describing that part of the Navy that consisted of the larger ships, such as destroyers, frigates and battleships. Laurie would have fitted in well whatever ship he was aboard; he was always well liked by everyone, and would have been a popular and efficient seaman.

It was when I joined HMS *Excellent*, situated on what was known as 'Whale Island' and reckoned to be 'the Gunnery School of the World' by all who had proudly trained there, that I learnt what those letters LC stood for, and that they covered all small craft: motor launches, motor gunboats, torpedo boats, harbour defence launches, and so on. It also emphasised that this course was not to be mistaken for the ordinary course undertaken by gunners who would serve aboard General Service ships, whose course was much longer than the three months taken to train anti-aircraft gunners for the 'light craft'. The efficiency of the qualified gunners in both instances was set to the same high standard, but the shorter course enabled the school to produce qualified men much more quickly. As events later would show, they were needed quickly, to fill the places left by those who were killed in action. Very soon the men serving in Light Craft, later to be officially known as Coastal Forces, would be engaged in actions against the enemy almost every day and night of the year.

After three months of concentrated training at HMS *Raleigh*, we were now as ready as we would ever be to take our places as part of what was still the greatest Navy the world had ever known.

Some would be joining ships immediately, others like myself would go to places like Whale Island for further training, and then to ships.

So it was then that Laurie and I parted. We never saw each other again until after the war had finished. It was 1946 when we met in Catford; I was going off leave, and he was just beginning his. He had not changed one little bit, but by then I had married, so although we did keep in touch a little the close friendship that we had enjoyed in the past was never resumed. He joined the Fire Brigade, where he went from strength to strength, eventually becoming one of the Brigade's most respected Fire Chiefs, in charge of one of London's most modern stations at Lewisham, south-east London.

## CHAPTER 2

# Not such an ordinary seaman

I T WAS now obvious to everybody that the situation was very serious, the war was not going to end for quite a while, but although we knew that we had our backs to the wall, only the most pessimistic thought of possible defeat, and they were always quickly told to shut up. To most people, both in the services and in 'civvy street', it was confidently thought that the war was going to end in victory for us, and meanwhile all that was happening was that we were undergoing a change in our individual way of life. This was true enough, so much so that most servicemen and women began to forget what life was like before joining up.

Because of the seriousness of the situation, at the end of our training at HMS *Raleigh* we were not granted leave to go home as had been usual, I was sent straight to the Gunnery school, at Whale Island, Portsmouth. At one time or another, men from almost every Navy in the world had trained here, and many foreign naval gunnery schools were modelled upon HMS *Excellent*.

The standard of discipline here was notorious and, mixed with a great deal of 'red tape', made life practically unbearable for many. You knew however that at the end of a course here, you were in peak condition physically, and if you had passed your course then you really felt good, and knew it.

Just prior to my joining, a young lad died from heart failure, after collapsing while drilling under punishment. It was said that his father was a Member of Parliament, and because of his position he was able to get the punishment routine modified, to avoid some other unfortunate youngster suffering the same fate. The actual modification was that lads, carrying rifle and pack, no longer had to run up and down the steep grass bank that formed one side of the parade ground. It was bad enough just to run around the ground on the level (the four sides of the parade ground measured exactly one mile), but to run up and down, zig-zag fashion, along this bank was nothing short of torture.

Whale Island had its own zoo. When ships returned from visiting countries abroad, they often brought with them various animals, usually gifts from the country of their visit. Sometimes of course the animals would be pets, for example HMS *Tiger* would bring back its namesake, as also HMS *Ocelot, Seal,* and so on. They were all housed here on the Island, lions, tigers, deer, fowl and reptiles, but the dangerous species were taken away at the outbreak of war, for very obvious reasons.

The length of the course was twelve weeks, and it was at the height of the Portsmouth Blitz, so I was now going to experience my third major air attack, three of the worst inflicted upon this country. First it was London, where we were getting used to the screaming noise of bombs and shrapnel falling from the sky above; then it was Plymouth, which was not quite so bad, but bad enough; and now Portsmouth. They say that bad luck goes in threes, how would we fare this time? Maybe it would be 'third time lucky'; time only would tell.

This time I was not involved in anything as spectacular as the earlier incident, which was just as well, because I would not have been so lucky a second time and the mind boggles at the thought of what would have happened if I had been brought before the officer commanding HMS *Excellent* on a charge so serious.

The duties when not at lessons were mostly humdrum, even boring, but you dared not show it. Night sentry in the officers' quarters was one boring duty, its only consolation being that it was inside and under cover. You sat at a small desk with a notebook, and were expected to record everything that happened during the four hours spent on duty there; when on duty between the hours of midnight and four in the morning, it could appear very spooky. The combined snores of the sleeping officers did not help time to pass easily. As their cabins were all heated, the warmth penetrated to the corridor; this made inexperienced men straight from civvy street, as I was, drowsy, and it was hard to keep awake.

A poisoned foot interupted my course; what caused it was never discovered, but it was bad enough to get me excused from doubling around the school until the ships's doctor passed it as cured. Doubling meant that during working hours nobody walked anywhere, you literally ran. Officers on courses were not excused, and the instructors ran with them. Yes, you were definitely fit when you left the Island. The condition of my foot meant that I was unable to attend classes for a few days, so I was taken out of the class I had been in and found other duties to perform. Immediately I was pronounced fit, I was enrolled into another class, and so started all over again. All this delayed the finish of my course for a further two weeks, but eventually I took my examinations and passed out as an AA3(LC), with pride I might add.

Most servicemen appear to dislike parade ground drilling, and I can understand, but I actually enjoyed it; it installed in me a feeling of pride and patriotism, a feeling that I belonged.

During our course at Whale Island we were denied long leave, possibly because it was felt that leave spent at home would interfere with our studies. We were, however, allowed short weekend leave, usually from 1200 hrs on Saturdays to midnight on Sunday. There were restrictions imposed: we were not allowed outside the boundaries of Portsmouth; this also applied to day or all-night leave.

While I was there, I made friends with two other seamen who came from Downham, a London County Council housing estate adjacent to Catford. They were taking part in a different gunnery course to me but we met quite accidentally one evening in the junior ratings' bar, so it was quite natural for us to be together quite often.

One evening in the bar, we discussed the possibility of making a short visit to our homes. We knew that there was no chance of travelling by rail, anyway we could not afford the cost, even if we managed to elude the Naval Patrols. London-bound trains did not stop at any of the smaller stations between Portsmouth and London so there was only one alternative, we would have to hitch-hike.

We decided on the following Sunday to make the trip home. We would have to attend the church parade, and make certain there was nothing to delay us, as time was all important.

The names of my two new friends were George Burtonshaw and Ivor James. Both were able seamen, a little older than I was, and therefore that much wiser in ways to cook up schemes.

Sunday arrived, we duly attended church and the parade that followed. Immediately it was all over it was one mad dash to our messes to collect any small items that we wanted to take home with us. Then we had to muster near the main gate, where we were inspected and briefly lectured as to how we were expected to behave while on leave. We were also warned that we were confined to the boundaries of Portsmouth.

We caught a bus to the northern limits of Portsmouth and began to walk toward London. Every time a service vehicle came into sight we had to hide. It never occurred to us that all vehicles were equally suspect, that any one could contain officers who would at once know what we were up to.

After walking for several miles, far enough to make us feel a little despondent, several cars had passed us without stopping, but the next one did. We were in luck, more than we ever imagined: the driver was going to his home at Bermondsey, south-east London, just a few miles further than Catford, and he was actually going through Catford, so he would be able to drop us off. George and Ivor would be dropped off by the Green Man public house, within walking distance of their homes, and he would leave me near the Town Hall in Catford, also within walking distance of my home. That was not the end of our luck. Bill, the driver, was also returning to Portsmouth that same night, so it was arranged that if we were all together at one point, he would pick us up and take us back to barracks. The time arranged was to be 2300 hrs, which was fine by us.

When our good samaritan dropped me off at Catford, I only just missed catching a bus that would have taken me the last half-mile home.

Not wasting any time, I began the final walk home, but lighter in heart than I had been when starting off at Portsmouth. In my mind I was imagining the expression of surprise that would appear upon my mother's face when she opened the door to me. I would have to knock at the door as I had given her my doorkey when I left home to go to HMS *Raleigh*. It was going to be only for a few hours that I would be home, but it was going to be worth it, as it was bound to please her.

Many thoughts passed through my mind as I walked, then, as I drew near to the second alley in Sangley Road, my pace faltered and slowed right down as I drew level with it. I glanced wistfully along the alley, hoping that someone might just by chance be walking towards me, someone who was so very special to me. It was not to be, the alley was empty, there was nobody in sight, so quickening my pace again I strode home.

The pleasure showing on my mother's face was a sight to behold, marred only when she was told how we had managed to get from Portsmouth to Catford, and how short the visit was going to be. Despite her meagre ration allowance, and the tightness of her finances, when the time came to leave, she had prepared sandwiches and cakes for me to take back. I said a sad farewell and left for the meeting place with George and Ivor.

My two companions were already waiting at Catford. For some unknown reason Bill had insisted that he picked us all up at Catford. This was fine by me, but it did make the visit shorter for the other two.

We never realised when the time for the return journey was arranged, that it coincided with the closing time at Bermondsey pubs, allowing just enough time for Bill to say his goodbyes and make the journey to Catford. 2300 hrs came, no sign of our good samaritan; 2330 hrs came and still no sign. We were then beginning to get a little panicky, so we began to discuss possible ways and means of making our own way to Portsmouth, not very enthusiastically it must be admitted, and the thought that we might not get back at the allotted time made our future look very bleak.

Then at 2345 hrs, Bill arrived, very apologetic, but also well under the influence of drink. Into his car we climbed, and so began one of the most hair-raising drives by car that I was ever to experience.

Bill's speech was somewhat slurred, at times we found it difficult to understand him. He thought we were 'taking the mickey' out of him; we were not, and would not have dared, our only thoughts were to get back to Whale Island in time, and we knew that in the condition that Bill was, it was going to be a gamble. There was also the fact that while we were waiting at Catford an air raid had begun. It was still in action and we had to cover many miles before we were out of the danger area.

Bill had been visiting his family and friends. Because of his work, it was necessary for him to work at Portsmouth, leaving his family at home in Bermondsey. At least, being a civilian, he could go home every weekend to see them. In true Cockney fashion Bill and his family had had a good typical celebration. He assured us that he nearly did not meet us as apparently everyone had wanted him to stay there and not to return, and Bill, like many, could not say 'No' to a drink. It may have been the plight we would have been in if he let us down, or it may have been something else, but he did insist upon going back, fortunately, and so he eventually met us. We would have been in serious trouble otherwise.

As we drove away from London and its air raid, Bill's driving began to get more erratic. After driving through Croydon, Dorking and Guildford the skies began to get quieter, but Bill did not; his speech was well slurred now, and he literally covered both sides of the road as he drove. He blamed this on the fact that there were no street lights anywhere because of the blackout conditions existing, but there would not have been any lights outside towns and cities anyway. No, our Bill just could not see straight for other reasons.

Near to the town of Haslemere we ran into thick fog. Bill was not at all concerned, and by now had broken into song, not very musically it must be said, but at least he was happy, and if he was happy then we stood a good chance of getting back safely to Portsmouth, and in time.

Our worst moments were when Bill negotiated the road around the area known as the Devil's Punchbowl, when our nerves, already taut, almost gave out, but singing lustily all the time, he did manage to get us back to Whale Island. Not only in time for breakfast, but we also managed to get a couple of hours sleep.

The most important thing to be done that evening was to write a letter home, to reassure my mother that we had arrived back safely, for I knew that she would not stop worrying until she knew.

When George, Ivor and myself met that evening after classes, we discussed our little adventure in detail, but resolved never to chance anything like that again. For us, hitch-hiking was definitely out, the risk of getting caught was too great, it was to be by train only in future. In fact, the three of us were not going to make a trip home together again. George and Ivor completed their course before I did mine, so they were then drafted to ships. During the

1950s I met Ivor again, but not George, but I believe that, living quite near to each other, Ivor and George did meet again.

The 'days of days' arrived for me, the course had ended and I was now an anti-aircraft gunner, an AA3 (LC), and as proud as the proverbial peacock. I could not sew my badges on quickly enough. A red badge for my everyday suit, a blue on a white background for my overalls, and a gold wire badge for my best suit, known by all as 'the tiddly suit' or 'No. 1's'.

Now I wanted some leave to be able to show off my newly acquired glory, but it was not to be. The very next day, the ten of us that qualified were told to report to the drafting office, where we received instructions to pack our kitbags and hammocks the following morning, when we would be transported somewhere else. We were not told where, or if it was to a ship or a craft of any sort. We duly reported outside the drafting office, where a petty officer took charge of us.

We climbed aboard a lorry, and said farewell to Whale Island. We were then taken to the railway station; there we collected sandwiches and boarded the next outgoing train for London.

It had been hard and tough going for us youngsters while at the Island. We were still wet behind the ears when we arrived there, but they knocked some sense into us, and we now felt like trained warriors about to enter the fray. While at the Island we were not allowed to walk anywhere between sunrise and sunset, everything was done at the double; we were also critically inspected by everyone we met, with no exceptions. Voices would roar at you from the most unexpected places, places which you would have sworn on your life were empty before the voice sounded.

On the journey to London I carefully investigated the possibility of slipping off home, but we were met at Waterloo station by a Naval Patrol, who quickly took us across the city to Liverpool Street station, where we were ushered aboard another train. Still we did not know our destination. At Colchester we changed trains again; a very ancient locomotive pulled a couple of carriages with us inside along a quiet local track to a place called Brightlingsea. I had never heard of it before, so frankly did not know what to expect.

It was a very small seaside town, with a small but useful harbour, which was now being used by Royal Navy craft. At this time it was too small to be an established base and had yet to be given a name.

It really was only a number of terraced houses that the Navy had taken over, and if there was more to it, then I missed it, because next morning, along with five other lads, I was put back upon a train heading for London. All I ever saw of Brightlingsea were the terraced houses, and the nearest pub, which we all made for during the one evening we were there.

An able seaman in our party was put in charge of us. All he really had to do was make sure that we kept together, a responsibility that he did not really want, but was stuck with until we reached our destination, which turned out to be HMS *Attack*, the former submarine depot that had been called HMS *Osprey*, and was now a Coastal Force base.

Living here was luxury compared with what we had already experienced. It was only going to be for three weeks, but although situated at Portland, it was conveniently near to Weymouth, where we always went for day or night leave.

It was an enjoyable stay, comfortable billets, and the food was good. To combat that old saying, that idle hands make mischief, those in charge would find us rather mundane and silly work to do during the daytime. My daily job was to cut the grass on slopes outside the officers' quarters, a very boring task that was only offset by chasing and sometimes capturing grass snakes, which were in abundance here.

The weather was kind to us, very hot and sunny. This did not help those of us who were grass cutting on the slopes as there was no shade nearby at all. Two of our party had to report sick with sunstroke, and only then was the cutting temporarily suspended.

There was one consolation with being at HMS *Attack*, weekend leave was granted to us, but the journey would have taken so long by train that it really was not worth it, and there was the added risk of trains being attacked by enemy aircraft. This made long journeys in the southern counties very dangerous, apart from increasing the length of time a journey would take. We learnt from other sailors on the base that it was not unusual for a train to take twelve hours just to travel from Weymouth to London, without an air attack.

Three weeks I was here at Portland, and just as I was beginning to feel at home, it happened. It seemed at the time such a great moment. I was to be drafted to a boat, His Majesty's Motor Launch 216, lying at anchor, mid-stream, at Burselden, a small village on the river Hamble, only a few miles inland from Southampton Water. The main road from Portsmouth to Southampton ran through the village. It boasted an Admiral as one of its residents, and contained several small boatyards, which was one reason to base Coastal Forces craft there. The journey from Portland by lorry took a mere two hours, which passed happily enough as there were several other ratings on draft there also.

# CHAPTER 3

# *Down to the sea in ships, well, boats anyway*

H IS Majesty's Motor Launch 216 would not have inspired fear
in the enemy as she lay at anchor. To be truthful, she did
not inspire me either, but at least she was afloat, and might actually
go to sea one day. In fact it must be said that 216 did spend a great
deal of time at sea, doing various duties, efficiently, and also
gallantly.

The launch was 112 feet in length, with an 18 feet beam. She
was Canadian built, had two Hall Scott engines and was reputed
to do 20 knots at speed. Personally I rather doubt this, 16 would
be more like it, although as I never sailed in her I cannot be an
authority on the subject. The weight of ship's stores, provisions,
guns and ammunition would not have been conducive to that sort
of speed.

Her armament at that time I was aboard was not impressive
either, consisting only of a three-pounder manual loading gun
mounted on the foc's'le – this gun was used as a saluting gun in
peacetime – and two sets of twin Lewis guns mounted on the
bridge, plus a quantity of depth charges for anti-submarine warfare.

One of the pair of Lewis guns would be mine, so I was informed
by the cox'n. The boat was so basic that heating and cooking were
by coal-fired ranges.

I was aboard 216 for about two weeks only, and during that
time she never even weighed anchor. I am now certain that I

probably would not have enjoyed serving aboard her for any length of time, especially as she hit a mine in the North Sea in 1944, and foundered. I am inclined to think that it was not intended for me to form a permanent part of the 216 crew, I think I was there simply to make the numbers up while she was at Burseldon, and so back to HMS *Attack* I went.

Thankfully this time it was only for four days, then another draft with eleven other lads to Littlehampton in Sussex, to commission a new motor gunboat just completed at William Osbourne Ltd., a peacetime yacht and motor boat builder now building 'little ships' for the Navy.

When we arrived at the yard, HMMGB 320 was not even afloat, but was still on the stocks. Not knowing much about boats and boatyards, I looked somewhat sceptically at her, and did not feel too happy that I would be working and sleeping aboard her where she was.

Our arrival at the yard was greeted by the cox'n, Petty Officer Peter (Sharkey) Ward, who proved to be an outstanding seaman, completely devoid of fear, but also very understanding towards those of us who lacked experience. The compassion that he showed towards us made him ten feet tall in our estimation, but it also obtained our loyalty to him, and a willingness to carry out his orders without contradiction. Petty Officer Ward never refused advice or help when it was needed, and there were many times when he took the blame for mistakes that we made; I am certain, however, that our officers knew this, and consequently he was never reprimanded for it.

Our boat was to be commanded by Lieutenant Peter Loasby RN; he was to be the Senior Officer in charge of the soon to be formed 12th Flotilla of motor gun boats, which would operate from Great Yarmouth on the east coast.

Peter Loasby, although only twenty-three years old, was already a Coastal Forces veteran, having commanded the 2nd flotilla of motor launches previously, operating from Dover. He had already experienced plenty of action, and was a very respected name amongst those who manned the little ships. His reputation was somewhat awesome to us. The fact that the rings upon his uniform sleeves were straight ones showing that he was a regular officer also helped to create the impression that he was going to be strict, but it always seemed to me that perhaps his bark was worse than his bite. Secretly I grew to like and respect him, and in later years when we were both civilians, we were to meet and become friends.

The other officer on board was then Sub-Lieutenant Bob Goodfellow RNVR. A tall quiet man who had grown up amongst boats, he was an excellent seaman and navigator, who did everything conscientiously, and loved boats and the sea. Bob perhaps was not as strict a disciplinarian as our Skipper would have wished, but he more than made up for that in many other ways. Efficiency was not impaired, and his attitude went a long way towards making 320 a very 'happy boat'. Our Captain never said much to us, but his eyes were everywhere; he missed nothing, and you could safely bet that if something was wrong, he would know. When this happened it was Bob who received the rough end of our Captain's tongue, but he never took it out on us, and was quick to show his sympathy if deserved.

The 320 was something special. Of the latest design, these boats were destined to make their mark in the increasing fight against the enemy's E-boats. They were 110 feet in length, with a 17 feet beam; they had three Hall-Scott engines that were supposed to give us a speed of 26 knots maximum and an average speed of 23 knots. Once again, when stores etc. were on board such speeds were impossible, but we were able to make 18 knots comfortably.

The armament was good for the size of the boat. On the foc's'le we had a two-pounder manually operated pom-pom, on either side of the bridge, slightly aft of it, there were power operated twin .5 machinegun turrets, and aft we had a two-pounder Rolls-

Royce gun, plus a supply of depth charges. Midships, there was an ejector for hand grenades, called a Holman projector. The idea behind it was good, but in practice less so; often when fired the grenade would fly a few feet into the air and drop back on board, which was far from being popular. In fact, although a rating was detailed to fire it in action, ours was not in use very often.

In rank and responsibility our cox'n came next, followed by the Petty Officer motor mechanic, I do not remember the man who held this position when I first joined the boat, but it was not long before he was replaced by Ralph Puttock from Guildford in Surrey. Not only was Ralph a first class mechanic, he was also an expert photographer, eventually becoming the official Royal Navy photographer for the base at Great Yarmouth once his talent was recognised.

The rest of our crew were a motley throng. Ldg. Stoker Stan Hubbard, Stoker Jeff Goodey, and Stoker Len Downs made up the rest of the engine-room staff. Ord. Tel. Standley was our wireless operator and the remainder of the crew were seamen Taff Johnson, Monty Mortimer, Vic Copeland, Ernie Nunn and ordinary seamen Ross, Millington and myself, with two more whose names I am unable to recall. Later a lad by the name of Jarrett would join the crew when we became the first Coastal Forces craft to have radar installed: RDF as it was known then. In all, they were a fine bunch of men, and when I eventually parted company with them I did so with a heavy heart and a large lump in my throat.

When the final check by the boat builders had been made on the 320, it was handed over to Lieutenant Loasby, and preparations made to leave Littlehampton as soon as possible. We had some stores on board, a little fuel, enough to reach our next port of call, and some ammunition for our guns, not enough for a concentrated fight with enemy boats or aircraft, but enough to be able to put up some sort of defence at least.

We sailed then for Burseldon where we were going to carry
out various trials and to store ship.

During the journey we encountered rough seas; on occasions
we had to steer head-on into the oncoming waves, some of which
were thirty feet high. Although it could be described as a rather
unpleasant experience, it was also a very thrilling one for me. It
was, after all, my very first time at sea. I do not think that anyone
was really worried about the rough sea and waves, unless our
Skipper did a little; after all he had just taken possession of a brand
new motor-gunboat, and here he was, under way with at least half
of his crew inexperienced, I do not know if this was true, and it
is pure supposition on my part but Peter Loasby never appeared
to worry about much.

We arrived in Burseldon, and those of us who were allowed
ashore made ourselves acquainted with the local pubs, of course!
Before we were allowed to go ashore, we were warned by our
cox'n to be on our best behaviour as several Naval officers lived
in the vicinity, at least one being an Admiral.

On one occasion when out in the Solent completing a trial,
thick fog came down suddenly without warning, as if someone
had dropped a blanket over us. We could do nothing, we could
see nothing, we were literally helpless. We could only drift with
the tide, sounding the ship's bell every few minutes to warn other
shipping where we were. The Solent being a very busy shipping
lane even in wartime, we were in danger of being run down,
especially if destroyers were called out in an emergency; racing at
full speed they would be on top of us so quickly we would stand
no chance at all. As luck would have it, conditions were quiet and
there was no shipping in our vicinity. These conditions lasted for
about an hour or so, then as suddenly as it fell, the fog lifted and
we were able to return to our moorings at Burseldon.

It took a week to complete our trials, sailing up and down the
Hamble, out into the Solent. Usually we had Admiralty civilian

staff on board, who were experts in something or other. One evening however, we sailed into Ryde on the Isle of Wight, and moored alongside a destroyer, remaining there all night. I believe the Captain of the destroyer was a friend of our Skipper and they chose this opportunity to spend an evening together. It was fine for us too as we were able to go aboard the destroyer for the evening, play tombola (nowadays called bingo in civilian life), and generally enjoy ourselves mixing with the destroyer's crew. Although the main purpose of going aboard was to enjoy the visit, it was the first opportunity I had had to go aboard a 'General Service' ship. I was not impressed and much preferred being on board the 320.

Everything proved satisfactory during the trials, so we sailed into HM Dockyard, Portsmouth, where arrangements had been made for us to fill our tanks with fuel. To obtain the fuel we had to tie up alongside a large floating container, lying at anchor a mile or so out of the actual dockyard. This was a safety precaution, as if the dockyard was hit by enemy air attack, the explosion from 100% octane fuel would be terrific and the damage catastrophic. Situated where it was however meant that it could only be pumped into our tanks by hand, approximately 1800 gallons of it. It was not only going to take time, but it was also going to be hard work, consequently the work had to be shared by us all, stokers and seamen alike. When the fuelling was completed we returned to Burseldon for the night, no leave being granted, and the following morning we set our course eastwards, bound for Great Yarmouth, on the east coast, which was to become our home base, along with the rest of the 12th Motor Gunboat flotilla.

The trip to Great Yarmouth was quiet and really uneventful, which was a good thing so far as we youngsters were concerned, as it was going to take time to get used to each other, and in those conditions you did not have a lot of time to spare. It also gave us the opportunity to acquire our 'sea legs', which proved quite a

*Stoker Len Downs and myself.*

thrill at first. To walk around the deck of a motor gunboat
travelling at speed is quite something, as not only does the boat
roll, there is a tremendous thud as she hits oncoming waves head
on, combined with the loud throb of the engines and their vibration. It all gave you a feeling of pride and power, never to be
forgotten.

Fortunately the weather was kind to us, a little choppy maybe,
with a few 'white horses', the sailors' description of waves that
were large enough to create a white feathery effect when they rose
and fell. The older and experienced members of the crew delighted
in pointing these out to us novices, saying that they were the sign
of rough weather to come.

Because none of us were seasick on this journey, it lulled us into a false state of well-being, and we now began to consider ourselves to be real sailors, and to think that the dreaded tales we had heard about sea-sickness were all a fallacy, and nothing to worry about. How wrong we were, and it was not going to take long for the truth to hit us.

# CHAPTER 4

## *E-boat Alley, here we come*

OUR arrival at Great Yarmouth was quiet and unobtrusive; certainly there was no fanfare of trumpets. Immediately upon arrival our Captain had to report to the Base Commander, and make arrangements to discuss our future operations.

Three other boats belonging to our flotilla were already there, and cheerful greetings were exchanged between their crews and ourselves. Two more boats were expected to arrive soon, thus completing the flotilla.

Our base, our new home if you like, was named HMS *Midge*. Before the outbreak of war it had been where trawlers from the North Sea landed their catches and this was where the fish were sorted and graded, then put up for auction. The shore-base consisted of several large draughty sheds built along the north side of the river Yare and although it was now over two years since the last catch of fish had been landed there, the smell of fish was so ingrained in any woodwork that the place still stank.

Minesweeping trawlers were also based here, but not with us, their moorings being nearer to the harbour mouth. We were situated close to the town centre, for which we were very grateful when staggering back after an evening sampling the local brew.

One of the stokers became my closest friend or 'shipmate', the term usually used by sailors. We regularly went ashore together, and quickly established ourselves as regular visitors to local dance halls. On some occasions Jeff Goodey and Stan Hubbard would join us, and I found myself envying Jeff for his dancing ability, which of course helped him make friends easily with the girls.

There were two dance halls in the town; one, which was also a cinema, was called the Aquarium, and the other was at Goodes Hotel, where they preferred to call it their 'ballroom'. Both were on the seafront. The Aquarium is still there today, both as a cinema and a dance hall, although the dance hall is mostly used for bingo now. Goodes Hotel has been knocked down, unfortunately, but I was able to stay there as a paying guest during the 1960s before this happened.

The regular dance band at the Aquarium noticed that I was a frequent visitor. Sometimes I went there on my own if Len was on duty and not allowed ashore, and when they sighted me entering the hall they would play the first few bars of the song popular at that time, called 'The Sailor with the Navy Blue Eyes'. At first I found it embarrassing, but realised it was meant as harmless fun. After a few occasions I began to enjoy it, and on the rare occasions when they missed my entry, I would feel quite hurt. It also helped Len and me to become quite well known amongst those who used the hall often.

This friendly liaison with the band did, however, lead to one major embarrassment for me. On one particular evening, owing to fog, their drummer had not arrived, and they were reluctant to attempt to start without him. Because they now knew me very well by sight, the band leader decided to ask me to take the drummer's place, all his kit being there. I was very reluctant to do so. I was aware of my limitations in the field of music, despite being Welsh by descent, but they insisted that I could do it, so I tried. They quickly realised their mistake, and told me not actually to hit the drums, but just go through the motions, which I did. Then, fortunately for the band and the dancers, somebody entered the hall who really could play the drums and, having seen the predicament I was in, he offered to take my place. I was much

happier down among the dancers; after all, you cannot hold a girl
and wield a drumstick.

Great Yarmouth, being a fishing town and port, naturally and
quickly welcomed its adoption by the Navy for use as a base for
the trawlers and gunboats. The residents found places in their
hearts for the many young seamen, most of whom were really
only boys, and very new to the sea. The RAF personnel who
visited at weekends were also made welcome, but it was only
natural that the folk of Yarmouth, being mostly descended from
sea-faring stock, should lean more favourably towards the Navy
lads, which did incite some rivalry between the two services. Of
course the situation with the Waafs was different; here the only
rivalry was for the company of the girls by the sailors.

About this time, the Naval bases were beginning to be staffed
by Wrens, and HMS *Midge* was no exception. It is only a guess,
but I feel certain that these girls were either asked or told not to
mix with us ordinary sailors, and in the main they did not.
Consequently, there seemed to be a distinct lack of Wrens at the
local dances; this was noticed by the Waafs who did not mind
at all.

The saloon bars and lounges were used by officers on their
evenings out. Although the Royal Bath Hotel and the Grand were
their favourites, some did frequent the saloon bar at Goodes. When
their visit to Goodes coincided with a dance, they did take part,
and we would see the occasional Wren there too. Although the
management of Goodes preferred to call their dance-hall a 'ballroom', so far as sailors were concerned, it was simply a rose by
any other name, and most certainly the girls all smelt as sweet.
Dances at the hotel were by far more popular than those at the
Aquarium, possibly because the Aquarium was twice the size of
the other, thereby giving a slightly less friendly atmosphere.

Goodes Hotel had a distinct advantage over any other pub or
bar in the town. It had working for them Tessie Barwick. Tessie

ran the saloon bar adjacent to the ballroom. Tessie was never seen to be miserable, she had a laugh, a joke or a smile for all the lads, perhaps partly because her own son Jimmy had joined the Navy. She was of Irish stock and was an extremely capable and efficient barmaid, very well liked by everyone, always ready to lend a sympathetic ear to anyone with trouble, a veritable asset to the hotel. Tessie was as straight as they came, and often lent money to servicemen when they were broke; unfortunately some of it was never repaid. If there is a heaven, I am sure that Tess earned herself a place there. She was still working as a barmaid in the town in the 1960s, and looked unchanged in her appearance and her ability to run a sucessful bar.

When Jeff, Stan, Len and I managed to get ashore together on a dance night, because of Jeff's popularity as a dancer, we were quickly joined by a group of four girls, three were Waafs, the fourth a Wren; they were four very lively girls, single, and knew how to look after themselves.

The girls were all wonderful company, they all loved dancing, and were good at it. At first when they began to seek our company we thought that it would cramp our style, but very quickly this was forgotten when they proved to be such good company and equally good at dancing. Furthermore, they did not sponge upon us for their drinks, which was more than a blessing for me, as the lowest paid of our group. The three Waafs had been together for some time, and had proved themselves to be very entertaining by singing as a trio, their favourite song being 'Roll a silver dollar down along the ground', and their rendering of it was really very, very good. We could never persuade them to get up upon the stage and sing, no matter how hard we tried, but towards the end of the dance, in Tessie's saloon bar, they would suddenly burst into song, encouraging everyone to join in, which everyone did without much persuasion. They also had another 'party piece' that was very popular, and one that I remember very well to this day.

It was not a song this time, but verse, and the words were as
follows:

> The girl of my dreams,
> Has bobbed her hair,
> and dyed it a fiery red.
> She drinks and she smokes,
> and tells dirty jokes,
> and hasn't a brain in her head.
> She thinks alcohol makes the world go round,
> and drinks even more than I,
> But the girl of my dreams,
> is a cigarette fiend,
> And the sweetheart of some other guy.

Not exactly William Shakespeare, but it always raised a good
laugh.

One of the Waafs in particular attracted me. I knew that if I
were to get interested to a greater extent it would come to
nothing, as she was far more interested in Jeff than was good for
her; that too could only end in tears. However, my interest was
roused because she reminded me of someone special at home; she
was of average height, slim, darkish as a red English rose would
be, and with looks good enough to turn anyone's head. Sometimes
the reminder brought a touch of sadness, but mostly it pleased me.

The company of the girls was good for me, curing some of the
shyness I still had, but all the time something made me fight shy
of any serious attachment.

Life aboard the 320 had become more settled, a daily routine
when in harbour had been drawn up by the 1st Lieutenant and
the cox'n, and we were all justifiably proud of her appearance. I
had been allocated the portside .5 twin machine guns, the turret
was power operated, and I was at my happiest when seated in the
turret, almost completely alone with my thoughts.

We had now begun patrolling the North Sea at night, keeping

watch on the sea lanes for signs of either E-boats or U-boats. Every so often we would receive a signal informing us that E-boats had been detected in a certain area, so off we would dash in search of them. Too often it would be a wasted effort, but if we managed to frighten them away then it was a good job done, and many merchant ships had cause to thank us for doing this.

The E-boats were often very difficult to detect, owing to their habit of lying alongside buoys; this made them impossible for radar to detect, or even for us to see from a distance. When discovered they seldom stopped to fight; having superior speed to us they quickly managed to outdistance us. On some occasions we would be able to exchange a few shots, but although when we opened fire we were serious about it, I suspect that many times the Germans were teasing us, knowing that they had the advantage of speed.

During normal weather conditions, the boats in our flotilla operated in pairs. Most operations were at night; we would leave about dusk and return after dawn, depending upon circumstances.

Although there were six boats in the flotilla, it usually meant alternate night patrols, one pair out at sea patrolling, another pair resting in harbour, with either one or both of the remaining boats on stand by. Often neither would be available owing to engine trouble and sometimes three or more could be unseaworthy for some reason; when this happened it would mean extra patrols for the boat or boats available.

Apart from the patrols, there were exercises and various man-oeuvres to practise; we also had to keep practising with our guns and depth charges. If we sighted a floating mine, it usually meant that it had broken away from its mooring, and was a danger to shipping. If on exercise we could take our time and sink it ourselves, but if on patrol it was sometimes difficult. If we failed with our first few shots we would radio its whereabouts to Admiralty, and a minesweeper would be sent to deal with it.

One of the exercises meant that we would be out on our own, hunting a 'mystery submarine', which meant that we would be exploding a depth charge. We found the area where the submarine was reputed to be, supposedly located it and dropped the depth charge – bingo! We chalked up a hit but, better still, the explosion stunned or killed hundreds of fish, which were now floating on the surface ready for us to collect. The Skipper gave his permission, and except for Vic Copeland and myself in our gun turrets, it was all hands to the task of collecting the fish. Vic and I were not allowed to take part but we had to stay at our guns in case of a surprise attack from the enemy. One never knew, it could come from the air or the sea; we had to be prepared.

As we were in the luxurious fishing grounds of the North Sea, our catch was very good. Under the watchful eyes of the cox'n the lads sorted the fish as they brought them inboard. Fish that were only stunned and unharmed were thrown back into the sea, where they were expected to regain consciousness and swim away; any damaged fish were thrown away too, and although we were far from land, it was amazing how quickly seagulls came from nowhere after the fish.

Naturally we were going to have fresh fish on our menu for days to come. Some would be given to the other boats in our flotilla, and the remainder of the catch, the bulk actually, would be given to local hospitals.

This was the first of many depth charge practice runs. The hospitals were very grateful for the gift of the fish, so at varying intervals of time, charges were dropped, and a welcome addition to the hospitals' diet was established.

Our patrols were often boring and unexciting and there was always the danger that lack of action could make crews lethargic and careless, so our officers were always looking for ways to keep us active and on our toes. Lieutenant Loasby thought he had the answer. Our fishing spree gave him the idea: we would fish the same way as trawlers did. From somewhere our Skipper begged, borrowed or maybe someone even stole? some trawler's nets, which with the co-operation of another gunboat, we could drag behind us, in effect, sweeping.

So with another boat, out to sea we went, officially on patrol. Once we were far enough away from base, and our radio operator told us conditions were quiet, we dropped the nets into the sea and began to trawl.

We had been towing the nets for about half an hour, when we received information that E-boats were in our area. Without hesitation our Skipper gave instructions to the crew of our accompanying boat and ourselves immediately to cut loose the trawler nets, and we made all haste to where the E-boats had been reported.

As usual, nothing was encountered. If the enemy had been there, he was now long gone, so there was nothing we could do except cruise around to make certain. We were angry, we had lost our nets, and therefore caught no fish, but there had been no alternative, the loss of the nets counted for nothing against the possibility of foiling an attack by E-boats upon our convoys. We never learnt where our Captain obtained those nets. If the loss ever worried him, he certainly never let it show. What happened did stop any future use of nets being contemplated. It had broken the montony for us, which needed doing, but as our Skipper explained to us, we would have been at a disadvantage had the enemy managed to get close to us while we were trawling, and that was a possibility that could not be ignored.

The local hospitals did not miss out on fresh fish, as at least once a week depth charge practice was carried out by a Yarmouth based boat, whether it was one of our flotilla or one from another, including the mine-sweepers, some of which were based also at Lowestoft, and were equally enthusiastic about supplying the hospitals with fresh fish.

It was not long before we had our very first taste of action. We were out on patrol on our own as the other boat had developed engine trouble soon after leaving harbour, and rather than upset the schedule, our Skipper had decided to carry on alone. Although by this time the stretch of the North Sea from Dover to Grimsby was now known as 'E-boat Alley', because of the frequency of enemy attacks upon our convoys, we knew from past experiences that there was little hope of getting close enough to an enemy boat to enable us to engage it in combat. When these fights did occur, they often happened by chance. The E-boat crews did not go to sea looking for fights as we did, they wanted more valuable targets for their torpedos, our merchant ships. They were also well aware that we were more heavily armed then they were, so in a fight their chances of survival were much less than ours, but to offset this disadvantage their speed was greater, enabling them to evade action.

We had been at sea for almost three hours. It was a dark and cloudy night, the moon breaking through for short periods every now and then. The sea was choppy, but not really rough. So far it had been a trouble-free patrol again; we were quite happy with this, but were not lulled into any sense of false security.

Then unmistakably we heard the steady throb of aircraft engines approaching us. Our cox'n, Petty Officer 'Sharkey' Ward, was acknowledged to be the only man aboard with any experience of aircraft recognition, so it was left to him to decide whether or not any aircraft was friendly or not.

With conviction the cox'n stated that the approaching plane sounded like a Dornier, possibly one that was based in the Netherlands, where the Luftwaffe had many such planes in operation against us. Immediately the sound of an aircraft had been heard, we had assumed action stations, this was always carried out as a precaution. So confident were we that it was an enemy plane, that instructions were given to all guns' crews to open fire immediately the plane came within range of our weapons. There was one restriction however, as is normal with all engagements: the plane would be challenged by Aldis lamp from our bridge. If it was an enemy there would not be any reply except possibly a hail of machine-gun fire, or even a bomb or two. I was tense with excitement. Nowadays they would describe my condition as 'the adrenalin was running high'. There was only one thought in my mind, I must not miss; it was my first chance to prove myself and I was determined not to 'blow it'.

The challenge by our signalman went ignored and by this time the plane was right above us, slightly perhaps to our port side, so that I had an excellent view of it. The sound of our klaxon horn told us to open fire, and we did. Shells from the two pounder on the foc'sle, manned by Taff Johnson and two others, hit the plane, and my machine guns raked it from nose to tail. Only then did the crew of the aircraft come to life, and a somewhat angry signal was radioed to us stating that the aircraft was British, and was returning to its base somewhere in East Anglia. Why they never responded to our challenge in the correct manner and at the correct time we were never told. Perhaps our officers knew, but if they did they never passed on the information to their crew.

When we returned to base next morning, we received a signal from Admiralty, via the Commander-in-Chief, Nore Command, praising us for our speed in opening fire, and the accuracy of our gunfire. Although this was meant to make us feel good, the fact that it was one of our own aircraft dispensed with any pleasure in being told.

It was anticipated that there might be trouble between Naval personel and the RAF men when they met in the local pubs and dancehalls, and there was; it lasted for some time, in fact, although the truth of the situation was made known to everybody. The RAF lads just would not accept it, or the fact that in our position we could not take the risk when our challenge was ignored; to have done so would have been courting sudden death.

Fortunately, although badly damaged, the aircraft, a Lockheed Hudson bomber, made it safely back to base, and none of its crew were badly injured. Only their pride suffered.

Shortly after this incident, the 320 became the first Coastal Forces craft to have radar installed, RDF as it was then known. We were instructed that if any questions were asked by anyone regarding the strange aerials fitted to the top of our mast, on no account were we to attempt to explain what they were there for. At first our telegraphist had the responsibility of operating the set, but it was realised that it was too much for one man, so Ordinary Seaman Jarrett joined, having qualified as an RDF operator. He was an extremely nice fellow, and fitted in very well with us all.

Once the various tests with the RDF had proved successful, we were instructed to leave Yarmouth for Weymouth. Why this was necessary I never knew, but I was still as keen as ever, so it never bothered me not to know every why and wherefore. I had a job to do, and I intended to do it as well as I could.

Since starting operation in the North Sea, I had learnt what it was like to be sea-sick, as before joining the Navy I had not even crossed the river Thames by means of the Woolwich Ferry. It did not come as a surprise for me. It really is the most dreadful and unpleasant experience that anyone can have; it is also true that when undergoing seasickness death seems very close, and at times even welcome.

On one patrol, I was particularly ill. I had been sick inside my gun turret, and over my clothing, and despite the wind and salt air, everything simply stank. I was very, very unhappy, wet, cold, and convinced that I did not have long to live. Then a voice spoke from nowhere. I had been so engrossed in my own misery that I had not seen our Skipper come down from the bridge and cross the deck to see me. Peter Loasby said to me, 'Don't worry, Davies, the first six months are the worst, after that you will never be seasick again.' Despite the condition I was in, those words gave me no encouragement at all. The one thing that stuck out in my mind was the fact that Peter Loasby, Lieutenant RN, a regular Navy man, was sick every time we put to sea, after many years of experience; how on earth could I be expected to believe him?

But I accepted that he meant well, and it was good of him to bother about me to that extent. He was right, though, six months later I ceased to be sick when at sea, and never was again. That really made me feel good. I was now accepted as a real sailor by almost everyone, but it was as though I had passed a test, and could now be relied upon in all weathers.

CHAPTER 5

# There were changes ahead for us

ALTHOUGH bound for Weymouth, HMMGB 320 headed for Dover, where an overnight stay had been arranged, for reasons unbeknown to us, the crew. We did not moor alongside any other boats, but well away from everybody and everything normal; the walk into the main part of the harbour was long and miserable and as we walked we were exposed to all the elements, and soaked by the huge waves that seemed to come from nowhere.

Leave was granted to three-quarters of our crew. It was until midnight only, but this we did not mind, anything to get ashore and mix with others in the pubs.

Despite the constant shelling of Dover by the German guns at Calais, the public houses in Dover were lively places; most had non-stop music and a limited amount of beer that ran out very early in the evening, but no spirits to drink at all, although I expect they could be had from the black market that was now operating up and down the country. This did not bother us, at the tender age of nineteen I preferred to drink beer anyway, but there were girls galore, and in pubs this of course usually meant trouble.

Also in Dover harbour at the time were motor gunboats manned by Norwegian sailors, and a fine bunch of lads they were too. Unfortunately they were too popular with the local girls, and this was not appreciated by the local based troops, as I was about to discover.

My sailor's collar was a well-washed one, consequently it had become a very light shade of blue, very similar to the colour of Norwegian sailor's collars.

After a few drinks, I found it necessary to use the outside toilet, and wandered out to it on my own. That was a bad mistake. While in the process of doing what comes naturally, four English soldiers entered, slightly the worse for drink, of course, but that did not bother me and neither did the fact that their abuse was directed at me, although I was very puzzled as to what I had done. Then it was obvious that their intentions went beyond verbal abuse, and I began to get worried. It was trouble with a vengeance, and I did not know what to do. Fortunately, help was at hand; several of the Norwegians came in, and after a few empty threats by the soldiers, the situation cooled, and they left. One of the Norwegians explained what had happened. They had seen the soldiers follow me out, and guessed their intentions. They themselves had learnt the hard way not to venture out singly, so when they saw what was going to happen they decided to help me out of what would have been a very uncomfortable situation, to say the least.

They earned my undying gratitude by their actions, so, having come ashore on my own, I spent the rest of the evening in the company of my new-found friends. A very enjoyable one it was too.

The next morning the 320 sailed for Weymouth, where I hoped no similar situations would arise.

The pier at Weymouth was being transformed into a Coastal Forces gunnery school and general training base. As it was still in its infancy, it could not cope with too many crews at the same time. In any case we were apparently not there for further training.

Weymouth was, and still is, an attractive town. It was clean, and there was very little rowdyness from any of the services based there.

Sometime before the outbreak of war, there had been an unpleasant development between the town and the Royal Navy.

*MGB 320, July 1942.*

*Signatures of the crew of MGB 320 at the time of my leaving the 'Lucky Lady'.*

According to stories told by sailors who were there at the time, the local pubs and hotels barred sailors from their saloon bars when the Fleet had called there. The Home Fleet at that time consisted of a very large number of ships; there were more in that one fleet than we now have in our whole Navy put together. The Fleet had anchored just off Portland; the first few sailors had come ashore, visited Weymouth and found to their surprise notices banning gypsies, dogs and sailors. A signal was hurriedly sent to the Admiral in command of the Fleet, informing him of what was happening.

When ships from the Royal Navy visit anywhere, the places concerned spend a great deal of money in making preparations for the visit, and to provide entertainment. Of course they benefit themselves as well, so one can imagine how much Weymouth was going to gain, with the whole of the Home Fleet about to visit the town.

Unfortunately for Weymouth, the Admiral concerned considered the town's action to be an insult against the Royal Navy, so he gave orders to all ships to 'up anchor and leave for another port of his choosing'. This taught the town councillors a lesson they would not forget for a very long time. It proved a very expensive one for them, as they had no returns for money spent.

This time there was not going to be a repetition of what had happened earlier, and the townsfolk really went out of their way to make sure the Navy knew that they were welcome.

They wanted to make amends and they did. Of course most of the sailors based there knew nothing about what had occurred, and could not care less anyway; there was a war on, and that was why there were there, so their only concern was to make the best of their stay. However, some of the older men still remembered, and on a few isolated instances angry words in a pub would open up old wounds, and the unhappy publican, who probably was not there pre-war anyway, would suffer in retaliation.

The 320 entered the harbour at Weymouth, and moored alongside the quay, almost alongside the Sailors Rest, which was a small hotel converted into a hostel catering for the needs of the seamen. It provided tasty meals at very low prices, bed and breakfast accommodation, snooker and various other indoor games. It was managed by a very attractive young lady whose name was Victoria, or Vicky as she preferred to be known. I am sure that every visiting sailor to that establishment fell in love with Vicky, unsuccessfully, because she was already engaged to a very lucky Petty Officer cox'n, serving aboard one of our motor torpedo boats. Vicky was not a girl who would play around anyway; a nicer young woman would have been very hard to find.

Nevertheless, Vicky was well worth looking at, she was fun to talk to, and she did a great deal of good work looking after the visiting sailors. There must be many men who remember her even now, and appreciate how welcome she made them feel when they first arrived at Weymouth.

Our stay at Weymouth was not a long one. We carried out various exercises in the bay, evidently to the satisfaction of the powers that be, for we were then declared as officially ready for active service. We then set sail on our return journey to Great Yarmouth. It was always nice to visit these other ports, but there is no place like your own base in the end.

To most of us aboard, this visit seemed totally unnecessary and very much a joke. After all, we had already found our sea-legs, we had already spent many hours at sea and even experienced a little action, but who were we to dispute the whims of their Lordships at the Admiralty?

Our voyage back to the base at Great Yarmouth was made in one go with no problems encountered on the way, and even the sea and weather were exceptionally kind to us.

Our Captain never seemed to leave the bridge, and apart from being a regular Royal Navy officer, the fact that he was the senior officer commanding our flotilla made him seem to us a little awesome. We had to live up to a high standard, and be more than proud that it was our Skipper that was the senior officer commanding the newly formed 12th Motor Gunboat flotilla.

Although Peter Loasby proved to be a strict disciplinarian he was also a very fair man. He understood what we were capable of, and saw that we were not pushed too hard. He realised that many of us would appreciate encouragement, and harshness could do more harm than good. This did not mean that he was going to be soft in his handling of us, this was made quite plain, and both the 1st Lieutenant and the cox'n fully understood.

Our life aboard the 320 was made easier for us, as in Bob Goodfellow, our 1st Lieutenant, we had probably the kindest and most understanding officer in Coastal Forces. As our Captain was unapproachable most of the time, Bob was always there when needed. He was ready to give advice on any subject, personal or otherwise, and as a seaman none came better. Bob's mild manner and appearance deceived all those who came in contact with him, for under it all was a very brave man, as soon we, his crew, were going to discover.

Next in line of responsibility came 'Sharkey' Ward, our cox'n. Now that we had been at sea under him we appreciated what a fine seaman he was. His calm nature and efficient handling of the 320 impressed us all.

At the time of joining the 320, I still knew very little about the kind of work that she and similar boats were expected to carry out. It was some time later that the title 'Coastal Forces' was officially recognised as being a separate and independent branch of the Royal Navy, in the same way as was the submarine service. Once this recognition was acknowledged by the media, the newspapers and radio publicised the activities of Coastal Forces craft daily, as a boost to civilian morale.

It was no exaggeration to say that our boats were engaged in battles with enemy forces every day or night, and often both.

It was also true that unlike the great ships of the Home and other Fleets, who often never actually saw their enemies, we in gunboats and torpedo boats could boast that 'we only opened fire when we saw the whites of their eyes', just like the cowboys fighting the Indians on the screen at a cinema. We fought that close to our enemy on many occasions.

Of course this gave us a certain amount of glamour, in addition to the thrills, not all of which came from actual combat. One thrill that stays with you in your memory for ever, is to be on board your boat when it is sailing as part of a flotilla. The sight of a number of fast, well armed small craft heading out to sea, ready for anything, is really impressive.

The loss of life among Coastal Forces men was very high. It was inevitable with the risks they had to take. Our officers in the main were dare devils; they were not called 'death or glory boys' for nothing; and when it is taken into consideration that most officers in Coastal Forces had, only a while before, been in civilian jobs, such as insurance, banks, solicitors and accountants, their bravery and the way they handled their boats was nothing short of magnificent. They would go to sea looking for action, and as the war progressed, they mostly found it.

It was not all action though. The largest part of our operations were often boring and dull, also very uncomfortable. Because of the kind of conditions we lived under, their Lordships at Admiralty kindly paid us a trifle more than the men serving in 'big ships'. We actually received the princely sum of one shilling per day extra; sixpence of this was supposed to be 'danger money', the other sixpence was to compensate for having to live on board our boats in such cramped conditions.

There were other benefits too. Aboard our boats we were always issued our daily tot of rum neat, whereas aboard the larger vessels, below the rank of Petty Officer, rum was always diluted with two measures of water to one of rum, generally known as 'grog'. There was a useful aspect to the rum: after drinking it you were ready, willing, and able to eat almost anything, however badly it was cooked, or whatever the condition it was in.

Despite this rude aspersion about our food, where small ships were concerned another advantage was how well we were fed. The cox'n would received an allowance for each man on board, he was then allowed to purchase our food from wherever he chose. Some things were better value from Naval stores, but mostly food was better value if bought from civilian shops ashore. These shops would value the trade given to them and they would see that whatever we bought was the best in quality, and often throw in a little extra of something. So almost always we enjoyed fresh, good, wholesome food.

Sometimes the cox'n would ask for a volunteer to handle the buying of food and accounting for the money. The volunteer would then act as mess caterer. If he was good at his job, by careful housekeeping he would be able to feed us on the very best of food, and still have money in hand at the end of the month. This spare cash would then be shared equally among us all.

Having returned to our base at Great Yarmouth, it was accepted by us that we would simply resume our normal routine and patrol the sea lanes as before. For a while this is what we did, but when we arrived, soon after having moored at our usual berth, Peter Loasby slipped ashore to take part in important discussions elsewhere, and when he returned aboard everything was as normal, and for a few days nothing seemed to change.

On Sunday November 23rd 1941, after the usual church parade and service, leave was granted as usual, as from 1200 hrs, and after Len had shared his rum with me and we had eaten our dinner, the pair of us went ashore and into town. Len had shared his rum with me almost immediately we had become friends; officially it was not allowed, but our cox'n was prepared to turn a blind eye to it, so it was the accepted practice. Len was two years older than

I was, and married, I was nineteen years old, and had to wait until I reached twenty before I would be legally entitled to draw rum. Now and again, the other men who drew their rum would give me a sip of their tot, but usually I had done something for them to have earned it.

Sometimes Len would express regret that when on leave we had to go without our rum, and it started me thinking of how we could overcome this problem. Whatever we decided would of course be unlawful, and be very risky. We would also have to make certain that the cox'n did not know about it, not because we thought that he would report us, we were sure that he would not, but he would most certainly prevent us from smuggling rum ashore. Our concern was that we should not involve him in any way, as he had so much to lose if disciplined.

After thinking about the problem I came up with an idea. Ginger beer was sold in those days in stone jars, with screw stoppers. A little drop here and a little drop there, and we soon had a jar full of neat rum. Carefully I wrapped it in the cotton waste that was used to clean the guns and engines. We tested a jar wrapped in this waste and it stood up to being dropped and knocked about very well.

We carefully wrapped it again in brown paper, and addressed it to my home at Catford. Getting it past the base sentries was not a problem, so we made straight for the post office in town, where we managed to post our parcel without questions being asked.

It was decided that my mother should not be told what was inside the parcel, so that she would not worry unnecessarily, but I had to write to her immediately to prevent her from opening the parcel, and to let me know when it arrived. In due course a letter arrived, asking what she should do about the parcel. It was decided that more rum would be sent home, and Len and I would meet in London, to share it when next we had some leave. We sent a second parcel, then later two more; now we were happy, we were not going without our rum while on leave.

On this particular Sunday, the two of us went to the local cinema, saw the films through, and made our way back aboard.

On boarding the 320 we were surprised to learn that we would be putting to sea immediately. Len and I had not heard anything at all; recall messages for our crew to report back aboard had been sent out all over town, but the cinema that we had been in had not shown the message on their screen until after we had left the premises. The time was 1830 hrs, it was now dark, and we cast off from our moorings and slowly made our way towards the harbour entrance.

We gunners were already closed up at our guns, and seated inside my turret, I was not able to see anything that was happening on deck, but I was most surprised when the 320 slowly drew alongside the jetty where trawlers usually berthed. We never actually stopped, and all I was aware of was that several shadowy figures were waiting on the jetty for us. They immediately leaped aboard and quickly disappeared below decks. All very mysterious, and we were still moving out to sea. It all took only seconds for this to happen, and we were well out to sea before our mysterious visitors were seen again. It was not until I came off watch that I learnt a little about them.

Once we were well away from land, the only gun that was not manned was the Rolls-Royce gun aft. This was because as we were travelling at speed, the sea was breaking over that part of the boat, and not only would the gun crew be soaked through to the skin, but they would not have been able to see a target if they looked for one. Nevertheless, all guns, including the Rolls-Royce, had been tested to make certain they were in firing condition.

Everything was satisfactory, guns were OK, and our engines were running as sweetly as could be. We changed watches, and I went below to have my evening meal, anxious to learn what I could about what was going on.

Our speed was increased to twenty knots, and was maintained at this for the next five and a half hours.

When he regarded our position as being safe, our Captain called nearly all of his crew together on deck behind the bridge. He then revealed exactly what was going on, why all the secrecy, why the mysterious departure from Yarmouth, who our visitors were, and where we were going. There was going to be a need for complete secrecy, he said, even when we returned to base; we were to tell nobody about this trip or any others that we might make. We must, he said, be vigilant at all times, very shortly we would all be at action stations, and would remain as such for several hours.

As we continued our journey, nothing much occurred. The sea was choppy, the sky cloudy, we saw an occasional ship on the horizon which would thankfully turn out to be one of our destroyers guarding a convoy, and single planes would be heard, but not seen. When we heard the planes we kept radio silence; we could not risk being identified by either friend or foe, such was the nature of our journey. By now our visitors had appeared on the bridge with our officers. They appeared not to be happy, the reason was of course sea sickness, and they were not enjoying it.

Not everything was to run smoothly, and I suppose it would have been too much to expect, although I am sure that our Captain and his visitors had hoped that it would. Our steering developed a fault, which meant that the rudder could not be operated from the bridge. The only method of steering the boat was for a man to be strapped securely on deck above the rudder, to which a handle was fitted, then two lengths of mackeral line ran from the bridge to the rating's thumbs, and he knew that when a thumb was tugged, he had manually to turn the rudder in that direction. This was a real stroke of bad luck, but we were by now not far from the Dutch coast, so we had no alternative but to carry on with our mission.

It was not to be our night. Only twenty-odd miles from our

destination, the sea grew rougher and below the bridge, the charthouse was wrecked by a freak wave, so navigation was now impossible. That together with the faulty rudder created an impossible situation, and there was no alternative but to return to England. Our visitors were landed ashore at the same place as we had collected them, and we returned to our normal berth, where we were swamped with maintenance staff from the base, and an all-out effort made to put us right as quickly as they could.

A few days later, we collected our visitors again and set out to sea. This time the sea was quieter, not so cloudy, with much more moonlight. This was not so good, for it meant that the risk of running into E-boats was greater. Guns were exercised, and we were all at action stations, under the same instructions as on the last journey. Our visitors were happier with no signs of sea-sickness, and even singing to themselves; the signs were good.

Eventually land came into sight. We were now running on one engine only, one which had a silencer fitted to it, but even so, it sounded terribly loud to us on board. We had been reassured that despite what we could hear, it could not be heard ashore, I did so hope it was right; we had been warned not to drop anything because the sound could be heard ashore so this made us doubtful about engine noise.

The sky was now cloudy again, so it seemed very dark. All this time we had been slowly approaching the shore. Conversation on the bridge seemed a little agitated, and afterwards I learnt that we were slightly off course and our position was several miles out. We altered course, and slowly made our way to the agreed rendezvous point. Despite the darkness our visitors were able to discern and recognise the silhouettes of a pier and various buildings, so knew we were correctly placed, and all that was required was a light to be flashed a certain number of times, to indicate that it was safe to land. Now we had to wait. Nothing happened, we were getting restless, our nerves were taut and near breaking point.

Peter Loasby suggested that we could go alongside the pier, and our Dutch friends could walk ashore but after serious consideration this was decided against.

We had been told that the enemy had no heavy shore batteries at this part of the coast, but that there were anti-aircraft guns and searchlights in abundance. If by a stroke of bad luck we were discovered, our task was to put out the searchlights as quickly as possible, then concentrate upon the guns. It seemed that even under those conditions, we would still land our friends, and only then would we make haste back to England. There would be even greater dangers then, because nearby E-boat bases would have been notified and boats would be sent out after us. Fortunately this did not happen.

We slowly headed out to sea, and lay drifting with the tide about two miles out from shore, apparently still waiting for that signal from shore.

Suddenly, while drifting, a light appeared off our starboard bow. It was now very misty so we could not be sure as to what it was. We all held our breath . . . what was it? . . . an E-boat or what? Although the nearest E-boat base was actually thirty-odd miles away, it was always possible for one to stray our way. We drew slowly nearer and nearer to the light. When we were on top of it we discovered to our great relief that it was only a buoy. It was not marked upon our charts, so we were completely unprepared for its appearance. Blimey! we were so pleased to see that buoy.

The relief felt by everyone at seeing the buoy was immense, and shared by us all. It almost seemed to take the edge off our nerves, and relaxed us. We now resumed our wait for the signal from shore. Shortly afterwards, a light was seen ashore, wildly flashing. Our Captain passed a message to us that it was probably a coast patrol going their rounds, but not to worry, as he was sure that they could not see us. The light disappeared from sight, another fifteen minutes passed, and a single light flashed ashore. It was repeated at intervals, and we thought that it must be our contact ashore.

Our dinghy was lowered into the sea, near to our stern, then Bob Goodfellow and the three Allied officers climbed down to it and slowly rowed toward the shore.

We all waited in dead silence, our nerves once again highly strung. We were all tense and highly excited. For most of us this was real danger, made more so because we were not able to take any action to ease the situation. We could not describe it as 'action', because action suggests movement, and movement was something only being done by Bob Goodfellow, who was now rowing towards the shore.

Never having been of a religious mind, it came as a surprise to find myself mouthing a silent prayer, and I firmly believe that there were quite a number of prayers quietly said while we were lying there, within a couple of miles of the enemy.

In later years a certain politician was to utter a remark that would go into history: that 'a week in politics was a very long time'; maybe so, but ten minutes in our situation seemed like a lifetime, in other words – endless.

How long we lay there I cannot say, truthfully, we lost count of time. Maybe those on the bridge of our boat, and of course the wireless operator, kept a check on time, but the rest of us simply waited anxiously.

Then we heard the splash of oars, and very soon the dinghy was back alongside. All four officers clambered back aboard. The dinghy was hauled on board on our starboard side, and we heard to our bitter disappointment that the landing had been unsuccessful again. Once more we were in the wrong place, despite the flashing light. However, now that we were so near, Peter Loasby was not giving up, so with the agreement of the Dutch officers, another attempt was going to be made before sailing for home. We all must have sworn softly to ourselves, we had been so confident that this was the right place, but it was a sheer coincidence that we saw that flashing light at that particular time.

Our position was becoming more and more dangerous all the time. For all we knew the nearby E-boat base could have been alerted; God only knew how many boats they could be sending to deal with us. Then we were told that owing to the three o'clock curfew that the Germans had imposed along this coast, we had to wait until after then before we could make another attempt to land.

The place that had been earmarked for our landing was Scheveningen, a small port and town near to the homes of our three Dutch officers, a place they knew very, very well.

Our centre engine was then started again, and because of the now highly strung condition of our nerves, the sound was like all Hell being let loose. We were reassured by the behaviour of our five officers; they never turned a hair, a good word to describe them would have been 'imperturbable'.

Slowly and quietly we made our way to what should now be the right place; we stopped engines and drifted with the tide, almost lazily it seemed, just as though we never had a care in the world. At 0300 hrs Bob and the three Dutchmen were ready to make the final attempt, so the dinghy was again lowered into the sea, all four men climbed down into it, and off Bob rowed. This time the landing was successful. Thank God for that, our nerves could not have taken much more; we had been at action stations for over five and a half hours.

We on board the 320 had the soft part of the operation. Bob Goodfellow had to row the dinghy with three passengers for a good two miles, not knowing what might be waiting on land for him, then he had another two miles or so to row back, yet, when he did climb back on board, he was no more put out than if he had just taken his wife for a row on a local boating lake.

Enemy troops and guns were very near and our first task now

was to get out of their range before daylight when we would have been the proverbial sitting duck, and our mission no longer secret.

Only one officer had been left on shore, so before we could leave we had to wait for a signal from him to indicate all was well. The signal came, and thankfully we could then leave the area. At first we ran on the one silenced engine for about ten miles; ironically, while we had been near the shore, this engine had broken down, and only hard work by our very skilled engine-room crew had managed to get it going again.

The Dutch officer who had been left ashore was Peter Tazelaat, a wild dare-devil of a man, completely fearless, who, it was reputed, never really settled down to civilian life when the war ended. The other two officers were Erik Hazelhoff and Chris Krediet; the latter died a few years after the war ended but Erik enjoyed a successful career as an author, and now lives in Hawaii.

Just prior to leaving the 320, Peter Tazelaat, already resplendent in full evening dress, white tie and tails, was doused thoroughly with the contents of a bottle of brandy, so that if by bad luck he was challenged, he would pretend to have been to an all night party. He certainly smelt like it as he passed me on his way to the dinghy. It was said that Peter insisted that not all the brandy was poured over him, he had to drink some; if he was able to give an impression of being drunk as well as he smelt like one, then I am certain that he would have very little to worry about.

Despite the fact that Peter was being landed so near to his home, it was still a very brave and dangerous thing for him to do.

Peter carried a small automatic, concealed I believe in the tail of his jacket, which was only to be used in an emergency. I do not think that he ever had to use it but I am certain that he would not have hesitated had an opportunity made it necessary.

Making my way past the bridge during our journey from England, despite noise from our engines, I could hear Chris Krediet singing a popular song of that time called 'My Sister and

I'. Whether it had any significance or not I never knew, but it made me wonder, having a sister of my own whom I cared for, what would my feelings have been if I had left England and my family, as so many men from the Nazi occupied countries did. Did Chris leave a sister behind? He certainly appeared to be singing that song with feeling, and looking back and recalling the words, it could have been written by a Dutchman, the words were so appropriate.

When I mentioned this in a letter to Erik Hazelhoff, in later years, he was none the wiser, but remembered fondly that while on the bridge he also used to sing to himself. His choice was the one that Vera Lynn made famous, one of the most popular songs ever written, called 'Yours'. When Vera sang that song over the radio, every member of the Allied Forces took it as being personal. As for myself, I loved all the songs of that era and alone in my machine-gun turret I would sing them all, not very well it is true, but it helped keep me awake.

As soon as we reached the imaginary ten-mile limit, all three engines were put into operation and the course plotted for home. The return journey was uneventful, but the night had been a busy one. There were several of our destroyers patrolling the area, which was unusual there, but we were soon to know the reason why. Very soon we came across one destroyer standing by a merchant ship that had obviously either hit a mine or been tor- pedoed; only its bows were above water, and an anti-aircraft balloon was still flying above it, creating the impression of being unconcerned, yet, ironically, performing the function it was meant to. Within the next thirty minutes or so, the merchant ship sank completely, and the destroyer sped away to rejoin the remainder of the convoy.

At 11.45 a.m. we sighted land, and slowly drew nearer to it. We were a very tired and dirty bunch, most of whom had only slept for one hour during the whole escapade, while a few of us had also kept watch (sentry duties) during the previous night in harbour. Ths sight of land was a joy to behold. We were looking forward to turning into our bunks again with the greatest anticip- ation, but our luck was out, for just outside the harbour entrance we ran out of petrol, and had to lie there awaiting a tow by another vessel. Going to the wrong landing places had used up more petrol than had been allowed for and we could only be thankful that we had enough to get us this far.

Because of our condition, it seemed an eternity from when we signalled our predicament to our base and when a motor launch arrived to make the tow at 1400 hrs, we were taken straight to the fuelling berth. Here we filled our tanks and made our way to our usual berth at the base. Never had the sight of that cold bleak jetty looked so good. The worst part was now to come, but it was unavoidable of course. Before anything else, we had to clean and lubricate our guns, the deck had to be washed and cleaned, the engine-room too, nobody was allowed to dodge responsibilities. Ropes had to be stowed away, and the 320 had to look as though it had just come from the boatyard, brand new. Only when it looked 'shipshape and Bristol fashion' did our 1st Lieutenant allow us to relax and go below. Then everything was one mad dash, everyone wanted to have a bath and sleep. A few, who were entitled to, went ashore, claiming that they were now beyond sleep, but they did not stay ashore long, they had to give in and return to their bunks. We were all very fit and healthy and in our prime, but this escapade had taken its toll; rest and sleep were more important to us right now than entertainment.

It seemed hard to us that we had to clean everything before we could rest, but this was just good seamanship, and the condition of our guns could determine whether we lived or died, so they had to be a priority. There was another reason too; once we had docked, the Dutchmen having been put ashore by the trawlers, Peter Loasby had to visit the Base Commander and make his report as to how the trip had been, and any other information that could be used. Then during the afternoon, the 320 was visited by some other officers, who were probably involved in the espionage side of things.

Nothing of any importance occurred, so we settled down and resumed our place in the flotilla, carrying out the normal routine of patrols, chasing away marauding E-boats, but in reality not even seeing one on the horizon. We began to feel as though we had never done anything else.

Great Yarmouth was now well known to the Germans as a Naval base, and in consequence attacks by Nazi aircraft were frequent. Fortunately for us, their bombers' aim was not all that good, so there were not many direct hits on our actual base, and none on the boats themselves.

To me, painting ship was probably the most boring and arduous task of all. Our cox'n Sharkey Ward kept us at it, and ignored pleas from the gunnery ratings that keeping their guns clean, oiled and in good working order came before painting ship; he still made us do our share along with the rest of the crew. He even managed to get the motor mechanic to spare the stokers for a day or so to help.

All kinds of small repairs were carried out by civilian tradesmen employed by Admiralty, they were quickly referred to as 'dockyard maties' likening them to the men employed at the main Naval dockyards up and down the country and who were generally referred to as being lazy and natural work dodgers. This description was unfair; most men who worked in our dockyards were hard-working and honest, and often did many favours for the seamen on board the ships or boats they were working on. Of course there were the exceptions; it would be a strange world if there were not.

Working on the boats at our base was one carpenter, a 'chippy' in Naval parlance, who was particularly good at his profession. If work had to be carried out and the officers of a particular boat knew this man's reputation, he was always asked for in preference to anyone else. He was also well versed in possible ways in which he could benefit personally, and would make all sorts of personal things for the lads in return for payment of tobacco. He made a very fine ditty-box for me, in return for two tins of cigarette tobacco, properly dove-tail jointed it stood up to a lot of wear and tear. It went with me everywhere, including to bases in Algiers and Italy, and it is still in my possession today. On the inside of the lid of my ditty-box I wrote the following words that I had read somewhere, words that had a meaning, and that I felt appropriate, perhaps even to be my epitaph when it is time for me to go. These words were as follows,

'Rien ne trouble sa fin,
c'est le soir de beau jour.'

In English they mean, 'Nothing troubles his end, it is the evening of a beautiful day.' I know of no nicer thing to say and there is a ring of truth about it that appeals to me so much.

Life ashore in the pubs and dance-halls carried on just the same, and I made friends with a Yarmouth girl named Peggy. As soon as my shipmates knew about her I was constantly teased and tormented about her; a walk on the upper deck would suddenly start off a rendering of the old song about 'Peggy O'Neil', which may not have been too bad except for it being a rather bawdy version. The friendship did not last long. I suppose it was really a non-starter from the beginning, as she reminded me too much of the girl at home, who also had a sister named Peggy. To be honest though, it was pleasant and interesting while it lasted.

We youngsters in the crew, quite apart from our sea experience, were still learning to look after ourselves properly, without the help of 'dear old Mum'. To some it came easily, to others it did not; some were too used to mother cleaning up after them, putting their clothes away, and looking behind their ears, that having to do all these things themselves was hard work to say the least.

When a group of men are forced to live together in a confined space, as the crews of Coastal Forces craft and of submarines had to, unhealthy conditions can easily develop. Fortunately aboard every boat the older or more experienced men would take charge and guide the youngsters, sometimes forcibly, showing them what was expected of them, what they had to do, and where hygiene was concerned no mercy would be shown. Everyone was made to toe the line in this respect, and often one sure way of enforcing it was ridicule. Once a man experienced this he did not want it repeated.

Hygiene became a matter of personal pride, shirts would be 'whiter than white', collars and uniforms pressed to perfection, and the sailors' trousers had the creases depicting the 'seven seas' for all to see. When 'Jack' went ashore the girls couldn't help but notice. Army and RAF uniforms looked dowdy and even shabby against the sailors' freshly laundered 'navy blue and white'.

On board the 320, life was made easier for us all by our leading stoker Stan Hubbard and Jeff Goodey. They created a laundry service on board; for a small sum of money they would do all our washing for us, and when it was returned to us it would be nothing short of perfection, spotless and perfectly ironed. It was inexpensive, certainly most convenient, and a Godsend to us all. Even our officers were known to take advantage of it occasionally. At first it seemed strange to the seamen at first, that the two stokers would happily take on all our washing, normally referred to in the Navy as 'dhobeying', a word coined by sailors who had in the past served in the Far East. The real truth was that because working in an engine-room was often the dirtiest work of all, the stokers had a need to become very clean, sometimes to the point of fussiness, and it paid dividends when ashore with the girls, another fact that did not go unnoticed by the competition. By doing all this washing, it made certain that their hands were spotless, with not a trace of dirt under their fingernails.

Jeff Goodey was also a popular choice for cook's duties. Our crews, and this applied to all Coastal Forces craft, were too small in number to merit qualified cooks to be allocated to each craft, so everyone except the officers, both commissioned and non-commissioned, took their turn at being duty cook. Sometimes a crew would be lucky enough to have someone volunteer to be the cook permanently, but usually it meant taking your turn at it for a given period, mostly for a week. Jeff's popularity was due to his being able to make some of the finest pastry the lads had ever tasted, he was absolutely top class. Before he joined the Navy, he had worked as a boy in a bakehouse, and what he learnt there stayed with him always, much to our delight. Making pastry came naturally to Jeff. Jokingly, he always maintained that he only did it to keep his hands soft and clean, but we knew this not to be true, as he was an exceptionally clean person at all times.

Along with being able to buy fresh vegetables, and all types of food to our own choosing, our mode of life was vastly improved by men like Jeff Goodey. Unfortunately Jeff's skills and experience in the engine-room came first, so he was not allowed to cook regularly for us. We had to be satisfied with him being able to sneak away from the engine-room to make pastry for us, and for him to keep a watch upon the efforts of the duty cook when preparing our main meals.

Attempts by our Captain to obtain leave had been unsuccessful, but a signal was received instructing us to sail to a small boatyard just outside Lowestoft, where work was to be carried out on the 320. We had no idea as to what the work was, but it raised a great deal of speculation as to whether we could get some leave at last. We all nagged the cox'n until he agreed to have a word with the 1st Lieutenant on the subject. We then learnt that our 1st Lieutenant had already discussed possible leave with the Captain, who in turn had made the necessary application to the base Commander, and it had been granted. All but a skeleton crew could go on a week's leave almost immediately we arrived at the boat-yard.

So we set sail for Lowestoft. It was only a few miles down the coast from Yarmouth, so it required no special effort, no dangers, and with the prospect of leave we would have been willing to sail there in the worst gale conditions. The sea and weather were favourable, and we entered the boatyard without any problems.

At 1200 hrs, leave was piped. We mustered on the deck, where we were lectured regarding the need for secrecy in respect of what we had been doing recently. When this was over, there was a quick inspection of our dress. A search should have been made to see whether any cigarettes or tobacco were being taken home, but this search was given a miss, so it is best left to imagination as to whether it was taken advantage of. Len Downs and I were not too concerned; we had ample rum already waiting for us at home anyway, but we did take extra cigarettes.

We learnt that the work that had to be done would have only taken a couple of days, so to ensure that the leave would be at least a week, arrangements had been made for our engines to receive a complete overhaul. We had experienced trouble when near the Dutch coast, so to have them overhauled was more than just an excuse, although it must be admitted that it could have been carried out at our base in Yarmouth.

# CHAPTER 6

# *We decide that the 320 should be called 'The Lucky Lady'*

ON arriving home, things were more or less normal. Several bombs had fallen locally, but our road had escaped so far; my mother seemed no different and insisted that she could manage well enough. She was naturally very pleased to have me home.

There was, however, some bad news to tell me. My mother had received news from the Admiralty that my brother's ship had been torpedoed and sunk. There were no survivors, but my brother's body had not been found, so he was presumed dead; probably he had drowned. How she really felt will never be known, she had the strength to give me the details as far as she knew them. I can only assume that she did her grieving when she first received the bad news.

The family, all on my mother's side, were sympathetic and supporting; apart from that there was nothing else that could be done. As one of my mother's sisters lived nearby, at the top end of the same road, I knew that it would have been she whom my mother would have shared the information with first.

It would not have been too difficult for the family to accept, as Alan had spent most of his life away from us all. He lived in Suffolk for some time before joining Captain Watt's training ship at East Dereham, Norfolk. Following that he joined the Navy as a boy, completing his training at HMS *Ganges*, the boys' training ship near Ipswich.

For me it was different. Had I not also joined the Navy it would have been harder, but I now had proof that although the Admiralty made decisions that were often unpopular, behind their reasons often lay good, sound, common sense. When Alan heard that I had been accepted by the Navy, he requested that I should be sent to the same ship as himself, so that he could look after me. The Admiralty refused his request, stating that it was not approved that two members of the same family should serve together on the same ship. Lucky me! Had I been on Alan's ship with him when it was torpedoed, my mother would have lost two sons, not one.

In fact, I was fifteen years old before I even knew that I had a brother, but after a difficult start, we became closer than most brothers ever do. It was Alan's influence upon Laurie and myself that encouraged us to join when we did. Alan, in his letters, told me which were the best Naval tailors, he also taught us about other aspects of life in the Navy, and he helped prepare us for life in the Service.

So at the age of nineteen, I had become used to the knowledge that death was no longer restricted to the old and sick, and because of the ferocity with which Nazi Germany was attacking us, here at home as well as at sea, I even had the feeling that I probably would not survive the war. Morbid? Yes and, fortunately, wrong. Experiencing the Blitz upon London before entering the Navy, then Alan's ship being sunk, was mainly responsible for this attitude. The rest, I suppose, was down to my serving in the Coastal Forces, on a motor gunboat built entirely of wood, and the tremendous activity by the enemy by sea and by air, in that stretch of the North Sea now known as 'E-boat Alley'.

One very important thing helped me to disregard that morbid feeling: comradeship. All the danger that I had known, and all the danger that might come in the future, would be shared by others, my shipmates aboard the 320. If they were not worried, why should I be?

While on leave, everyone was as helpful as they could be. I need never have been alone; in fact, I found it hard to be just that. Mother's cooking made a very pleasant change, and although food rationing was very severe at that time, local tradesmen helped a lot. The shopkeepers all knew me. I had grown up in front of their very eyes; most likely there had been many occasions when they had cursed me, but now things were very different. Our country was at war, and Jack Davies was a sailor in the Royal Navy, perhaps not a hero, but he was out there doing his bit on their behalf. So those tradesmen helped, with a little extra here and a little extra there; the local baker even cooked hot cross buns early, so that my mother could post them to me wherever I was stationed. Even in later years when I was at Algiers, his hot cross buns arrived in time to be eaten on Good Friday: co-operation between the baker and my mother ensured perfect timing.

There were opportunities to visit my local pub. Here I received the finest possible reception, which included, quite naturally, plenty of free beer. Juke boxes were the big attraction in every pub and club in those days and, loving music as I did, I spent more time and money on these machines than I ought to have done.

Time was found to visit a local dance hall, but I found that I knew nobody there. The one person I badly wanted to see was just not around. I actually considered calling at her home, to ask if she would come out with me, but, despite the courage my uniform instilled in me, this was one kind that I was still short of. Had my leave been longer, maybe I would have managed it, but Fate stepped in. A telegram arrived, delivered by the police, instructing me to report back to the 320 immediately, so after a moist-eyed but not tearful goodbye from my mother and neighbours, it was back to my boat, my guns and my shipmates and of course — the sea.

The journey back to East Anglia was average; the air-raid sirens had sounded, but during the first part of the journey from Catford to Liverpool Street station, no enemy planes came within sight. The train was almost empty, normal for that time of the day, and people just did not travel unnecessarily in times like these.

At Liverpool Street station the situation was very different; it teemed with people, civilians, railway staff, and of course, service men and women galore; the red caps of the Military Police were everywhere. Although their equivalent, the Naval Patrol, was unobtrusive by comparison, if an incident occurred that involved Naval personnel, it was amazing how quickly they were on the spot.

The train for Norwich was already almost full by the time I arrived; it looked as though a search for a seat would be pointless, and so when I did find one I realised how lucky I was.

The 'all clear' note of the air raid sirens had now sounded. On that occasion the German visit had been fended off by our fighters, and they had not reached London, but the respite was only temporary, for within a short while, when we were miles from London on our way, we heard the sirens sound again, followed soon after by gunfire. We knew then that the first Nazi planes had been merely a 'feeler', and this new attack would be the main one. As the target was obviously London, the enemy planes made no attempt to attack our train as it sped on its way, and about three hours later we had arrived safely at the Norwich mainline station, where we were to change trains to go on to Yarmouth and Lowestoft.

There was a lengthy wait before the next train for the coast was available, so we had to make use of the railway buffet to while away the time, not daring to go outside the station to a pub, in case we missed our train. The train arrived; along with other service men and women I boarded it, and was taken to Lowestoft. There was no means of obtaining transport or even getting in touch with the boatyard, so I had to make the long, dreary walk on my own, in the dark as there were no street lights, and not a soul in sight. It was more by luck than anything else, that I found my way, but I did, and discovered that I was the last one to return. Of course everyone insisted that that was my intention, but as it really made no difference I took little notice of their banter.

Once I settled down, we all exchanged reminiscences of the leave, and a good moan about being recalled so soon. Then into our bunks for a good night's sleep.

The next morning we were in for a shock when we went onto the upper deck. There, midships, just aft of our machine-gun turrets, stood a large new fuel tank. We then knew that we had not finished with our espionage trips, as this tank was going to ensure that we did not run out of fuel again. The installation of the tank was why we had been granted leave, but the engine overhaul gave us those extra days. This tank, although a necessity, was an additional hazard for Vic Copeland and myself. Vic was the starboard machine-gunner, whereas I was situated on the port side: we would be the ones most at risk when under enemy fire. The Rolls-Royce gunner, Monty Mortimer, would not be much better off, as he was situated about thirty feet aft of the tank. Of course, with luck, plenty of it, we could be blown clear by an explosion, but we did not rate our chances as being very high; an explosion of a thousand or more gallons of 100 octane would be pretty lethal to say the least. It must also be added that the engine-room staff would not escape scot free as the tank was situated immediately above them.

That morning we spent cleaning and tidying up, as the workmen had left the upper deck in an awful mess, wood shavings and sawdust everywhere, plus odd screws and nails turning up in the most awkward places. During the afternoon we set sail for our base at Great Yarmouth, and arrived in time to wave farewell to two of our flotilla just about to leave on patrol.

The base was now officially known as HMS *Midge*.

There were not many of the boats' crews on the jetty when we arrived, otherwise the sarcasm and catcalls would have been louder and greater in number. There was no anger or resentment from anyone; they accepted that we had been lucky to get leave when we did, and merely hoped that their turn would soon follow. At least when it did, they were likely to enjoy their whole leave and not be recalled as we were. The work we had carried out and would be doing again set us aside from the rest of our flotilla, as being special, but being special meant more little aggravations and restrictions to endure. In this we had no choice.

Of course, while we had been absent on our espionage runs, and on our short leave, the rest of our flotilla had had to do our share of patrols, unfortunately much more often than before we went our separate way. The enemy had stepped up its attacks on our convoys, so our boats had put to sea more often. Our Skipper, always fair if possible, to the other crews as well as his own, made certain that we took part in as many patrols as possible; he could have excused us on the grounds that we had other more valuable work to do, but he felt obliged not to, out of fairness. In any case the fact that we were taking part in patrols meant that it was less obvious that we were carrying out other work.

Night leave was granted whenever possible, mostly when the weather was too rough to put to sea. When any of the lads had a date with a girl on a particular night, they would pray for a gale to blow, knowing that they would then be able to keep it. Selfish? – maybe, but we knew that if the sea was too rough for us, it was also too rough for the Germans.

In the main, the people of Great Yarmouth enjoyed having us based there. Although they missed the visits of the herring boats, and the prosperity they brought with them, the Navy was there all the time. This meant that the town continued to be prosperous, and not only the pubs either. Len Downs and I were out together a great deal, the two stokers also, but they used to disappear elsewhere, often to Norwich, so we never met up with them on most of our runs ashore.

Aboard most of our boats, if three stokers comprised the entire engine-room crew, plus the motor mechanic, all three were not usually allowed ashore together. Our three were lucky; the motor mechanic, Ralph Puttock, Petty Officer, rarely left the boat at all. It was true that he enjoyed his own company, but by no means was he either 'stuck up', or a recluse. He was simply a very nice person who preferred to spend his money more wisely than the rest of us. Ralph spent his on his hobby, which was photography, at which he excelled, and 'his' engine-room served as a darkroom for developing and printing the photographs he took.

The amount of money paid to British servicemen did not allow much in the way of luxuries. This was partly the reason for the popularity of American troops when they arrived; our lads just could not compete with the money and 'goodies' that the Yanks could throw around. Shortage of money also meant that often we could not afford the train fare home, so that except when free travelling warrants were available train journeys were limited. The warrants were usually kept for special occasions. I seem to remember that there were three free warrants per year, so if going home on weekend leave we either paid our own fare or found an alternative method of transport.

Hitch-hiking was of course the most common method, and on the roads in those days there were not many drivers that would not stop and pick up servicemen or women. It often proved, however, to be most time-consuming, because it usually meant obtaining lifts from several vehicles; only on rare occasions would anyone be lucky enough to cadge a lift all the way home in one.

Many would risk travelling without tickets. It was a fifty-fifty gamble, and most considered it worth taking. If caught, it was always possible that a sob-story would persuade the railway official to let you off; if not, he would eject you from the train at the next station. You would then try again, if successful in getting back onto the station. Railway officials were wise to most stories, they heard so many, but I think that in most instances when they let us off, it was out of sympathy because we were in the Services, and not because they believed the story told.

Another means of getting home on the cheap, was with forged or altered tickets. Often when travelling in those days, at the end of your journey, there would not be a porter on duty to take your ticket, so you saved the ticket, and with the use of an ink eradicator, purchased at any good stationer's, it was easy to remove the date stamp, and so be able to present the ticket again. I learnt about this upon my first stay at Whale Island, and became quite adept at removing the dates. In fact I used to get asked by my shipmates if I would alter a ticket for them and in return they would give me a drop of their rum. Although to the best of my knowledge, my efforts were never discovered, I always looked for means to improve my work. The actual dates were not a problem as a suitable date stamp could be easily bought at a stationer's or purloined from an office, but it was the removal of the old date that let most men down. Sometimes the eradicator would remove some other words, or too much chemical would make the ink from the new date run or smudge. I found what appeared to be the answer, and all the time my hands were steady I was able to get near to perfection. It was so simple; merely with the use of a safety razor blade, patience, and enough time not to need to hurry, a near perfect ticket would be produced. In those days, the tickets were of a fairly thick, soft cardboard. Some were dyed right through but some only upon the surface, the latter were the most difficult and needed the most care. The final result was an apparently new undated ticket, which could then be used at will. The lads loved them; many tried to do tickets themselves, but usually botched them up by leaving scratches or digs that eagle-eyed inspectors quickly spotted. To me it was all done in fun, but it helped some to see their families more often at a time when they needed to most.

At small stations, a group of men would rush onto the platform at the very last moment before the train left. They would shout at the railway staff on duty that there was no time to buy a ticket but that they would do so at the other end. Whether this was believed or not, I do not know, but it often worked. Of course, when the trains arrived at the other end, all sorts of dodges were used to get through the barriers without being stopped. Many would get off the train at a station before their destination and not give their ticket up, stating that they were going to rejoin the train after a drink, or some other excuse.

There were other risks taken to get home. The first train of the day, what was known as the 'milk train', usually left the station at around 3.30 a.m. and filled up very quickly, so seating was at a premium always. Nobody looked forward to standing all the way for fifty or more miles, so one had to get on to the train first. The trains used to stand just outside the stations in sidings; to get aboard the men had to cross electrified lines, and we did just that. Naturally when the trains pulled into the station to take on passengers, they were already practically full. Upon looking back I can see what fools we were to take such risks, but at the time they were risks worth taking in order to get home to your family.

Considering how often we were cheating death, what was one more risk, or one more, or one more? We all knew that we would have to meet our Maker some time, and when did not seem all that important at the time.

Early in December 1941, we put to sea again, collecting our Dutch friends as usual, on the way down river to the harbour entrance. We were again bound for Scheveningen. Later we learnt that this town was very near to the homes of our three friends, which would have been the reason why it had been chosen as the most suitable landing place. It was never said, naturally, whether any visits were actually made to their homes, it was most probably forbidden anyway, but who could condemn them if they did? The

town was also the headquarters of the German coastguards net-
work, which I understand stretched from Denmark all the way to
along the French coast. It was naturally a very busy place, yet we
were so close on one occasion we almost crashed into their pier,
and later, when Bob Goodfellow and the Dutchmen had rowed
ashore, they were actually challenged by a German sentry, who,
although he had not seen them, had heard the sound of splashing
oars in the water. The sentry was obviously satisfied that all was
well when Chris Kredeit replied in German; it was a very near
thing though.

We were all aware now just how dangerous this situation was
for us all. The only small consolation was that where we were
making the landings was within comfortable swimming distance
of the shore, but at the same time we knew that should the worst
happen there would not be much hope of surviving such a swim.
German sailors would probably have given us a sporting chance,
but we did not put their troops in the same category, and we could
expect to be machine-gunned while in the water.

Once the dinghy had returned, and Bob Goodfellow and the
remaining Dutch officers had clambered aboard, we set sail again
for home, following the usual pattern, on one engine for the first
ten miles, then all systems go until we reached base, at least that
was how it should have been.

Unfortunately Fate had other plans for us. We were approximately seventy-five miles from Great Yarmouth when the motor
mechanic reported to the Captain that the Stuart Turner engine,
used to pump out the bilges, had broken down, and although they
had been trying to mend it for some time, they had had no success.
This meant that the bilges were now full of water, and the
engine-room staff were standing in water above their ankles. At
the rate the water was pouring in we would sink very soon. The
Stuart-Turner engine was a small but vital part of the engine-
room, it supplied the power for the ship's lighting, but its most

valuable operation was to pump out the bilges which always filled
with water. Our boats, being built entirely of wood, always leaked
to a certain extent as no boatyard was able to build a completely
leak-proof boat and the weight of the powerful engines tended to
make any leaks worse. The next report I heard was that the water
had now reached the tops of the stokers' seaboots.

After inspection by the 1st Lieutenant it was decided there was
no alternative but for us to bail out by hand. It was not the best
solution but it was the only solution, and nobody was the least
enthusiastic about the prospect. Every available member of the
crew lined the deck with buckets, I did not realise we carried so
many on board, but it seems that a good cox'n always makes sure
that he has enough to put all the available hands to work when
'cleaning ship'. The buckets were passed down into the engine-
room, filled with water, handed back up and the water thrown
overboard, and so this went on for seventy-five miles until we
finally berthed at Yarmouth. It was an extremely uncomfortable
and back-breaking job, and those that did the bailing out deserved
medals. In fact they should have received a rise in pay but this was
not possible, of course, and when talked about afterwards it was
said that it was just part of a sailor's life at sea.

During this incident, we machine-gunners were lucky. Because
we were in very dangerous waters, discovery by the enemy was
possible at any time, so the Captain decided that we two were in
the best position to defend the boat if attacked. We could also act
as lookouts, for between the two of us we could cover almost all
directions. One seaman was detailed to stand near to us, so that
he could pass any message from us to the bridge, as the ship's
telephone was also out of action. Reports of progress or otherwise
from the engine-room also could not be transmitted to the bridge,
except by word of mouth.

With all this dampening our spirits, there was one redeeming
feature: at least the hydraulic system that operated our machine-

gun turrets was not affected. It does not bear thinking about had they also been inoperable. It is this kind of situation that provokes fear in a man, the futility of it all, to imagine all that we had experienced and achieved would have counted for nothing had we sunk, and a watery grave would have been all there was for us.

Our wireless operator had already passed the details of our plight to HMS *Midge*, and they had sent two launches out to escort us safely back to base.

The following day, with the co-operation of the base staff, the Stuart-Turner engine was repaired. It was put to work immediately to pump out the remainder of the water left in the bilges. It had not been possible to do this the previous night; apart from it being very awkward to do, the lads were so tired that it would not have been fair to have asked them to do it, though I am sure had they been asked there would have been only one possible reply.

While we were eating our dinner that day, we were remembering all the mishaps we had experienced, and, taking it all into consideration, how lucky we had been. At this point, Jeff Goodey spoke up and said that because the 320 was a lucky boat, we ought to name her the *Lucky Lady*. We all agreed, and from then on that was how she was known. The name stuck, and those of us that were pleased to have served aboard her always remembered her as that. All things considered, if she had not been lucky, where would we now be? Although it is not known at this time what happened to everybody who had served aboard her at one time or another, and although no information was available from the Admiralty, it has been discovered that the *Lucky Lady* is still afloat even now. She is serving as a floating hotel and has been named the *Xoron Floatel*. She is berthed at Bembridge on the Isle of Wight. This one pleasant fact emphasises that she, at least, is still 'lucky'.

# CHAPTER 7

## *It was a good place, was Felixstowe*

W<sup>E</sup> were not given any chance to settle down after our unpleasant trip. A day or so had gone by, but we had not been asked to continue patrols of 'E-boat Alley'. It did not worry us, but neither did it give us cause for thought, when perhaps it should have done.

Then one afternoon, when our thoughts were on what we were going to do ashore that night, the cox'n came to our mess-deck with the information that there would be no leave that day, and that we were sailing at about 1800 hrs. He said that that was all he had been told to tell us; if he knew more, and I am sure that he did, he was not going to pass on the information. So, at 1800 hrs exactly we set out to sea and a few miles out from the harbour we turned the boat to starboard and headed south. Soon afterwards, word was passed around that we were heading for the port of Felixstowe, where we expected to remain for the night at least.

Felixstowe had became an operational base for flotillas of what we called 'seventy-footers'; they consisted of both gunboats and torpedo boats, but were much faster than our C-class boats, and up to that time had probably carried out more actions against the enemy than any other class of boats. From here operated such famous names as Lieutenant Commander Robert Hichens DSO, DSC, RNVR, Captain Peter Dickens DSO, MBE, DSC, RN and Lieutenant Ian Trelawney DSC, RNVR, and many other famous Coastal Forces names. At the time of our arrival, these men and their crews were just beginning to have their exploits noticed, and the Admirals at Whitehall were beginning to sit up and take notice of what Coastal Forces were doing.

When we berthed at Felixstowe, it was at a mooring well away from the base where the other Coastal Forces craft lay. It was a most inhospitable part of the harbour, but it had been arranged this way so that nobody could see who came aboard us, who came off us, or even whether or not we were there at all. So we became 'the mystery boat', much talked about by Naval staff and civilians at the base. The boats' crews never mentioned us, except at first when they attributed our being berthed away from them as being because we were stuck up or thought we were better than them. This was not so, of course, as eventually they were to find out. At first the atmosphere was awkward and unpleasant when we met ashore, but it never developed into anything serious, I am pleased to say.

We arrived too late for leave to be granted that night, so reluctantly we all spent the night on board.

Next day began as normal with maintenance of our guns, engines, and various other small tasks that the cox'n said needed doing; mostly it was a case of keeping us all occupied, because of the well known theory that 'idle hands make mischief'.

Not having been officially told why we were at Felixstowe, rumours were rife; the famous 'bush telegraph' was working over-time. When time began to get near to 1600 hrs, it was no real surprise to learn that shore leave once more was not going to be piped. While we were having our evening meal, the Dutch officers slipped on board again and the cox'n came to give us warning that within the hour we would be casting off, destination probably as before. This time we did not do so happily, and there were many moans and groans, chiefly because we had not had an opportunity to go ashore and discover Felixstowe. Jeff Goodey, whose home town was Colchester, not many miles away, knew Felixstowe well enough to extol its virtues; he would also be able to slip home to

*Bob Goodfellow in 1993.*

his wife when night leave was granted. I do not know if he ever did while we were there, if so he kept quiet about it. He always did keep personal matters very much to himself, which we quite understood.

So under the cover of darkness, we cast off, and our 1st Lieutenant plotted a course for the Dutch coast that he now knew so well, as indeed we did too.

Once we were at sea, and had exercised our guns, we were now used to the idea, and settled down to what we hoped would be a quiet night, with everything running smoothly. Although we understood the dangers we could encounter on these trips, our hearts really went out to our 1st Lieutenant, Bob Goodfellow; he had the hardest work of all, having to row our dinghy single-handed, with three passengers most of the time. He probably did not have time to think about the consequences if discovered, but then he most likely never gave discovery a thought. He really was a 'Goodfellow', but it is a safe bet that when a boy, he never thought that he might one day have to justify his surname. He did exactly that, over and over again, earning the gratitude of Queen Wilhelmina and her Dutch resistance fighters. He was awarded the Military Williams Order, which was presented by Her Majesty the Queen of the Netherlands herself, this order being the Dutch equivalent of our Victoria Cross, both only awarded in exceptional cases of bravery. Bob was the first Englishman to receive this award since the Duke of Wellington, after the Battle of Waterloo.

Until now all the trips had been very similar, the only differences being the mishaps. There now existed a friendly feeling of comradeship between the Dutchmen and ourselves. Whereas at first they had kept to the bridge of our Skipper's cabin and never spoke to any of us, they would now wander around the upper deck while we were at sea, examining and asking questions of us. Their moods were no longer as serious as they had been, but Peter Loasby did not encourage them to become too familiar with us, and rightly so.

As usual, we kept away from the normal sea lanes and encountered no opposition from the enemy. Planes were sighted every now and again, but they were too far for us to discern their nationality, and probably had more important targets than the small and insignificant looking gunboat 320.

When we saw these planes in the distance, it meant that we would have to increase concentration and awareness. There was a possibility that they were enemy planes, and although we were 'small and insignificant' an enemy plane would report our whereabouts to the nearest E-boat base. As this apparently never happened, it must be assumed that the planes up to now had been our own. Our Captain, via the telegraphist, probably knew this, but did not tell us, in order to keep us on our toes.

*Eric Hazelhoff.*

This landing was made successfully, without any challenge from a German sentry ashore, and several further trips were also made, with various different stories. On one visit, we were actually in the mouth of the harbour before we realised; Erik Hazelhoff quickly spoke to our Captain, and we speedily made our way back out to sea. Although Erik had not actually seen any E-boats then, he remembered having seen rows of them moored in this little fishing harbour of Scheveningen before escaping to England, and he was taking no chances on this occasion. On another occasion, the landing had been made late, and dawn was breaking, so the Dutch agent had to telephone his contact. He found a telephone kiosk and made his call. On this occasion the agent was dressed in a British Naval officer's uniform, but although German troops did see him, they must have mistaken the uniform for a German one, because nobody challenged him. He was able to make his call, and the visit was a success. On another occasion, Erik Hazel-hoff was the one ashore. Although late at night, he met, face to face, a Dutch policeman who had known him. Apparently they looked each other in the eye, said not a word, and walked past each other.

At a later stage in our operations, we took another boat from our flotilla with us, the idea was to 'break it in', so that if anything happened to us they would be able to take over the operation; the boat was MGB 326. We rendezvoused at sea, and made our way to Holland, 326 following in our wake.

We made the landing successfully, with 326 drifting nearby. Unfortunately, to everyone's horror, she struck a sandbank, and lodged securely upon it. There was nothing we could do to help, although we had been in exactly the same spot many times; the state of the tide on this occasion had fooled us all. This time it was not at all favourable, and 326 was unable to move. To move her, it would have meant putting all three engines of both boats into use; the noise would have been deafening and the whole of the Dutch coastline would have been alerted. Because of the need for secrecy this risk could not be taken, and the only alternative left was for us to leave her there, and hope for the best.

So we did just that. It was a sad, moving occasion and all of us aboard 320 felt very badly. Very soon dawn would be breaking, and discovery imminent; what would happen then could only be pure speculation.

We moved off, and made our way back to England. When we were three-quarters of our way home, we heard the good news: the tide off the Dutch coast had changed just in time, not long before dawn, enabling the 326 to float off the sandbank and sail as fast as she could for home. At a later date, when we were both at Great Yarmouth, there was a distinct air of hostility between the crew of 326 and ourselves, because of what had happened. The crew had not been told the whys and wherefores, they did not know how important it was that the Germans did not know about us. However, we understood, and thought that in the same situation our attitude may well have been the same.

These were just a few of the situations that occurred, and I am certain that Peter, Chris and Erik have many more they could tell. In fact Erik has written a book, called *A Soldier of Orange*, in which he relates stories of these trips, along with many more, from the days when he and his friends were students under the occupation of the Nazis, right up to the end of the war.

Once we returned to Felixstowe, and our isolated berth, our visitors disappeared, and we set to cleaning guns, engines and the boat in general. When all this was finished we were allowed to fall into our bunks and sleep.

Shore leave was now granted to us, and after our evening meal around two-thirds of our crew made their way into town.

It was much smaller than Yarmouth and it had a cleaner appearance. Not that Yarmouth was dirty, but it was an older town and the houses were different. Felixstowe did not have the huge 'herring sheds'. I suppose the overall appearance of Felixstowe was more affluent, yet it would be a safe bet that Yarmouth had seen more money pass through it in one year than Felixstowe did in ten.

Len and I soon found that there were two dance-halls. One, at The Cavendish Hotel, was within walking distance of the base, approximately two miles, not much when one was sober, but much more after a few drinks. The Cavendish was also renowned for having two beautiful barmaids. As far as they were concerned, admiration across the bar was one thing, but it had to stop there, and it can be said with all honesty that all the lads that went there, did just that.

As with all good class and properly run dances, they were organised and controlled by a Master of Ceremonies, and a good MC would contribute a great deal towards the popularity and success of a dance, so much so that it was almost unheard of to start a dance without one.

Except for the occasions when Jeff would be missing, visiting his home at Colchester, Len, Jeff, Stan and I would all be found at the Cavendish dances. We would mostly be together, and when not dancing I would be watching Jeff's prowess on the floor with a fair amount of envy, he was so very good. Watching him I learnt a great deal.

To my delight, there was a girl who did not mind how many times I would claim a dance with her. She was a lovely girl, something like the Hilda I knew before joining the Navy. She was petite, that being the right expression to a 'T'. Her name was Della, delightful to look at and talk to, slim of figure and an exquisite dancer. Dancing with her always made me feel on top of the world.

The slow fox-trot was our favourite dance, with an occasional waltz or tango. I never bothered with quicksteps as there would then be too many on the floor to be able to enjoy the dance properly. So I would leave Della for others to enjoy; she never missed a dance as she never lacked for partners. I considered myself extra lucky to be able to dance with her as often as I did.

While at Felixstowe I could almost forget the feelings I had for that 'someone else'; almost, but not quite. My thoughts were concentrated upon her most when alone in my gun-turret at sea. With only the vast limitless sea around you, it needed thoughts and memories, and the prospects for the future, to keep you sane.

There was nothing serious between Della and myself. This was accepted, as we never knew how long we would be at the Felixstowe base. After all, Peter Loasby was still Senior Officer in command of the 12th Motor Gunboat flotilla, and until Admiralty decreed otherwise, it was still based at Great Yarmouth. Ultimately that was where we would return to, so not knowing what each day would bring, I was determined to enjoy as much dancing with Della as I could.

The weather on the East Coast was now becoming unreliable. Several times our excursions to Holland were called off at the last minute because of gale warnings. Planning ahead became almost impossible, both for the espionage angle and for our social life. We had to accept each day as it came. We never knew where the Dutch officers stayed overnight, they may even have returned to London, as we soon learnt that they liked the bright lights. Behind the black-out curtains of course.

It was uncanny, however, that no matter what, when a decision was made to make another trip, those officers would be on board, raring to go. I think they took an almost fiendish delight in seeing the disappointed looks upon our faces when we knew that shore leave was out of the question, and that we would be putting to sea. To ease our hurt feelings, we tried hard to convince ourselves that our disappointment was on behalf of the local girls, and what they would be missing.

One particular Friday, the wind was blowing gale force, with no prospect of it abating, night leave had been piped, and after our evening meal most of us would be making for the Cavendish Hotel. Friday nights were always special, and looked forward to by all, we would have money in our pockets, and so would the girls. Not that we ever took advantage of that, nevertheless, having money of their own made them a little independent, they could pay their own admission fee, and those that were without partners could even buy their own drinks, not that many ever had to.

The bars, all of them, were already full, Navy lads, RAF lads and lasses, soldiers, they were all there on Fridays. It was the big night. The dance hall was open, with plenty of would-be dancers standing around in groups, the dance band was practising a few bars to warm up, but there was no sign of the dance beginning.

The four of us entered the hall, after collecting drinks from the bar, so, like everyone else, we just stood at the edge of the floor waiting. We watched with curiosity the activities of Mr Eaton, the proprietor, who was walking round the hall talking to every man present, until eventually he reached us. Then we were told that the MC had not arrived, and possibly would not be able to, and without him, Mr Eaton could not allow the dance to go on. He then asked if one of us would volunteer. Apparently he had asked just about everyone else and we were his last hope. 'Yes,' said my so-called shipmates, 'Jack will do it,' and gave me a quick push forward. At first I angrily said, 'No', but gave in when Mr Eaton said that he would have to cancel the dance.

In return for my efforts, and I made it plain that this would be my first attempt, Mr Eaton would pay me the sum of five shillings, plus two free pints of beer; this made me feel really wealthy, and on top of the world.

The duties of an MC were not difficult, and I soon began to enjoy myself; the dance then began to go with a real swing.

To my surprise I found sudden popularity with everyone; as a dancing partner I was in constant demand, and so were my shipmates, they were benefiting from being with me. The dance was a huge success, and Mr Eaton was overjoyed. He came to me with a proposition: every time our boat was in Felixstowe, he would be very much obliged if I would come along and be his MC again, he even offered to increased the five shillings, he never actually said what to, and add an extra pint of beer. No doubt I would have taken advantage of his offer, but it was just our luck that this evening was going to be our last at Felixstowe, and we would be on our way to Great Yarmouth, as because of weather conditions there would be a temporary suspension of our espionage activities.

The Cavendish Hotel was still in existence right until the 1980s. Mr Eaton's son Russell was the proprietor, and I was able to stay there, enjoying excellent food, drink and company; the two barmaids however, were no longer there.

That winter of 1941–2 was probably the worst one of the war, weatherwise. While we were at Felixstowe, it was so cold one night that the sea froze over in the harbour and the seventy-foot boats had to break the ice so they could proceed to sea. The ice stopped us totally from going to sea, but the other boats had to go out on an emergency call.

We returned to Great Yarmouth, as soon as the weather permitted, but the base was not the same as it was when we left; it was no longer the 'free and easy' establishment we had known.

At this period in time, radar, RDF as it was then known, was still in its infancy. The equipment was large, and took up a great deal of space; consequently until now it had only been put into 'big ships' and bases. We were then ahead of the Germans with radar, and foresaw with greater vision its potential. Then our scientists produced a version small enough to be added to Coastal Forces craft. Our *Lucky Lady* was to be the first boat to have it, at first on trial, but it soon became an established part of our equipment, and put to very good use.

At first the operation of it was down to our 'Sparks', the wireless operator; the Navy had been training operators for radar for some time, but none were available yet for our boats. Our telegraphist had to undertake a crash course in operating the set, getting extra pay for doing so. He quickly mastered the technique, returned aboard, and tests and trials were then under way. Sparks never complained about the extra work and responsibility but perhaps the extra pay had something to do with that. Personally I prefer to think that it was down to his devotion to duty.

The other boats in our flotilla were glad to see us back, though there were still sarcastic remarks made about the incident with 326; it had not been forgotten. Everyone agreed that 320 had been exceptionally lucky so far, and it was living up to the name of *Lucky Lady*, and we all felt that with that reputation we did not have much to worry about. Such is a sailor's faith in his ship, in our case, his boat. Sharkey Ward, our cox'n, was particularly happy about the name. The 320 was his pride and joy, it was as if he were married to it; it was more than a boat to him, it was his life, his world.

As security had been tightened at the base, so had discipline in general. Before, we had been allowed to go into town dressed in our white submarine sweaters, and wearing sea-boots (Wellingtons); now any visit into town meant wearing full uniform. This did not go down very well, but it was something that we had to get used to. It applied to everyone, our boats, minesweepers and all. Once, we had a surprise visit from a submarine, but they stayed no longer than a few hours, then left, never to return. It was never known why the submarine visited Yarmouth on that occasion but the crew walked around the town dressed as they would normally, in white submarine sweaters and sea-boots. If there was a reprimand given then it was safe to assume that was why their visit was so short. There must have been some red faces at the Coastal Forces offices when they learnt the submariners had been walking around dressed in the way we were forbidden to.

Because of the great rise and fall of the tide on the river Yare, all boats had to have sentries on duty at night, primarily to watch the mooring ropes, to tighten or slacken as necessary; during the day this was carried out as part of normal duties, so an actual sentry was not necessary. The Base Commander decided however that all boats' crews should share sentry duties at the various entrances to the base. This led to disagreements all round, and our Skipper said, 'No.' He regarded this as being unfair to the crews, who, after a hard night at sea should not be expected to stand guard as sentries immediately they returned to harbour, and therefore he would not allow us to take part. It is understood that an exchange of words between the two officers became quite heated, and played a part in Peter Loasby being relieved of his command, and being posted to the Admiralty as a Communications officer. This could well have been true, but it must be taken into consideration that Lieutenant Loasby was highly qualified in communications and valued as such by Lord Louis himself.

Peter Loasby's crew regarded what happened with considerable anger and dismay; he was a good, efficient, capable officer and to lose him in this way was nothing short of pettiness and stupidity, and that view was shared by many others. However, he had made his point, and we were not forced to take part in sentry duties on shore.

Something else happened to add fuel to the fires of our anger. Someone, believed to have been possibly an enemy agent, spread the story around that German E-boats crews did not have to live on board their boats when in harbour; the story went on to state that they only manned their craft when going to sea while all cleaning and maintenance work was carried out by base staff. In this way it was guaranteed that boat crews were always fresh, relaxed and in tip-top condition. Whereas we would return to harbour, possibly exhausted, then have to carry out cleaning and maintenance work before going to our bunks, sometimes only having a few hours sleep before setting out to sea again.

Attempts were made to suppress the story, but it was too late, and it all made sense to us. We believed it to be true and to some extent the story made us feel disgruntled, especially happening as it did on top of the sentry fiasco, until someone bright pointed out that we would have more confidence in our equipment etc., when having personally maintained it. This was very true, and evident by the high standards that crews kept when looking after their guns or engines. We also knew that the E-boats experienced break-downs just as we did, so if the rumour were true, it never made the E-boats any more efficient than us. Speaking for gunners, we had more confidence in guns we had looked after ourselves, and when and if we experienced a breakdown, we were competent to deal with it. Mind you, we would have liked to have been pampered a little.

The increase in discipline at the base also meant that each flotilla had to appoint one of its officers as the 'flotilla gunnery officer'; he was supposed to be responsible for everything connected with guns, guns crews, ammunition, and supply aboard all the boats in the flotilla. In theory it was not such a bad idea; it only fell down when the officer concerned was resented as an 'interfering big head', because he came from another boat and not your own.

In our flotilla the officer appointed as gunnery officer was the Captain of another boat. He was well liked by his own crew and his fellow flotilla officers, but not everything can be perfect, and unfortunately he and I simply did not get on. It was as simple as that, and it happens all the time; often it begins without apparent reason, men meet and their dislike is mutual, they do not even have to speak to each other, the instinct is already there, and that was how it was for us. Although probably not true, he seemed to seek me out, to find fault with anything that I did. There was nothing that I could do about it, except to do my best to keep out of his sight, which I managed fairly well considering.

The story about the German crews' welfare was circulating about the same time as the flotilla gunnery officers were appointed. One morning this officer came aboard, immediately we had arrived alongside the jetty, after a night at sea, when we were bitterly cold and tired and my fingers were actually frozen. We had made our guns safe, but needed rest before being able to concentrate on maintaining anything, but His Eminence would not allow this, not at all; after a good dressing down from him, we had to strip and clean our guns before we could do anything else at all. My face clearly showed my anger and frustration, so he described my attitude as 'insolent', and reported me to our Captain, who gave me a simple rebuke and left it at that. Despite our condition, the guns were thoroughly cleaned etc., but I cannot help thinking that there must have been many instances when because of the tiredness something would be overlooked or even not done properly, and a life or even lives could be lost because of it, whereas, after a little rest it could have been done thoroughly to everyone's satisfaction. During the rest of my days in Coastal Forces, no other officer ever brought out this reaction in me, and certainly none ever called me insolent.

Christmas came, and weather conditions allowed us to have leave granted. Except for a few volunteers, leave was granted to the whole crew; the volunteers would take their leave when the rest of us returned.

Len Downs and I travelled together to London. When we parted at Liverpool Street station, he was going on to north London and I to the south-eastern part but we made arrangements to spend at least one evening together, with his wife as well. In any case, we had to meet in order to split our rum supply again. We chose the Lyceum Ballroom, at Covent Garden, as the best place to meet, which we did on the following evening. I found

Len's wife to be a delightful person, attractive, and very good company, she was also a very good dancer. She was prepared to share her dances between Len and myself, but I would not allow this, and enjoyed watching the two of them much more than any dancing that I did with other girls. This was not much, as practically everyone there came with partners.

Various visits were made to uncles living within reasonable distance of home. It was understandable that they would want to hear stories of my life in the Navy but they could only hear part. Because of our espionage exploits we had been sworn to secrecy; to my mind this did not leave much to talk about, but I was given to understand that they were quite happy with what I could tell them.

Of course my thoughts would often turn to one person in particular, but although being in the Navy had done a great deal for my self-confidence, I could not bring myself to call at her home. I thought, mistakenly perhaps, that it would be wrong to cultivate her friendship when there was the possibility that I might not survive the war. I also knew that there was every chance that she had a 'beau'; I had been out of touch with life in Catford, and it could well be another case of 'out of sight and out of mind', and in the past on the occasions we met, I had not declared my hopes and intentions.

Very quickly the day came to return aboard the *Lucky Lady*. As there was still considerable rum left, I told my mother that when the weather was very cold, she could give my sister's husband some, to warm him up. This she did, and whether his visits increased by coincidence I never knew, but another supply would be necessary before my next leave.

By arrangement, Len met me at Liverpool Street station. This time his wife was there to see him off; she fought hard to stem the flow of tears, but could not hide them all. I thought at the time that had I not been there, there would have been a real deluge. I was glad in a way that nobody was there to see me off, as any similar demonstration would have had me in tears as well.

The train was almost full, but we were lucky enough to be able to find seats. Conversation in those travelling conditions was very difficult, so we slept most of the journey. After changing trains at Norwich, we arrived at Great Yarmouth in no better condition than when we went on leave. Although the railway station was within comfortable walking distance, there was a lorry waiting to take us to the base, supposedly another example of the way in which the base had altered. I do not think for one moment the transport was out of consideration for our welfare, more likely it helped the Transport Officer to justify his position.

Weather conditions were still bad, much too bad for our boats to put to sea. In an unpatriotic way, we considered this to be too good to be true, yet deep down inside us all, our feelings for our country were so strong that we would have put to sea with the Devil himself had it been necessary. It was understood that where the weather was concerned we were beaten every time. Old Mother Nature did what she wanted when she wanted, and she did not give a damn for the war, but when it was a straight-forward case of going out to fight the enemy, nobody dared try to stop us.

When at sea, the crews of motor torpedo boats, and those on motor gunboats often appeared to spend more time wet and under water than submariners. It was a frequent experience to find that not only were we soaked to the skin while on duty, but when we came off duty and went below decks, we would find that every-thing would be saturated by sea water. Our bedding, and all our clothes would be soaking wet, not a dry piece anywhere; there would be no alternative but to remain wet and bloody miserable for the duration of the patrol. We could only remedy this when we returned to base, where there were drying facilities for all boats' crews. There was, however, one thing that we often did, with the permission of the motor mechanic: we could hang our clothes in his engine-room, where the heat of the engines would dry some of them.

A signal was received by our Captain, to make the necessary arrangements for ordinary seaman Allen to leave us, to go for an officers' training course; he was to leave right away. 'Darby' Allen was an extremely nice person, rather on the quiet side, softly spoken, but would help anyone if needed. His relief was on his way, another ordinary seaman, like Darby, from London, but that was where any similarity ended. The relief, known to all his friends as 'the Duke' Dewey, came from the Lambeth Walk area of London; he was the genuine article, a big, warm hearted Cockney, who very quickly became liked by us all.

That afternoon the sirens were sounded, and enemy aircraft were reported to be heading for Yarmouth. All guns ashore and afloat were manned and ready for action. We waited; there was not a sign of any aircraft, friend or foe, but we had to remain 'closed up' at our guns until the all clear was heard, almost two hours later. Slightly relieved, but also disappointed, we all resumed our ordinary duties. The joke then went around that the enemy turned back because they did not know what rotten marksmen we were. It must be stressed that the remark was totally untrue.

## CHAPTER 8

# The entrepreneurs of the
# Lucky Lady, our stokers

A RARE sight was to see stokers on the upper deck at any time. They always seemed to have a natural aversion to fresh air, perhaps it was just as well in view of the work they had to do. Fortunately most stokers enjoyed their work, which no doubt helped them to cope with what were, in my opinion, unpleasant and unhealthy conditions.

On this particular afternoon all three of our stokers were deep in earnest conversation together on the upper deck. Something, I said to myself, is up, but what? As I came into their sight, they beckoned me over to them. A rather prickly sensation at the back of my neck suggested that there might be trouble in the offing: a kind of foreboding.

There was a surprise in store for me, but unbelievably it was not an unpleasant one at all. It was totally unexpected, but we had been together now aboard the 320 for some time, and I both liked and trusted all three men. They were all older than I was, so enjoyed higher rates of pay, but, as most of our servicemen did, they were always looking out for suitable opportunities to make some more. It seemed, according to them, that I was going to make their fortunes for them.

It was our visit to Felixstowe, and my being MC at the Cavendish Hotel dance, that had given them the idea. They intended to hire a hall and a dance-band, and I was to be their

Master of Ceremonies at these dances. It all depended now on my decision. They would do all the financing and arrangements necessary; they realised that I was unable to chip in on the expenses, but they would pay me ten shillings each time I officiated for them, plus a few drinks, and the three of them would share any profits made. Not being of a mercenary nature I readily agreed. In any case, the ten shillings made it worth my while. Pleasant memories of the Cavendish were still with me. It was odds against me returning to Felixstowe, but I could envisage something similar taking place here at Yarmouth.

It was going to be a big gamble, the lads knew this; what if everything was arranged and paid for and we had to go to sea? Jeff and Stan were confident that they would be able to arrange for someone to take over if this happened, but at this time of the year, the weather should prove a valuable asset in favour of their venture. Jeff had one answer to any doubts: 'Start praying, and keep on until the dance is over.' He refused even to contemplate losing his money; always an optimist was our Jeffrey.

It was not only we who were on tenterhooks, it seemed that every sailor in Great Yarmouth was. Most wanted our dance to be a success; a few were hoping for a failure, but they were only a tiny minority. The three girls: the Waafs and their Wren friend Geraldine from Chingford in Essex, were all enthusiastic about the dance; they notified all the other Waafs, and Geraldine even persuaded some of the Wrens to attend. What was even better was the fact that they even sold tickets in advance. Although the number of tickets sold in advance was not great, it helped to boost our confidence. The hall was booked at the Goodes Hotel; posters were put up around the base and wherever possible in town; the band, a Royal Air Force dance-band, was hired, tickets printed and already in circulation; so it would be all systems go when Friday night came around. In those days we were not able to get advance weather forecasts, so everything now depended on how the day dawned.

The great day arrived. Friday at the Goodes Hotel was 'Jolly Jack Night'. The decision to call it that was Jeff's; he reckoned that I would be the Jolly Jack, my name being what it was. They all agreed that it had a happy, jolly sound to it, and if the first dance was a success, Jolly Jack Nights would become nights to look forward to. I was beginning to get a little concerned, and wondered if their faith in me was going to be justified. I need not have worried. Jeff and Stan drifted around the hall and bars, ready to act as bouncers if the need arose; fortunately it did not. Although the dance was packed, there were many more than should have been, everyone was happy, and friendly, and there was only the odd drunk, who was quickly encouraged to leave. Len had the task of selling tickets at the door, and once he was sure that they were well in profit, he would slip me an extra ten shillings.

Jolly Jack Night was here to stay, so it seemed. My friends were happy with their profit, my reputation as an MC was established, and with this came an increase in popularity with the girls who came to dance. I was loving every minute of it all. It appeared to be the thing to do to dance with the MC; I was expected to dance with every girl that asked, and when the band struck up for a fresh dance I was expected to lead the floor. All this practice helped to improve my dancing, but I was never going to reach the same standard as Jeff.

The next day the four of us sat down for a serious discussion. The decision was that we should hold Jolly Jack nights once a fortnight, on Fridays, in for a penny, in for a pound. All three wanted to take the gamble. It was not up to me, it was their money, and their risk; they were going to increase my ten shillings to one pound, so I was well content. There was going to be a trial period agreed with the hotel proprietor. As the weather was expected to have improved by then, the future of our dances would then be entirely dependent upon Fate, but Jeff was even optimistic that far ahead.

Arrangements were agreed with the dance-band. They had in their own way enjoyed our dance so much that they would have been very disappointed had we not organised more. I believe if my memory serves me well that their band was named 'The Spitfires'; we knew how good the planes were, and we were of the opinion that in the world of music, our band was equally good.

We thought it would be impossible, but somehow it must have been the influence of the *Lucky Lady*; some of her luck was rubbing off onto us. Irrespective of weather conditions, the 320 never went to sea upon 'Jolly Jack Nights'. Even now, looking back, it is unbelievable, but true. Of course in winter the North Sea is never the best place to be, and in our case Fate never let us down. Sometimes the weather was in our favour, sometimes we had been to sea the night before, or we were on stand-by. Stand-by was the biggest gamble: leave was allowed, but we could be recalled in an emergency at any time, so this could spoil a dance if it happened, but it never did. The stokers were making money, I made a little with my MC's fee and what Len slipped me on the side, but more than anything else the important thing was that life had become very enjoyable for me.

The fact that we never went to sea on our dance nights did not go unnoticed. There were many stories in circulation about how we were able to manage it. Some were openly accusing, even to the extent of accusing our Skipper of collaborating with us. This of course was absolutely ridiculous: Peter Loasby was too honourable an officer for anything like that; he also had his future to consider, as the Royal Navy was his career. Many years after the war had finished I met Captain Peter Loasby and his wife Rosemary. Peter and I discussed those dances, our luck, and the rumours that grew around the fact that we never went to sea on dance nights. Peter laughed at my obvious discomfort, and assured me that he knew about the rumours at the time. He considered making us cancel them, but decided against this sort of action, it might have fuelled the fire, but they were unfounded and totally untrue. He made it quite plain, that had the 320 been called to sea, or if for any other reason leave was refused, the dances would not have been considered at all, and most definitely he would not have involved himself in our activities. I was aware of this but such a run of good luck was still unbelievable to me; I had to broach the subject, and am very glad that I did. I had the pleasure of getting to know Peter and Rosemary very well, and Peter insisted that I stopped referring to him as either 'sir' or 'Captain'. 'Jack,' he said, 'we are both civilians now. Please, in future, I am Peter to you, and I hope you will not mind my calling you Jack.' I cherished those kind words greatly.

So far as Len Downs and I were concerned, we spent most of our evenings ashore either at one of the dances or in the saloon bar at the Goodes Hotel where Tessie Barwick was in charge. Tess always had a smile of welcome for us, and when we held our dances she would bring her daughter Vera, whom she always kept a very watchful eye over. Rightly or wrongly, it depends upon whose view, Tessie trusted us with her daughter; perhaps some hidden instinct told her that Vera, young and pretty as she was, was not interested in Len or myself anyway.

'Home is where the heart is', is a popular saying that is, even today, prominently displayed in many homes; to us aboard the 320 the *Lucky Lady* was home now to us, she was much more than just another wooden 'man 'o war'.

Jolly Jack Night had now become an established event in Great Yarmouth, not least by the proprietor of Goodes Hotel, who had a packed ballroom on those Fridays, and very full bars too. The other members of our crew were most co-operative. If we had to ask for favours in connection with the dances, they were rarely refused; there was never any sign of resentment or envy, and we all shared the same feelings about the 320. She was now the *Lucky Lady*, and we were all confident that her luck was to our benefit.

Together, Bob Goodfellow and Sharkey Ward did a good job of blending our crew together. We were a very mixed bunch of men, from various walks of life. I have already described those I knew best, but the remainder were no less important. The eldest was Vic Copeland, my opposite number of the .5 machine-guns. He lived then at Southend-on-Sea. When Dunkirk was imminent Vic and his father sailed their small pleasure-boat across the Channel to help with the evacuation. Vic was an excellent seaman and a very competent machine-gunner. He was married and had a family and probably because of his family obligations he much preferred his own company, and enjoyed a quiet pint on his own somewhere, where he could sit and smoke his pipe. Vic died I believe in the seventies, just before I tried to make contact with him.

Our most effective weapon was the two-pounder pom-pom mounted on our fo'c'sle. In charge of it was able seaman 'Taff' Johnson, his home was at Milford Haven in South Wales. Taff had joined the Navy before the war began and so he was more experienced at getting out of trouble than the rest of us; when the more menial tasks were being given out, Taff managed to be elsewhere. Reluctantly he would advise us youngsters on the devious ways of able seamen, but made sure that no blame could be attached to him.

Taff was also a very patient person. Someone made a bet with him that he could not catch a seagull. To win that bet he spent hours upon our fo'c'sle, near his gun, with a piece of string, and it did not take him long to catch a gull. As soon as he found someone to verify his catch, he let the bird go, none the worse for its experience.

Mounted upon our stern was a strange looking gun. This was our Rolls-Royce two-pounder. It fired the same shells as the pom-pom and, as with all Rolls-Royce products, it was a masterpiece of British engineering. It was extremely accurate and unlike any other gun that I knew of its shells when fired had no trajectory. After a few useful years' service it was phased out of use aboard Naval craft, because the salt in sea spray caused the gun to jam too easily, so fine was the engineering workmanship. This gun was the responsibility of able seaman Ted 'Monty' Mortimer, whose home was at Manchester. Monty was very conscientious in everything he did, he neither smoked nor used bad language, and drank very little. He lived for his music, and was passionately fond of Glenn Miller. To Monty there was nothing else in the world that compared with the famous Glenn Miller sound, and I was in complete agreement.

There were four other seamen. Able seaman Ernie Nunn, from Ware in Hertfordshire, was our torpedo man, although we never carried any. He looked after our depth charges and electrical equipment. He also acted as steward to our officers, and for a while he was the boat's cook, and was quite good. In fact Ernie was a useful chap to have on board. Then there was Ken Ross, an able seaman from Leicester, but the special character on board us was ordinary seaman Ted Millington; his home was in Nottingham. Ted was a very sincere and genuine person, and his sincerity regarding Nottingham was one hundred per cent, including the legend of Robin Hood. His fervent upholding of the legend made him the butt of much leg-pulling, especially by Jeff Goodey who loved to get Ted going, relentlessly attacking the character of Robin Hood, who was quickly reduced to 'Robbing So-and-so', although 'so-and-so' were not exactly the words chosen at the time.

The teasing of Ted would go on until his patience ran out, or until the cox'n intervened. It was a shame that he was teased so much, but unfortunately this is bound to happen when a group of men live together in confined spaces such as we were subjected to. Ted was a good worker, and a willing one. Later when made able seaman and if drafted to another boat he might have escaped further teasing.

Our RDF operator was Bill Jarrett from Bristol. He fitted in quite well with us all but was a more serious type of person than the rest of us. His closest friend was our telegraphist who was of a similar disposition.

John Standley was our telegraphist, our 'intelligencier'. John knew everything that went on, he handled all signals both incoming and outgoing, he was often in the position of knowing something before our Captain did but, like most members of his branch, he knew when to keep a still tongue in his head.

There were two other members of our crew, one I regret escapes my memory completely. The other was a man from Liverpool, not one of our original crew; he joined us at a later date. He was something of a mystery, always cheerful, but most of us felt uneasy in his company. He was the cause of an unpleasant incident that affected the entire crew, officers as well.

On one occasion when weekend leave had been granted, I arrived home to find my mother in a very agitated frame of mind. She had recently been visited by the local police. Armed with a search warrant they had searched our home from top to bottom. Once they were satisfied that there was nothing there, they told my mother that a service revolver, belonging to our Captain, was missing from the boat; they apologised for inconveniencing her and left.

Of course I had nothing to do with the theft, and had a clear conscience, but there had been Navy rum at home, and my spare white submarine sweater. The latter was there legitimately but, like most mothers, mine wondered if I was entitled to bring it home. The police in this instance were kindly and courteous, they had seen these things but were not concerned; they were looking for a revolver and nothing else was of consequence.

The homes of the entire crew with the exception of the Captain were searched, nothing was ever found, and the incident died a natural death in due course. Three years later, in Italy, I met Taff

Johnson again, and the subject of the revolver came into our conversation. He disclosed that he knew who had taken it, although not at the time. It was the one who had been most suspected, but against whom nothing could be proved. Taff never said how he knew, so I can only think that the certain somebody told him himself.

By this time Duke Dewey had settled in well. He kept everyone amused with his stories of life in and around the Lambeth Walk, his exploits with the girls in that area were uncountable. Perhaps they were not all completely true, but he made them sound as though they were. There was one girl in particular: she was, he boasted, the best dancing partner ever. He suggested, because of our dance exploits, that I should take Eileen dancing when next on leave, he would fix things up for me, he said. After seeing a photograph of Eileen I was keen, so the Duke accordingly made arrangements for me to meet her during my next weekend leave. The Duke was on duty that weekend, so there was no hope of him being able to introduce us in person. So, dressed in my best No 1's, I set off for Eileen's address, where she was waiting for me. We then took a taxi to the Hammersmith Palais de Dance. For some reason she would not go to the Lyceum; I suspect that there might have been someone there she preferred not to see her with me. It did not matter.

We had a very enjoyable evening, I could not say otherwise. She was an excellent dancer, never put a foot wrong, I could not have wished for a better partner, but the atmosphere was wrong; we did not 'click', I can explain it no other way. Eileen seemed to know everyone there, she was obviously a popular girl, and I of course knew nobody there at all, I could not really say that I knew the girl I was with. Truthfully I was relieved when the dance ended, a feeling completely alien to me. A taxi took us to her home and we said 'goodbye', then I caught the next train home to Catford, resolving never to do that kind of thing again. Eileen was very nice though.

Partly owing to that unfortunate experience the weekend went far too quickly, and Monday morning I was on my way back to Great Yarmouth and the *Lucky Lady*.

The weather was normal for the time of year, so we knew that there would not be any espionage trips in the offing. Any attempt even to make the journey across the North Sea would be impossible, so it meant a return to anti-E-boat patrols, along with the rest of our flotilla.

*Winter, 1941, patrolling 'E-boat Alley' in the North Sea. HMMGB 320. AB Vic Copeland in starboard .5 turret; me in the port turret; AB Millington in foreground, with AB 'Monty' Mortimer on Rolls-Royce gun aft.*

It was normal practice for us to leave harbour at dusk, and return soon after dawn, unless there was still enemy activity at the time, but mostly the E-boats returned to their bases by dawn as well, because it was too dangerous for them to operate in daylight, as then they became perfect targets for our destroyers, apart from obvious conflict with our boats.

Sometimes when we looked back at our patrols, they appeared to have had negative results. Hours had been spent at sea, sometimes in atrocious conditions, with no sight of the enemy, perhaps not even a friendly greeting from one of our own ships. In reality this was not so, the patrols more than served their purpose. Our mere presence was often more than enough to deter any attack, and because of our superior armament the E-boats were not keen to indulge in open conflict as it seemed we were. Consequently once it was known that we were patrolling in a certain area, and they had means of knowing this, they would keep well away.

In bad weather of course, like us, they would be 'harbour bound', probably enjoying shore leave in much the same way as we did. I wonder if they had 'Jolly Jack Nights' too?

Usually, when out on sea patrol, life was much the same for each trip; a routine would be adhered to, so we knew what to expect, unless the enemy interfered with our peace and quiet.

My own little world consisted of two-hour watches between the hours of 1600 and 2000 hrs, and then four-hour watches after, until we returned to harbour. Seated in my machine-gun turret on the port side of the 320 constituted my be all and end all; there was not much room inside that turret, and apart from being on the lookout all the time, all I could do to break the monotony was to operate the hydraulic system and move the turret around, and my guns up and down; nevertheless, my guns and turret were my pride and joy.

The roar of our engines made conversation upon the upper deck difficult at any time, but when under way it was downright impossible. After being at sea for several hours, during the hours of midnight and four a.m., keeping awake would often be a problem; at these times I would be shouting the words of popular songs to keep awake mistakenly thinking I was singing them. In this way I learnt the words of all the popular songs of the time; what a pity I could not sing!

Sitting in that turret also gave me plenty of time for thought. I could mull over my deeds of the past, the present, and possibly the future; there would be things I would regret and things I was pleased about and sitting alone in that turret could have helped improve me in some ways; whether it did or not I never knew. Naturally my thoughts turned mostly to home, and my family. I wondered about my brother and what had really happened when his ship was torpedoed. I would think about all the friends that I had grown up with and went to school with, where were they now? Then my thoughts were dominated by one girl in particular, where was she? What would she be doing? I did not wonder this during the early hours of the morning of course, but on watch before midnight I would. I would wonder if I was ever going to see her again, and many times I would make plans to try to see her when next on leave, but something always happened to prevent my doing so.

Before joining the Navy I was very finicky where food was concerned; you could even say that I was spoilt, and you would be right, but every mother has the right to spoil her children when at home and, not being from a prosperous background, mostly our choice of food had been very basic. One of my dislikes was soup, there was no way in which I could be encouraged to have it, so my mother stopped trying to persuade me. Out in the middle of the North Sea, when cold, wet and miserable, sitting in my turret, the voice of Ernie Nunn would sound in my ear, and a mug of hot, steaming soup be thrust into my hands. It was a Godsend. I drank it with the utmost gratitude and pleasure, and from then on

I became a devotee of soups in general. When we returned to harbour, Jeff Goodey and Ernie started up a stock pot which was added to daily, and was one of the most enjoyable soups I ever tasted. Naturally it was chockful of nourishment, so it did us the world of good. It was a little difficult to keep going at sea, but somehow Ernie managed it with Jeff's help.

At the outbreak of hostilities blackout conditions were enforced throughout the British Isles. Everything was also removed that would identify the area or help the enemy should they attempt a landing on our shores, particularly signposts. It was also possible that they could have been a valuable assistance to any spies that were landed. There was one thing that puzzled most of us that sailed from Yarmouth: right at the very top of Goodes Hotel was a large gold coloured sphere, and when out at sea this ball could be seen from miles away, plainly. In fact when the sun shone this ball literally lit up; it especially looked beautiful to us when returning from a patrol. One would have thought that the authorities would have insisted that the ball be painted over, possibly with black paint, because if we appreciated the sight of it, informing us that we were within sight of Yarmouth, then it would have served the same purpose for the enemy. This ball was still there, still shining in the sunlight, many years after the war. Now it did more than act as a landmark; it served to remind many that beneath it was where so many service men and women enjoyed themselves during a bitter war against Nazi tyranny; and for many it would have been a last fling before the expected invasion of Europe.

When we were not at sea and money was in short supply, as it so often was, passing the time became a problem. Our boat's radio would be tuned in to BBC programmes as often as possible, but when our telegraphist was ashore on leave himself, this became a real problem, because nobody else was allowed to interfere with the ship's radio and quite rightly so. At this time, Vera Lynn was delighting us all with her singing and Anne Shelton too. The

American band leader Glenn Miller had now reached the pinnacle of his success, and we had our own big bands: Joe Loss, Henry Hall and Jack Payne, to name but a few. Music to the service-folk meant everything, and the entertainment world was determined to give it to them. One day, when discussing the world of music in the mess, we came to the conclusion that what was missing was a gramophone. If we had one, Monty would take charge of it, and bring some of his own records from home.

After a lengthy discussion, it was left to me to obtain a gramophone from somewhere, so I decided that I would try an appeal to the readers of a newspaper, who might just have one somewhere that was not wanted. I chose the *Kentish Mercury*, a very fine local newspaper that covered a large part of south-east London, where my home was. The editor responded magnificently and they printed my letter in full, in their very next edition. To their amazement as well as my own, they were flooded with offers to give us a gramophone.

The editor wrote to me immediately, and suggested that I call to see him at his office when I was next on leave, and between us we would decide which offer would be accepted. This would be the difficult part as the editor had to make certain that none of his readers would be offended if their offer was not accepted; after all, he had to keep an eye upon his paper's circulation figures, even though there was a war on.

It was arranged that the very next weekend, depending on weather conditions of course, I would have leave, whether I was entitled to or not; the subject had been discussed with the cox'n, who had informed our officers what was happening, and they were in full agreement. Luck was with us as usual, gales were blowing and there was no chance of any of our boats putting to sea that weekend, so off I set for London, my home, and the offices of the *Kentish Mercury*.

Upon the Saturday morning I duly called at the *Kentish Mercury* offices, which were then situated right on the border of Greenwich and Deptford. Without delay I was ushered into the editor's office, where I was shown the huge pile of offers that had been received from their readers. They were all put into a large cardboard box, and I had to pick one letter out. It was from a very nice family at Sandrock Road, Lewisham. The letter allowed someone to call almost at any time, so the editor made a 'phone call to them, and we set off in his car to the house.

Our visit to Sandrock Road was a short but pleasant one. It had been the young daughter's idea to give the gramophone, and her parents had readily agreed. After taking tea with them, they handed over the machine; the editor first drove me back to his office, and then to my home. During the journey home, we discussed what should be done with all the other offers. He explained that any decision must be partly mine, as all the offers were in response to my appeal. It was an easy one: an advertisement was put in his newspaper, offering gramophones to service units that were pre-pared to collect. I thanked everybody on behalf of the lads aboard the 320, and assured them that our machine would be put to very good use. It most certainly was.

Carrying the gramophone from Catford to Great Yarmouth via public transport was not the most comfortable of tasks, but it was a very proud moment for me when I finally struggled on board with it.

That gramophone remained the proud possession of 320 for years to come. It was not only enjoyed, it was treated with the greatest possible reverence and when we prepared to put to sea, the safety of the gramophone was of paramount importance. It was wrapped in waterproof coverings, and placed somewhere where it could not fall; that became Monty's job, and one he was only too happy to do.

There was one occasion however, when the machine was not molly-coddled. It was the very first patrol we were going on after receiving it when we thought how nice it would be, and how stirring it would sound, if we played a Glenn Miller record over our outside broadcasting system, the sort of thing that one saw happen on cinema screens. The Captain gave his permission and we sailed down the River Yare to the strains of Glenn Miller's orchestra playing 'Stage Coach'. It really was stirring and we all felt good as we listened to it and watched the people ashore, on both sides of the river, as they heard us sail by.

The crews from other boats in harbour all came onto their upper decks to see us on our way, and to give us a few cheers as well. What with our dances, and now this, I half expected someone from Equity to come aboard and demand to see our trade union membership cards.

Almost sadly – I say 'almost' because we knew the Captain was right when we thought about it – this was the only time that music was played over the broadcasting system. It was realised that playing it on these occasions would give the enemy vital information about our activities and operations. So Peter Loasby imposed a ban immediately, and instructed that in future gramophone renderings of any music whatsoever would be kept for our mess-deck only. Thankfully he had been amused by it all, and after the patrol, when making his report to the base, he successfully covered for us, and there was no trouble.

We were disappointed and disgruntled at first about the ban, but we could see that it was sensible, because along the southern bank of the river Yare ran the main road to Lowestoft. In many places the public could stand and watch our boats setting out to sea; any enemy agent could watch, and they probably did.

Life carried on much as usual with routine patrols, and I kept out of the way of our gunnery officer so successfully that he really had to make an effort to find me before he was able to criticise me. He probably could have found me quite easily, and it just may be possible that he could see a funny side to it all, and consequently did not put himself out too much. However, with the assistance of Taff Johnson, and co-operation from the others, I managed to keep out of trouble.

HMS *Midge*, now always referred to by name, was steadily growing larger. More boats were being based there, which meant more men and women, and more boats also meant more civilian maintenance staff. It also meant increased measures of discipline, because of higher ranking officers being appointed to the base, and this was going to put a damper upon our spirits.

# The Mess-deck Dodger

We were the mess-deck dodgers
Out on the MTBs
We never scrubbed the paintwork
or got upon our knees,
After we had our tot of rum,
Our work for the day
Was over and done,
We were the mess-deck dodgers,
Who cleaned the MTBs.

(Could be sung to the tune of 'Lilli Marlene'.)

JWD

The title of 'Mess-deck Dodger' was affectionately, sometimes sarcastically, bestowed upon the man made responsible for keeping the crew's living quarters known as the mess-deck, clean and tidy.

While in harbour he was excused all other duties, making it a much sought after job. It was usually given to the older and probably more conscientious able seaman.

# CHAPTER 9

## *Situations, like things, prove nothing is for ever*

THE disagreement that arose between our Captain and the base Commander over the 'sentry duties' for boat's crews, was never obvious enough to cause comment from us. In fact nothing was really known or even suspected until one day we learnt that Peter Loasby was leaving us and that another officer would be appointed in his place. It seemed that a reprimand had been given after the row had taken place, but the other officer concerned was not prepared to let it rest at that, and the story going around suggested that the other officer, being senior in rank, did all he could to make sure that our Captain was not going to remain in command of the 320 or the 12th Motor Gunboat flotilla, and so would be drafted away from Great Yarmouth.

Peter Loasby eventually retired from the Navy in the 1970s, as a senior captain RN. In my own opinion he should have retired as an admiral, and why he did not was probably because of the incident referred to. After leaving us, Lieutenant Loasby RN joined the Admiralty in London as a signals and communications officer.

A new Captain was appointed to the 320, a Lieutenant Hughes RNVR, and so we returned to normal patrols and duties, not quite as though nothing had happened. We knew that we had lost someone who had been prepared to stick up for us if the cause was just. This new officer, however, was understanding, and did

*Captain Peter Loasby RN retiring from the command of HMS* London, *in London, alongside HMS* Belfast, *1973.*

not push us too hard, as with that old saying that 'a new broom always sweeps clean', it was natural that there would be changes, so we were prepared for the worst. In truth, the worst never came; Peter Loasby had left a good, clean, efficient and, what is most important, a very happy boat; there was also Bob Goodfellow to take into consideration, the whole crew liked him, and would have happily joined another boat so as to remain with him.

On the day before Peter Loasby left us, he 'cleared lower deck', which is the Navy's way of saying that he called us all together, to say his goodbyes. He thanked us all, and expressed his regret at having to leave us. He had done a very good job with us; we were now far from resembling the new bunch of assorted men who first joined the 320 at Littlehampton. Although the two men that were in direct contact with us all the time, Bob Goodfellow and Sharkey Ward, did the actual shaping of our characters, on all boats, our conversion had to start at the top, and for us it was Peter Loasby who had been there.

As our assembled crew began to disperse after our Captain's speech, he instructed the two other ordinary seamen and myself, who had been with him when the 320 was first commissioned, to report to him upon the bridge. There he carried out his last duty as our skipper and confirmed all three of us as being able seamen from then on.

Appointment to able seaman may not seem much, but when it happens to you personally it is most important. There is an accepted saying in the Navy, that 'there is nothing lower than a Midshipman'. Very few would argue with that, but just one step higher is the ordinary seaman, and now we were one step higher than him. It meant more pay of course, but most important was the acceptance and recognition that came with it from the older and more experienced men you served with. There was only one ordinary seaman left aboard now, Duke Dewey; he had not been in the Navy long enough yet, but it was not something that would worry him, and he knew that his time would eventually come. To be absolutely correct, there was another ordinary seaman still part of our crew, Bill Jarrett the RDF operator. Although he had been in the service longer than the Duke, he was not yet eligible either. As he was never included in any upper deck duties we tended not to regard him as a seaman, but as a member of a specialist branch.

Under the command of Lieutenant Hughes, we seemed to carry out more patrols than ever and we sailed further afield in search of trouble, but the *Lucky Lady* lived up to her reputation and we carried on enjoying what can only be described as a charmed life at sea, with very enjoyable times ashore. Our dances were still as successful as ever, and remarkably, we never had any interference from higher up.

One afternoon, however, leave had been cancelled, and as we had not been detailed for a patrol, an air of hostility existed amongst us all. Uncertainty of any kind can be very demoralising, and this was no exception. Then the cox'n came down to our mess-deck, and informed us that we would be putting to sea within the hour, more than that he would not say. We then tried pumping our telegraphist, but unsuccessfully. His radio had been crackling away for some time, and he had kept disappearing in the direction of the officers' quarters, so we were sure that he knew what was going on. But, like all good 'sparks', he was not going to tell. Ordinary Seaman Jarrett was also very absorbed with his radar set, but we never thought of interrogating him, not that it would have done any good. Once again we recognised the symptoms, it was all very hush-hush, so we put to sea completely ignorant of what was going on.

Once again, normal routine took place. We tested all guns, and headed due east for several hours. 'Action stations' was piped for guns crews only; this was unusual, but it was not given much thought, and certainly did not concern us at all. The truth was, we did not know that only our guns crews were closed up; there was nobody extra on the bridge either.

No official information had been given to us at all, but a story was circulating that we were heading for the Danish coast to chart certain buoys. Being used to what we referred to as 'the usual mad ideas from Admiralty', we accepted this as being possible, and appreciated that, as with our trips to Holland, the utmost secrecy had to be maintained, and that we must escape attention from the enemy, again absolutely vital.

The reason why we gunners had been closed up at our guns so soon was because we had been told that at least two E-boats were reported to be somewhere in the area. Extra vigilance was expected from us because, having the extra fuel tanks full to capacity on board, meant that our maximum speed was considerably less than any E-boat, so we would stand no chance if attacked by several of the enemy boats.

Personally I had lost all count of time. It was a dark night and we could have been anywhere for all that I knew. Then our main engines were cut, and we were running upon the silenced engine only. It was assumed then that we were now somewhere off the Danish coast. There was absolutely no sign of a shoreline; naturally there would not have been any lights anyway, although there would have been a possible shore patrol as there had been on the Dutch coast, and an occasional show of headlights from a passing car, but we saw nothing at all.

On occasions such as this, seeing nothing, hearing nothing and knowing nothing, those were the times when you realised how much you were dependent upon the courage and wisdom of your immediate officers. You even prayed to God that they really knew where we were and that their navigation had been accurate. We, the crew, did not know where we were, we had seen lights from buoys, which lent credence to the story given to us, and we did have implicit faith in our 1st Lieutenant. All the time, ever since we cut out the engines, complete radio silence was maintained.

We gunners had been closed up for a very long time now; it was cold, the sea a little choppy, and we were not feeling all that happy. Ernie Nunn had been forbidden to heat up the stockpot, in case he might drop something inside the galley, which would have sounded across the sea like the sound of church bells. He was told to keep out of the galley and stay near to his depth charges. Had we all known of this instruction we might have guessed that there was more to this adventure than charting buoys.

Still no information was to be given to us, we seemed to do nothing but wait. Our RDF had been in constant operation, but there was still radio silence. A temporary panic occurred when a spanner was dropped down in the engine-room; despite the lack of knowledge, everyone held their breath, literally, maybe it was only for a few seconds but it seemed like fifteen minutes at least. The darkness remained undisturbed and there was no sound of anything, so we assumed that it had not been heard. To all of us aboard the 320, the noise made by our silenced engine seemed loud enough to wake the dead, even though the experts had assured us that in actual fact it could not be heard ashore. I could never rid myself of the doubt, but I was not prepared to go ashore to prove it.

The hours dragged by. Still nothing appeared to be happening, most of us were now thoroughly bored; at least the other gunners could move around their guns, but we machine-gunners in our turrets could only sit there, like stuffed dummies, dressed in our kapok suits.

We could not understand why we were still running on the silenced engine only. We had seen several buoys now, and naturally assumed the charting had been carried out, and the idea of becoming a sitting target for E-boats was becoming a very unattractive one, but nevertheless a distinct possibility. With great relief, a short while before dawn, the order was given to start all engines and we knew that we were heading for home.

As we left the area, radio silence was broken, and we could tell there was an enormous amount of radio activity. Although it was not possible for us on deck to tell, messages were passing to and from our bridge endlessly, to other ships and shore bases. Where we were situated in our machine-gun turrets, we could see there was plenty of activity on the bridge, and messages were being passed there from our telegraphist. We quite naturally assumed that our mission had been successful, and so were blissfully unaware of anything else.

A few hours later, we duly berthed at our usual place at the base, and it was not just our imagination that made us sense an air of excitement about. Not that we were going to take any notice; truthfully, we were far too tired to care and even if they had Hitler locked up in the Tower of London it would not have made any difference to us.

Later that day, however, came news that shocked us terribly, news that was impossible to believe. Not only could we not understand how it happened, but we were also very angry that it had. Had it been possible to detect any change of colour in the air in and around HMD *Midge*, I am certain it would have registered a deep shade of blue. We all cursed everybody imaginable, Admiralty, the RAF, the Army, and our own boats for operating from the Channel bases, futile and silly, yes, but what had happened that night to make us feel this way was even more futile and silly. However, it is too easy to apportion blame when you do not know the exact circumstances. Three pocket battleships, the pride and joy of the German Fleet, the *Prinz Eugen*, the *Gneisenau* and the *Scharnhorst* had actually sailed through the English Channel, our Channel, and now they would be in an ideal position to attack our shipping. The date was February 12th 1942 and they had sailed past Dover just after midnight on the 11th.

What on earth had happened? Torpedo boats had been sent out to attack the three ships, but those from Ramsgate discovered that their torpedos were not in firing condition, so they had to return to base disappointed and frustrated. The torpedo boats from Felixstowe, owing to a wrong signal given by a Wren at HMS *Midge*, upon leaving harbour headed north instead of south. This was catastrophic, but the other services apparently did no better, and the three German ships were soon through the Channel and into the wide open spaces of the North Sea. One can almost imagine the crews all lined up on their decks, thumbing their noses at us.

Weeks later we learnt the truth about our recent visit to the Danish coast. It was nothing to do with charting buoys; we should have known that our navigation experts would already have known about every buoy in the North Sea and beyond. We should have realised that all of our charts would be right up-to-date making the supposed survey not only unnecessary but a totally ridiculous idea. We had in fact been sent out to find the whereabouts of these three battleships, and send back to England details of their position.

Winston Churchill and their Lordships at the Admiralty had known that the three ships had left harbour, but they did not know where they were heading, so, being only 110 ft in length and built entirely of wood, it was possible that we could get near enough with our RDF to radio back sufficient information to England. We did exactly that. During all that time when radio silence had been imposed, our radar was in operation; that radio silence was broken just once, when we passed on the information required. How near we were to those three ships I never knew, but I am also sure that those ships never knew how close we had been to them. Fortunately for us, they probably never knew of our existence, otherwise they would have sent several of the E-boats that were escorting them to deal with us, and we would not have stood a chance. They might even have sent larger vessels, perhaps destroyers, to deal with us, but it was certain that one way or another, we would have been blown out of the water.

The odds were, I suppose, really in our favour. They might not have had radar on their ships at that time. Imagine how we would have felt had we known our true purpose, almost ridiculous: it would have been a 'David and Goliath' situation but we would not have had either a sling or a stone big enough.

As the years passed by, later in my life, it was easy to overlook what happened, and when I remembered, I even felt that it must have been a dream, I could not have been on the 320, out looking for three German pocket battleships, no, I must be mistaken surely! I would not dare relate the story to anyone, it was just too fantastic to be true. However, many years later, I told the story to Captain Loasby, with my thoughts on the matter, and how I had convinced myself that it was all a dream. Peter smiled. At first he corrected one fault in my memory, he had already left us and the *Lucky Lady* had been under the command of someone else, but it had all happened. He was able to verify it as he had been on duty at the Admiralty at the time. As a signals officer, he had seen the various signals passed, by all those involved; he also admitted that although having left the 320, he was still more than just a little interested in her activities, and watched her every movement with the greatest pride and interest. If he had not given me this information, I probably would not have repeated the story again, but now I can do so with equal pride.

I like to refer to all that occurred as 'the Channel Incident'; in reality it was much more, but unfortunately too much to sweep under the carpet. We aboard the 320 achieved something bordering upon being remarkable, almost unbelievable, but it also went unrecognised.

The achievement was a triumph for the German Navy, and it took a great deal of courage on their part to do what they did.

Nobody talked about anything else for days, but it did not

prevent us quickly resuming normal patrols and other very ordinary duties. Life is like that.

## ADDENDUM

The heroic dash made by the three German pocket battleships, and it certainly was 'heroic' by all standards, will go down in history as one of the German Navy's greatest achievements. To make the 'dash' was not an easy decision for their Admirals to make, in fact they were reluctant to attempt it, but it was Hitler's idea, and it was made upon his instructions, to consolidate his most powerful ships where they could do the most damage to our shipping.

On February 11th 1942, at approximately 2215 hrs, the battleships left the port of Brest in northern France. They had been seen by an RAF plane, but at 1219 hrs they were passing Dover, where they were fired upon by the Dover shore batteries, without apparent success. At 1245 hrs they were attacked by six Swordfish planes, all being shot down by the ships' anti-aircraft guns. At 1431 hrs a mine damaged the *Scharnhorst* but it was able to sail on; at 1955 hrs another mine damaged the *Gneisenau* but that too carried on sailing. At 2134 hrs the *Scharnhorst* was again damaged by a mine, but still it carried on to its ultimate destination.

On February 13th, the *Gneisenau* and *Prinz Eugen* arrived at Brunsbüttel, and the *Scharnhorst* at Wilhelmshaven, time 1030 hrs. The whole operation was code-named 'Cerberus' by the German Navy.

On February 26th 1942 the RAF bombed the *Gneisenau* while it was at Kiel, so badly that it had to be 'moth-balled'; another day the *Prinz Eugen* was torpedoed by one of our submarines, HMS *Trident*; this too was unable to take part in further actions at sea.

His Majesty's Motor Gunboat 320 left harbour just after dusk on February 11th, returning about the same time on the 12th. From the moment the ships passed Dover we were most vulnerable; anything could have happened. The escort of German fighter planes could easily have dealt with us, or the escorting destroyers and E-boats; only luck prevented our presence being detected, and helped us live to tell the tale. The information given by the 320 probably enabled the damaging attacks by the RAF and our submarine to take place.

# CHAPTER 10

## *A change of boats, and a complete change of life*

THE dances at the Goodes Hotel went on as usual, every fortnight, on the Friday evenings. They meant a great deal to the four of us. Being the lowest paid member, and not entitled to a share of the profits, I did not make much money out of the dances, but it never worried me; the entertainment they gave me, along with the company of all the girls, meant much more to me than money, although I readily admit that having a little more money would have made life even more enjoyable.

Our gramophone, already described as a Godsend, was always in use. We began to get short of records. We were never really bored with what we had on loan from Monty, but we needed more variety, but one weekend in particular solved the problem for us.

When at home on leave, I visited one public house more than any other, I had made it my 'local'. Its name was the Plough and Harrow and it was situated upon the main road that ran through Catford, from Lewisham towards Bromley in Kent. It was a small 'beerhouse'. The proprietor, Mrs Marriott, was priceless, she had a marvellous temperament and sense of humour, and she stood for no rowdiness of any sort in her establishment. She appreciated her regulars, and despite my youth and the fact that I was mostly away from Catford, she understood, and regarded me as being one of her regulars.

On this particular leave, I visited the pub as usual, spending a great deal of time and money playing records on their juke box; it was something I amused myself with when there. Sometimes Mrs Marriott would send a pint of beer over to me, as a friendly gesture. She did so now, so I left the juke box to join her at the bar. After a while the conversation turned to my appeal in the local newspaper for a gramophone, and how pleased she was that it had been so successful. It had been a talking point in her pub, and one of her regulars had offered to give their own gramophone. It was never said who that person was, and I never asked.

Merely as part of our conversation about the gramophone, I mentioned the shortage of records; no ulterior motive was intended, the conversation altered, and Mrs Marriott left me to go to her own private quarters.

When it drew near to closing time, Mrs Marriott called me into her quarters, and gave me a pile of records, possibly as many as thirty in all. 'These,' she said, 'are for you to take back to your boat, as a gift from the Plough and Harrow, you can tell your shipmates.'

It was a wonderful gesture on her part. I realised that the records would not have cost her anything, nevertheless, she need not have given them to me. On juke boxes, the records are changed frequently and mostly the old ones are taken away or destroyed. They would have served their purpose by enticing people to spend their money, and many would have enjoyed their music. Mrs Marriott explained all that, and that if she did not get rid of them they would only lie and collect dust before being thrown away, so I would be doing her a favour by taking them. Although she never actually said that more would be given later, at various times she did give more.

When I returned aboard with those records the enthusiasm shown was unbelievable. Someone even said that Mrs Marriott had restored his faith in Father Christmas.

It could never be said that I was a good seaman. Peter Loasby had made me an able seaman before he left the 320, but in reality there had been a lack of opportunities for me to indulge in real seamanship. Priority for the gunners was to look after their particular weapon, and in fact our cox'n was so proud of 'his boat' that he seldom allowed anyone other than himself to splice the ropes and wires; he would always insist upon doing it himself. On rare occasions he would get Taff Johnson to do some, and even Monty, but Vic Copeland, despite the fact that he was such an excellent seaman, would be kept maintaining his guns, like myself.

To Peter (Sharkey) Ward, Petty Officer, cox'n, the *Lucky Lady* HMMGB 320, was not just a boat, it was his home, his world, his family. He asked for nothing more, and I believe it is true that he died aboard his boat.

We were now well into 1942, without realising it. Time was not important to us, we had all adopted this different way of life, and it seemed perfectly natural. We never talked of our lives before in 'civvy street', and most of us never gave a thought as to what might be in store for us when the war eventually ended.

The only exception perhaps was Vic Copeland. He quite openly expressed his dislike of being away from home and his family, yet he was such a good seaman that one would have thought that he would have appreciated being in the Navy. After all, he was really a classic example of being a square peg in a square hole; he was where he belonged and had he been forced into any other service it would have been a terrible waste of his ability. He would have been even less happy I am sure, and later his ability was recognised, for he was promoted and became cox'n of his own boat.

The appointment of a new captain for the 320, once Peter Loasby had left, was almost like a deliberate attack on my personal happiness. I knew that life would never be the same again. The first officer appointed to replace Peter was quite good, but was unfortunately only temporary. It was the news that the man who was going to take over command of our boat was actually the officer who had become the flotilla gunnery officer, that made me think that my world really was about to come to an end.

What happened next might have been a coincidence, but in this instance I find it very hard to believe. Within days of the new Skipper's appointment, a signal was received aboard, and I was told to pack my kitbag and hammock, ready to leave the 320 next morning. Once again I was bound for HMS *Attack* at Portland. In later years I would realise that what happened was in fact Naval policy, and downright common sense. I had joined the 320 as an inexperienced ordinary seaman, on board 320 I had become experienced and to an extent had proved myself among men, now I was leaving to become the nucleus of another crew, aboard another boat, and my experience would hopefully help other youngsters who had just joined the Navy, and Coastal Forces in particular. My place aboard the *Lucky Lady* would be taken by some other youngster, who would benefit from the good friends and shipmates I was now leaving behind.

When it is decided that a man is to leave his boat, no time is wasted; to leave yesterday is never quite possible, but it very nearly is in the Navy. The signal was received in the evening, and I had to be on the jetty at 0800 hrs the next morning, with all my kit ready for transport, I have to consider myself lucky, I suppose; they could have drafted me that same evening.

The next morning I had sadly to say my farewells, with the largest lump in my throat ever, and verging near to tears. I had been so happy aboard the 320 that I was sure that I would never be so happy again. It was true to say that I was now looking at the future with dread; none of our escapades on board the 320 had ever filled me with fear as this draft did, I only hope that it never showed too much. I think that Len Downs also felt the same way about me leaving, so the parting with him was short and sharp. Jeff and Stan, both being older and having experienced

ADDENDUM to


JACK , THE SAILOR

WITH

THE NAVY BLUE EYES.


Insert page 130, before commencing

new paragraph.

# CHAPTER 10.

It was May 11th, 1942, Chris Krediet
and Erik Hazelhoff, Dutch Espoinage agents,
were again on board MGB 320, together they
had completed fourteen landings from this
same boat on to Enemy occupied land, their
'Homeland', HOLLAND.   Now they were about
to make their fifteenth landing, God willing,
and everything going to plan.
    The 320 on this occasion was commanded by
Lieutenant Pat Hall RNVR, a very capable
and efficient officer who had been appointed
to carry on the good work originally began
by Lieutenant Peter Loasby RN, who had been
transferred to Admiralty as he was a specialist
in communications.
    The boat's 1st Lieutenant, Bob Goodfellow,
had been the "mainstay" of all the operations
so far, personally rowing without help, the
Dutch spies, from the gunboat to the shore,
which was at least two miles, and often more
on the return journey.   Although he did not
know it at the time, this was to be his last,
and a very memorable one it proved to be.
    The journey from Gt.Yarmouth in Norfolk,
escorted by two other MGB's from our flotilla,
was eirily quiet, but it all seemed to be
going well and we were soon at our destination.
While the 320 went in closer to the shore,
the other two boats lay in wait a mile or so
to seaward.
    As Bob Goodfellow rowed the two Dutchmen
towards the beach a parachute flare was fired

from somewhere ashore, lighting the area
brilliantly.   Bob instinctively turned
the dinghy around quickly, and pulled with
all his might in the direction of where the
320 had been.   The other MGB's came in
closer to help, opening fire unnecessarily
they added to the hazards now worrying the
three men in the dinghy.   Tracer bullets
and shells from the shore were enough
danger, but fire from the other MGB's,
however well intentioned, simply added to it.

The 320 had moved from it's original
position but was now racing to the rescue,
the three men were quickly hauled aboard
and the dinghy hastily abandoned, then at
maximum speed headed out to sea, hopefully
out of range of the guns ashore, who were
now 'pouring shells at us.'

Somehow the 320 was separated from the
other MGB's, no longer illuminated by the
flare everything around seemed black, the
sky dark with dense cloud.   All of a sudden
there appeared lights, they formed a circle
with us, MGB 320, in the centre.  Outboard,
to seaward, appeared two huge searchlights,
sweeping the sea around us.  Lieutenant
Hall and Bob Goodfellow counted the boats
surrounding us, there were nine E-boats,
and two Nazi destroyers, the latter were
operating the searchlights.

Bob explained the German strategy to the
Dutch officers, each boat showed one light,
if any one light was extinguished from the
view of the other boats they then knew that
we were the reason, so being easily located.

2.

All nine E-boats would then 'go in for the
kill.'

By brilliant seamanship and clever
manoeuvering the two MGB officers managed
to avoid detection, the E-boats then switched
on all their lights and with the glare from
the two searchlights the area for a while
resembled a "film set", only this time it was
for real and not a 'mock-up.'

Several times the searchlights flicked
across us, how they missed seeing us we shall
never know.   On the upper deck we were all
rigid, not with fear but something else,
anticipation of a combined burst of fire
from the Enemy, we knew that if this happened
it would be the end for us all.  What I never
realised was that circling us in this way,
the E-boats had to be careful when opening
fire, otherwise they would have hit each other

A suggestion from our Dutch friends, that
we call for help from the RAF was rejected
by our officers, any planes would arrive too
late anyway, but our officers were confident
that we could still outwit the Germans.  Still
slowly and quietly easing the 320 inbetween
the Enemy boats we somehow managed to slip
outside the circle of E-boats, fortunately
the two destroyers were situated on the other
side of the perimeter from where we were.
Then without increasing speed and operating
only our silenced engine we made for the open
sea and home, praying that we had not been
seen and followed.   Our prayers must have
been answered for we had an uninterupted
voyage back to Gt.Yarmouth.

3.

Fortunately the Germans did not detect
our absence for some time, allowing us to
be far away when realisation hit them.
Later we learned that one of our escorting
MGB's had been destroyed by the E-boat pack,
presumably before we had been encircled.
It had not been a successful landing this
time; somehow Enemy agents had learned about
our trips to the Dutch Coast, and their
boats had been waiting, ready for us on this
occasion. When we decided to name our boat
"The Lucky Lady" we never knew then how apt
it was going to be, for "Lucky" she most
certainly was for us all, plus, I hasten to
add, the cool heads and bravery of our
officers.
The trips to Holland by boat were then
discontinued and future agents were dropped
by parachute from RAF planes, although still
dangerous it was less risky than by boat now
that the Enemy knew what we were doing.
Bob Goodfellow was an exceptionally brave
man, he was liked and respected by the entire
320 crew. With him aboard the "Lucky Lady"
the future held few worries for those who
served alongside him.
When we first left Gt.Yarmouth we tested
all our guns as usual, and 'action stations'
was piped almost immediately, this meant
that I, along with everyone else, remained at
my place of duty from then on, without a
break of any sort, but we were all now well
used to this.
Vic Copeland and I were the most unfortunate
as we were confined to our machine-gun turrets,

4.

we were unable to move around at all,
whereas the other crew members could stretch
their legs whenever so inclined, although
they could not leave their place of duty. In
fact, Vic and I were not allowed out of our
turrets until we were almost back in harbour
at Gt. Yarmouth.

When the flares were fired over us from
the shore, and when the Enemy guns bombarded
us, it was all fairly straight-forward and
we knew what was going on, we also had been
instructed, as with all our operations, that
we gunners were not to open fire under any
circumstances, unless authorised by our Captain
and this was no different under the command
of Lieutenant Hall.

The circumstances were changed however
when we were encircled by the Nazi boats, at
our guns we only knew that we could see
lights around us, and as these lights were
in most instances, a quarter of a mile away
from us, amid almost "pitch-black darkness",
we did not know anymore than that. Whatever
had been discussed on the bridge between our
officers and the Dutchmen could not have been
heard by members of the crew, except the Cox'n
and he would never repeat what he heard, even
when safely back in harbour.

The only deviation from usual procedure
was that when we were surrounded, even though
we did not know what was going on, all gunners
were told that if we were fired upon we could
then fire back. Machine-gunners were told
that if this happened they were to aim for the
searchlights, it would be very important to
put them out first. This at least gave me
an inkling of what was out there in the darkness, but the tenseness of the situation

5.

prevented me from imagining what kind of
situation we were really in.    This in many
ways was a good thing.
     There was a very good reason as to why we,
the crew, were not told more, the circumstances
were so volatile when we were surrounded by
the E-boats that had the seriousness of our
predicament become known to us all, there was
the possibility that one of us could have
"snapped." under the strain.    Then without
any doubt our "Lucky Lady" would have run out
of luck, in short, it would have been the end
for us all, boat included.
     Personally, even today I remember very little
of this particular incident, only those lights,
and when the E-boats turned on all their lights,
being on the port side of our boat I was not
able to see much of what was happening, and
shortly after that we were outside the circle
and on our way home.
     Once back in harbour there was too much to
occupy us for any discussion to take place
about what had happened, guns etc. had to be
stripped and cleaned before we could retire to
our bunks and sleep.    Our stokers would be
making plans for the next "Jolly Jack Night"
at Goodes Hotel, but there was going to be a
worse shock, especially for me, my life was
about to undergo what would be to me, a very
unwelcome change.

many such partings, showing no feelings; they simply said their goodbyes, and to them it was just another chapter in their lives coming to an end.

Altogether a party of twelve men left HMS *Midge* that morning. We had been issued with our railway warrants and meal vouchers, and instructed to report to Naval patrols at the various railway stations we would be passing through.

It did nothing to cheer us up to be told about a rumour circulating that the Navy was short of volunteers for the submarine service, and it was possible that we could be transferred into it.

Whether there was any truth in that rumour we never knew. It was just possible that some bright wit at the base had invented the story out of malice, just to make us uneasy, and to ensure that our journey to Portland was not an enjoyable one. If this was true, then I confess that with me he succeeded; the thought of being imprisoned in a submarine below or even above water simply terrified me no end. That prospect frightened me much more than having to face all the E-boats that Adolf Hitler could muster. Providing I had my guns at the time, of course.

A few days after I had left the 320, the *Lucky Lady* made another journey to Scheveningen, under the command of Lieutenant Hall. It was, according to the Dutch officers, a first-class trip. Despite my dislike for the man, I knew that he was an efficient officer, very competent, so I would have expected to have heard this, and that he would make many more such trips.

It must have worried the three Dutchmen at first, when they heard that Peter Loasby was being transferred to Admiralty. It meant placing their lives in the hands of someone extremely new to them. What a relief it was to discover that his replacement was equally as efficient as his predecessor, even though RNVR as opposed to RN.

Very little can be said about the rail journey to Dorset. The countryside between Yarmouth and London is very flat, and very uninteresting when seen from a railway carriage. The beautiful scenery depicted by Constable is hidden from view as the trains speed through Suffolk, and truthfully at times such as those, beautiful scenery is really far from one's thoughts.

We reached Liverpool Street station, during an air attack. The Naval patrol was occupied with other things, so we seized the chance to leave the station and spend our meal vouchers at a pub outside, the already famous tourist attraction Dirty Dick's in Bishopsgate.

We returned to the station, and found the transport waiting to rush us across London to Waterloo station, and quickly put us aboard the waiting train that was bound for Dorchester. On reaching that town, another lorry was waiting to take us the last few miles to Portland.

There was one attraction to joining HMS *Attack* again: it was the prospect of obtaining leave to go home, so after settling in our new quarters we all made arrangements to submit requests for leave to be granted. These requests would be considered the following morning, and hopefully we could be homeward bound by midday. Most of the requests were granted with any fuss or objections; no reasons had to be given, so we did not have to appear before the Commander in person. With the utmost haste, I packed a small case, mostly, I admit, with soiled clothing to be washed, I collected my free travelling warrant, and I was soon on my way home to spend my first real uninterrupted leave. I can remember how wonderful it felt to be boarding that London-bound train. After several stops because of air-raid alerts, some six hours later in fact, we arrived at Waterloo. It was then one mad rush across platforms, and I was aboard another train that would take me to Catford.

Not having a girlfriend to come home to, one leave was very much like another, except that this was a little longer, with no prospect of being recalled. A neighbour, who was a regular Navy man, having joined before the outbreak of war, was also on leave at the time; he was serving aboard HMS *Liverpool*. This was an older type of destroyer. In comparison with the men aboard those ships, I had been living like royalty. Jim was a few years older than I was, and of course vastly more experienced, but he accepted me with a certain amount of good humour and tolerance, and we did become good friends.

The usual rounds were made to visit family. No visits were made to dances, as Jim did not like dancing, so we visited many pubs, the Plough and Harrow included, and probably drank too much, but there was not much else for two young men such as ourselves to do in these times. If we tried to date girls, we could not have been very successful, as I have no fond memories to look back upon, at least not on that particular leave while with Jim. There would have been a lack of enthusiasm on my part anyway, as in reality there was only one girl who was always in my mind, and I knew that the kind of places that Jim and I were visiting were not the kind of places where she was likely to be.

As my sister and her husband knew the girl in question, I often used surreptitiously to ask them questions about her, but they were never able to tell me much. Sometimes, depending upon who I was talking to at the time, I would be encouraged to call at her home, but even though I could now be quite brazen at times, this was something I could not pluck up courage to do. I was able to brave the sea at its worst, I could face gunfire, and the hazards of espionage, but to make an impromptu call at the home of this very special girl, was simply impossible.

There had not been any further news about my brother. The family accepted that Alan had been lost at sea, yet my mother, for some strange reason, did not accept the report as final; her instinct suggested that there was still hope. Her sister Ethel also refused to acknowledge that Alan might be dead, and as she was a firm believer in spiritualism, she was certain that through it she would somehow find the truth.

During this leave, my aunt asked me to accompany her to a spiritualist meeting. She thought that there might be a chance of some sort of message being received from Alan. At that time I neither believed in that kind of religion nor disbelieved. The fact that she was well known to be a member of the spiritualist church was accepted by our family but she was also treated with quite a bit of humorous sarcasm that she would accept gracefully.

So I agreed to attend this meeting with her, and along to the church hall at Sundridge Park, near Bromley in Kent, we went, and took seats towards the back of the hall. My aunt would have sat right in the front row, but I would not agree, so she settled for the seats that I chose. To my way of thinking, if there was anything in this spirit business, then it would not matter where we sat; I thought that this was quite logical.

To my complete surprise, a message did come. It was never actually said who it was from, but this is how it happened:

It was similar to any other church hall; the audience − or if you prefer, the congregation − sat upon chairs, in rows, facing the end of the hall where there was a stage. Up upon this stage sat the medium, upon a chair, facing us all; she was introduced to us, and the seance began. There was nothing strange about it, no 'hocus pocus' as in magician's tricks; she simply sat there silent, until a message came to her. After giving several messages to others, she announced that she had one for a young man dressed in a blue uniform, no name given, this young man was fair, with blue eyes, then she said that it was from this young man's brother, she thought his name began with the letter 'A': Alan? Would the young man if present, stand up to receive the message. At first I was reluctant to stand, but after much persuasion from my aunt, I did, to be told that Alan was alive, he was a prisoner of war, he had not been injured when the ship he was on was sunk, but he had spent many days afloat in a rowing boat with others. I was not to worry, he was all right, and would soon be in touch with us.

Even then, I was sceptical. How could it be proved to be authentic? I wanted to believe, I probably did, I certainly do now.

We passed this information on to the rest of the family. It was received with mixed feelings and had I not been present with my aunt, they would have ridiculed it all, but my being there meant that they had to accept it as having taken place. The only one who was not doubtful was my mother; she merely shrugged her shoulders and said that 'time would tell'.

Six months, almost to the day, after my mother was notified of Alan's disappearance at sea, she received information from the Red Cross Organisation in Switzerland, that Alan was then a prisoner of war, and being held in Germany. A letter was enclosed to her from Alan, short, but enough to give exactly the same information as I had received at the spiritualist meeting. It was, as near as could be recalled, word for word. Any doubts that might have existed in my mind regarding this form of religion now disappeared.

Months later, when again on leave, I attended another meeting at that church when I think the same medium was in attendance. We were accompanied by young Frank Fiddler who was not old enough at that time to be in the services, but he was a member of the Sea Cadets, so he was in sailor's uniform at the time. Although he came with us voluntarily, he was obviously very nervous. No further message came for either my aunt or myself, but to Frank's horror, one came for him. Unfortunately he was too frightened to stand up to receive it. I understood it, but there was no way that I could take it, he had to stand up for all to see, and this is exactly what Frank was not prepared to do. By this time the medium was becoming agitated; she emphasised that it was a matter of 'life or death', and had Frank accepted it, there was the possibility that a life could have been saved.

The message from the medium referred to two young brothers who had lived almost opposite Frank and myself in the road where we lived. One was the same age as Frank, the other two years younger, Stanley, the elder of the two brothers, had died about two years previously; John, the younger one, was employed somewhere at Lewisham.

Shortly after our visit to the spiritualist church, John walked into a plate glass door somewhere in Lewisham, and was killed instantly. The question that remains now is, could his life have been saved if Frank had accepted the medium's message? I wonder!

A few days before this leave ended, I visited a private club close to the boundaries of Downham and Bellingham. There I met a young girl I took an instant liking to. Her name was Sylvia and she was sweetness itself, very pretty, and full of life, I must admit that I really enjoyed her company. We corresponded for a while, and I called to see her when I arrived home on following leaves, but I decided that enough was enough; she was four years younger than I was, and I thought that by continuing our friendship I was not being fair to her. Quite wrongly, like many before me and many afterwards, I thought that she was much too young for me, so I made it clear that our romance, such as it was, was over. It was not something that I enjoyed doing, and I felt guilty about it for some time afterwards. Ironically, when in later years I did marry, it was to a girl four years younger than I was. This time I did not consider the difference to be important, and it is said that women are mentally more advanced than men by four years, which would balance the ages.

After the end of the war, I did see Sylvia on one occasion, and I must admit that she had grown into a very beautiful young woman. She was smart, well groomed, in fact quite sophisticated in appearance, but the friendship would not have worked, as at the time I was thinking too much about someone else.

The leave ended, and I returned to HMS *Attack* at Portland, where, on the very next day, I was drafted to Weymouth, to join a 70-footer, HMMGB 84. It had a much smaller number of men in her crew, and although I was not aware of it at the time, this was going to be a similar experience to the short stay I had aboard ML 216.

She was berthed almost alongside the Sailors Rest, so I was able to see Vicky again. Conversation with her during daytime was always difficult as she was kept very busy, and of an evening she was nowhere to be found: I did hear that her husband was home on leave, so Vicky was sure to put his needs first, and who could blame her?

The rest of the lads aboard 84 were friendly enough, but my stay aboard the boat was very short-lived, only ten days at the most, so I really did not get much of an opportunity to make any close friends aboard her. The existing crew members had been together for some time and they may have known that I would not become a permanent member of their crew, or maybe they sensed it? Whichever it was, the parting with them was not a sad one as with the 320, so the return to HMS *Attack* upset nobody. The only difference between this and the short stay aboard 216 was that I did go to sea aboard her, one day only, and it was merely an exercise out in the bay. This was at the time that I was friendly with Sylvia, and I had a photograph of her with me when I left the boat. I never noticed that this photograph had disappeared, in fact I really thought that it was among other photographs I carried around with me, and it came as a surprise in 1945 when, in Italy, a former member of that crew came up to me and gave me Sylvia's photograph. Apparently one of the crew had light fingers where girls' photographs were concerned, and he had purloined this one while I was busy packing my kit. The fellow that gave it to me had carried it around with him ever since he took it away from the thief, hoping one day to give it back to me, which now he did.

It was looking as though Fate had decreed that I should not become attached to one boat or one place for too long for no sooner had I arrived at Portland, than I received orders to be ready to be drafted the following morning. This time it was to go back to Whale Island for a refresher gunnery course, just for the weapons in use aboard Coastal Forces boats. This visit, however, would be different, at least I hoped so, as I would be joining the school this time as an experienced able seaman, as opposed to the green kid that was still wet behind the ears when joining the school before.

Because of its fearsome reputation for discipline, plus more than its fair share of 'red tape', most men regarded the Island with a mixture of fear, dread and often pessimism. Only those with their eyes on future promotion contemplated the Island with relish. Perhaps I was an exception to the rule? I actually enjoyed my visits there, yet at that time I most certainly did not have any inclinations for promotion. To be perfectly honest, however, like so many others, I was glad when the course ended and I was on my way to another boat.

Life on the Island was better this time. Although the course would only be a short one, one week, the high standards set by the school remained the same. It was simply 'at the double here', and 'at the double there' between sun-up and sunset; only cripples were excused, and Whale Island did not accept cripples in their classes, except perhaps 'temporary ones' as I had been on my previous visit, when I had the poisoned foot.

Being a refresher course, there would not be a serious examination at the end, only a quick, brief test to prove that the course had not been a waste of time. There would be no winners and no losers, but not even God could help you if you did not pass with flying colours, and if He could not help? Well, an erring matelot might be forgiven for thinking that Hell could offer more hope than to remain on the Island.

The gunnery school, HMS *Excellent*, was actually built on an island that many years earlier had been the City of Portsmouth's refuse dump. In later years everyone would concern themselves about toxic waste and methane gases in connection with these dumps, but not so in those times. If anybody suffered from living upon the Island, nothing was ever said or reported, I suppose we were much too occupied with the war anyway. I do not know if the Medical Officers knew then about toxic wastes; if they did, they might not have cared anyway. Certainly, while I was there, no ill-effects were either obvious or noticed, and if anyone was foolish enough to doze off during a lecture, the instructor would make certain that it never happened again. Standing in front of a class holding a very large and heavy shell is not the most comfortable way of learning, but at least it encouraged concentration on both lessons and keeping awake.

The Navy had other gunnery schools which were all strict and very efficient as they had to be, but HMS *Excellent*, on Whale Island, was more than that. It was the 'Gunnery School of the World', there could not be better, and while there you were never allowed to forget it, and you never did, even years after when you had left the Navy for civilian life. You are still proud of having been taught there.

At the end of the week, kitbag and hammock were packed, and it was back again to Portland. This meant a journey spent in pure speculation. Where would they send me next? At least the prospect of submarines no longer haunted me, I felt certain that I would now remain in Coastal Forces where I would be of use, whereas aboard a submarine I would be a liability and not an asset.

Owing to the increased activity of the E-boats, who were now becoming more and more daring, and the seemingly everlasting presence of U-boats in home waters, life aboard Coastal Forces craft had become very exciting and very dangerous, so men like myself with experience were needed to man the boats and help create confidence in the new youngsters now joining.

This time I spent three days at Portland, just long enough to be able to spend two nights ashore at Weymouth, where I had now made friends with the people who managed the Globe Hotel.

*The author, in submarine sweater.*

The Globe was a small, comfortable, and very popular place, not actually on the harbour itself, but near enough to benefit from its situation. The actual proprietor had been recalled into the Royal Marines, but the wife and daughter of Sergeant-Major Dawkins were more than capable of running the place in his absence, just as efficiently as if he were still there. Both of the young women were very attractive, but to compliment them I must stress that patrons always received courtesy and first-class service, and if there had been an epidemic of fluttering hearts, then they did not go out of their way to cause it.

The daughter I recall, being a red head, and an attractive one, did object for some reason, if sailors sang 'Jeanie with the light brown hair' in her presence. She would tolerate it to begin with, but very soon when the singers became over enthusiastic she would insist upon showing them the door, never needing help.

It was being able to spend my leisure hours in Weymouth that helped to make my visits to HMS *Attack* at Portland more enjoyable. There was the occasional visit to the town of Portland itself, but I never felt comfortable while I was there, not as I did in Weymouth. There was nothing personal about the feeling, nobody ever did anything or said anything that might have upset me, and I am sure that the many sailors that did spend shore leave there, had most enjoyable times.

# Simply a Sailor,
# and not just a Number

He was not much of a sailor,
But proud to be part of a crew,
And if the enemy should attack,
He knew exactly what to do.

Sometimes at sea he would take the wheel,
On instructions he would steer,
Into waves unspeakably high,
But from dangers he would veer.

He would quickly curse an officer,
Who found him extra work,
But to defend that same officer,
No dangers would he shirk.

When in port he went ashore,
He always looked his best,
His happy smile and attitude,
Never failing to impress.

Back to sea and ready again,
To fight against the foe,
Against no matter what the odds,
Into battle he must go.

The enemy was not just humans,
The weather was always there,
It often helped the mighty sea,
Cause havoc and despair.

Yet, at times when peaceful,
The sea could soothe and charm,
That was when the sailor felt,
It never meant him harm.

So in his bunk, out on the sea
His thoughts would surely roam,
To friends and all his loved ones,
And a safe return to home.

JWD

# The boats are getting larger, and we have more guns

WHEN the day arrived for me to leave the Portland base, there were about sixteen of us altogether, all bound for the same place, Lowestoft, Suffolk, almost home ground for me, and I wondered if there would be an opportunity to visit the *Lucky Lady* again, assuming that she was still based at Great Yarmouth.

Travelling was no different. A Petty Officer was put in charge of us all, although he made it quite clear that he was not actually part of our party, but his destination was also Lowestoft, so he had been given the responsibility of seeing that we all arrived there without mishap.

There was of course the usual changing of trains in London, plus the mad dash across the capital, but this time there was not an air raid, nor was there the sound of sirens. Compartments had been reserved for us on the trains, so there was no panic over seats. The Petty Officer had our railway warrants and meal vouchers; the latter he gave us as soon as we boarded the first train, informing us that we could use them whenever we wanted to, but we were to make certain that we all kept together, as he did not want the trouble of having to search for missing 'bodies'. We did manage to keep together, and so kept him happy.

When we arrived at Lowestoft, the Petty Officer left us to report to a minesweeper moored in the harbour. There was an able seaman waiting to take us to our destination, and a RN lorry to transport us. We all climbed aboard, after excitedly discovering that it was taking us to a boat-builder's yard at Oulton Broads, a small yachting centre outside Lowestoft, but inland. There, we were told, was a brand new motor gunboat, sitting there waiting for us to be its crew.

The boat builders were Messrs Brookes Marine, famous for their boats world-wide, and when we climbed down from the lorry and walked inside the yard, there, waiting on the stocks, was HMMGB 611, in all her glory, and although her shape was strange to us all, she looked a real beauty.

There were already some crew aboard who had been there for a couple of weeks, helping to tidy the inside quarters, ready for when we arrived. The cox'n introduced himself to us immediately: Regular Navy, and his name was Smith. It was strange, but all the time I served aboard the 611, I never learnt his Christian name; he was always referred to as either 'Smithy', or 'the Swain'. Of course there were also times when other not so complimentary words were used, fortunately not very often, as he became very well liked by us all.

The 1st Lieutenant was also on board, he was Lieutenant Turner RNVR, slight of build, and a quiet man. I never recall him raising his voice ever, but that did not affect his efficiency, or our respect for him. We were also informed that our Captain was around the yard somewhere; this was an indirect warning to us, so that we would all be on our best behaviour.

The cox'n then directed the stokers to the engine-room where they would find the motor mechanic and a stoker working, and the rest of us he took to the fo'c'sle to introduce us to leading seaman Febry, who was the 'second cox'n'. He in fact did not remain with us for long, he was waiting to take a course to pass as a Petty Officer, but while he was with us he was well liked.

It was with some pride that I discovered that I was one of the senior gunnery ratings on board, but what was more important to me was that a month or so previously I had celebrated my twentieth birthday, so I was eligible for a rum issue. Aboard all Coastal Forces craft, rum was issued neat and not as the watered down version that was given in barracks and larger ships. Once we had settled down, a friendship developed between the cox'n and myself that lasted all the time I was aboard the 611. It was not a 'going ashore together' friendship as he was considerably older than I was, a family man, but he had to have someone on board experienced enough for him to trust. Apart from leading seaman Febry there were two others of a similar seniority as myself, which was to make the cox'n's life much easier.

The 611 was a much larger boat than the 320, and when all the crew were aboard we had thirty-three officers and ratings; later it was increased to thirty-eight after certain alterations to the armament.

We spent another week at the boatyard as there were various jobs that needed doing. Although they should have been done by the workmen at the yard, they were not of a technical nature, so our Captain apparently had suggested that we did them, so that the boat would be ready for service sooner.

After having been aboard for twenty-four hours, the cox'n assembled us all on the dockside, and our Captain came to be introduced to us all. He was a Royal Fleet Reserve officer, and had commanded an assortment of merchant ships before being taken into the Navy. With him, also being introduced to us all, were our two other officers, Lieutenant Turner RNVR, and Sub-Lieutenant Lewis RNVR. Sub-Lieutenant Lewis, who later after promotion commanded a similar gunboat, was a lawyer in civilian life. He lived in Essex, and during the 1970s, while walking along the High Street at Southend-on-Sea, I felt a tap upon my shoulder, and to my surprise it was him. He had recognised me and wanted to say 'hello'. We exchanged pleasantries for a while and parted, but I did call to see him at his offices on a later occasion.

The Captain never said a great deal to us at that first meeting, he simply told us what was expected of us. He did not intend to be a strict disciplinarian, but this did not mean that we could take advantage of him; he would be just as strict as any regular Royal Navy officer if it became necessary. His stay aboard us was not a long one, and while he was with us he became very well liked indeed, and nobody ever attempted to take advantage.

MGB 611 quickly became a happy boat I am pleased to say, owing to our Captain. There was only a minimum of red-tape, as our other two officers followed his example and contributed much toward the boat's atmosphere, as also did our cox'n and the motor mechanic. The entire crew appeared to mix well, but as the crew was much larger than that of the 320, it was going to take longer for us to know each other and become moulded into an efficient fighting unit.

The overall length of the 611 was 115 feet; she had a 21-foot beam, and was powered by four Packard engines, which gave her a speed of thirty-four knots maximum, but I very much doubt whether this speed was ever reached after trials. Built of wood, of course, she carried 5200 gallons of fuel, again 100 octane so she would be able to cover approximately 500 nautical miles while at sea.

On her fo'c'sle she had a two-pounder manually operated pom-pom; this was to be mine, I discovered. There were two twin .5 machine-gun turrets, as with the 320, but these were raised higher, alongside the bridge; a single 20 mm Oerlikon gun was mounted midships, and a manually operated six-pounder gun aft. There was also the usual Holman projector and depth charges, altogether making the 611 quite a formidable sight, yet this armament was to be altered and increased at a later date, and probably fitted with torpedos too. I am not certain that this happened to 611, but most of these 'D' class gunboats were converted to carry torpedos.

While we were still at Lowestoft, now moored in the river,

having been taken off the stocks, life was very free and easy. Food
was purchased at the village shops, all the best possible quality, and
plenty of it. This meant a great deal to our cox'n, for although
not a very big man, he loved his food, and had an extremely
healthy appetite.

With other members of the crew, I made a visit to Yarmouth,
pleased to be able to show the lads around the town. To my great
disappointment, the *Lucky Lady* was not in harbour. Nobody knew
her whereabouts so I assumed that she was away on another of
her espionage trips. Eventually I discovered that this was right, but
she was not going to enjoy the same amount of good luck as she
had been used to. On one occasion when on one of these trips
she was going to find herself among four E-boats, and only
narrowly escaped from them; at another time she would suffer
from a major explosion which would badly cripple her. Unfortunately I am unable to discover what actually happened to her then
and neither can I find out what happened to my friends aboard
her, despite attempts by Captain Loasby and myself. Another blow
was that the 'Jolly Jack Nights' had to be discontinued, so I
wondered how Jeff and the others managed to supplement their
income now that no money was coming in from the dances.

Naturally I took my new friends along to meet Tessie Barwick
who was still in charge of the saloon bar at Goodes Hotel. She
was delighted to see me again; in fact three of us stayed the night
at her home on one occasion when we were unable to catch the
last bus back to Lowestoft.

We were able to attend one dance at Goodes; there were six
or seven of us from 611. I had told them so much about the dances
that the lads simply could not stay away. We all enjoyed ourselves,
and I was pleased to have the three Waafs and the Wren join our
company. It was quite like old times again, for me at least. After
some persuasion I managed to get the girls to give their rendering
of 'Roll a silver dollar' for the benefit of my friends, but their

popularity was challenged to my surprise by able seaman Charlie Nesbitt, who sang the words of Rudyard Kipling's poem, 'The Ladies', a ditty that I liked very much, so I learnt the words myself, for use on social occasions. Both Charlie's contribution to the evening entertainment and that from the girls went down very well at the dance. In fact, the happy crowd there were so enthusiastic, in such a noisy manner, that the management became quite worried and concerned for the protection of their premises. They need not have worried really, everyone was very well behaved, and thoroughly enjoying themselves. When we returned to 611 at Lowestoft, everyone agreed that they had had a very good evening at Yarmouth, and would be looking forward to the next one.

The 611 was now ready to leave the boatyard. We had completed the necessary trials, our Captain was satisfied with everything, and now all that was required was instructions to leave Lowestoft, and where to go. During that day, a signal was received from HMS *Midge*, congratulating us on the completion of trials, notifying us where to fill up with fuel, and ordering us to sail for Weymouth, where we would carry out gunnery trials. Weymouth had now become the official Coastal Forces gunnery school, and working up base. We would be leaving Lowestoft the next morning.

As we left our mooring at Brookes Marine, the entire workforce came out to wave us goodbye. This never happened when the 320 left the yard at Littlehampton, and I confess to finding this send-off rather touching.

Once we were well away from land, we carried out the usual testing of our guns. After all, it would not have been impossible for E-boats to appear suddenly, they were cheeky enough now, so even though we were off to Weymouth for gunnery trials, it was necessary to be prepared for anything. To operate my pom-pom in any engagement required a gun's crew of four, including myself. I had for my number two an ordinary seaman by the name of George Hamblett who was the son of a Norfolk farmer, and a very conscientious chap, who followed any instructions given to him to the last letter. It was a combined effort by the two of us that would achieve any results; the other two lads were there to supply and feed ammunition to our gun.

The weather, although not good, was not too unpleasant. The officers on the bridge seemed to be enjoying themselves, the friendly attitude towards us won our respect, and we thought then that we were lucky to have these particular officers, therefore ensuring 611 would be a happy boat.

The young ordinary seamen who had never been to sea before did suffer discomfort and were naturally seasick; however everyone was sympathetic towards them, and I was in the position now of being able to advise them in the same words that Peter Loasby used when he sympathised with me, because he was right, after six months at sea I was never seasick again. Funny that, because Peter was, right to the end of his career in the Navy.

It was not long before we discovered that our 1st Lieutenant was a brilliant artist. It was rumoured that he was descended from the great English painter whose surname he bore but whether there was any truth in this I never found out.

We hugged the coast on our journey to Weymouth, probably because we had such a large proportion of inexperienced men aboard. It certainly was not because of any possible navigation errors, as Sub-Lieutenant Lewis proved to be a very capable navigator. Keeping near the coast also helped us to keep out of the way of passing convoys. This was very important, because if we happened to be challenged by an escorting destroyer we had to give the correct reply very quickly to avoid being literally blown out of the water. Our destroyers could not afford to take any chances even in home waters; as we were an entirely new shape of silhouette, other ships would naturally be suspicious of us at first.

We made very good progress, and we were soon skirting the

southern coast of the Isle of Wight. Our Captain apparently knew the various landmarks like the back of his hand, according to the conversation with our cox'n when we were off watch together. Passing the Needles was a thrill for the newcomers, and for the rest of us as we knew it to be a sign that our journey was nearing its end.

We had been informed of our destination, and the reason for our visit. Recalling the pleasant times I had enjoyed at Weymouth I was looking forward to getting there; there would be old acquaintances to renew, and maybe even some news of where the 320 was and what she was doing.

Our arrival at the base was unheralded. It now had a name, and it was known as HMS *Bee* and was a gunnery school in its own right. We moored at a berth further away from the Sailor's Rest than I would have liked, nearer to the harbour entrance and the pier, right under the noses of the gunnery officers, but fortunately they were always too busy to come along and annoy us. The inside of the pier now housed guns of every size and calibre suitable for Coastal Forces craft; it had become quite formidable in appearance.

It was no longer possible to slip into either the Sailor's Rest or the Globe Hotel during our dinner hour, which was not such a bad thing really, even though we thought so at the time; it meant that we had more money to spend of an evening.

During the next two days other boats from our flotilla joined us, all brand, spanking new, looking very capable and aggressive. At first we were under the impression that we would be subjected to a constant stream of gunnery officers and instructors, but to our surprise this was not to be so. The base gunnery officers did visit us, as we were new in design and it was natural that they would want to look us over, and of course to sample the hospitality of our wardroom. Wardrooms of Royal Navy ships and boats, all the world over, are noted for their hospitality, only to fellow officers and notabilities of course.

Our gunnery trials were carried out in the presence of Admiralty experts, civilians. Their tests involved seeing how the boats stood up to the engine vibrations at various speeds and what happened when the guns were fired. Everything must have gone well, as we did not stay out at sea for very long periods each day, and the experts soon packed their bags and left. We were then seemingly left to our own devices.

It was while 611 was moored alongside the quay that the unexpected happened. There was always work of some description to be done, and the cox'n had me hard at it. In this instance any excuses raised about giving my guns priority did not work, as it was getting near to 'rum time' followed by dinner. I was feeling fairly contented.

Two seamen were passing by, on the quay, just two or three yards from me. Without attempting to eavesdrop I could hear their conversation plainly. Then they mentioned a name, and I was all ears. They were discussing a member of their crew, his name was Danny Davies. My cousin, surely; there would not be many Danny Davies's in the world. Although I had not heard that he had joined the Navy – we never saw much of each other when we were younger – I somehow felt that it must be him. So I hailed the two men, and asked about this Dan Davies, and where was he from? He was a stoker aboard their boat, a seventy-footer, and he was a Londoner; they thought he might possibly be from south-east London. I was now sure about who he was, and asked them to take me to see.

Making an excuse to the cox'n and letting him know where I was going and why, I jumped on to the quayside, and hurriedly caught the two seamen in time for them to take me on board.

Once on board they made for the engine-room hatch, and called down to those below. Their message was then passed on to Danny who, wearing a very puzzled look on his face, came on to the upper deck.

At first he did not recognise me, but the penny did not take long to drop before he realised who I was. We sat together on the upper deck of that boat for quite a while, exchanging memories of home, and talking of how long we had both been in the Navy. In fact, even though Dan was about six months younger than me, he had actually joined the Navy, or rather, he had been called up, several months before I was. Probably it was because of the branch of the Navy he had chosen, the engine-room branch. Dan was a stoker. We parted company, said our goodbyes, and never met again until 1944 in Italy.

We were fortunate that our visit to Weymouth coincided with a very warm spell of weather. It became a habit of mine, that after having my rum and dinner, I would spend my time sketching and making notes about my gun. I had already put together a fairly comprehensive notebook, and was quite proud of it. When busily sketching or writing, I would be so engrossed that I would never notice anybody nearby. I had started the notebook when at Whale Island, during the very first course, and it was now resembling something that I could be proud of. In fact it did become the envy of many gunnery ratings as time went by. I did keep it, until about ten or more years ago, I lent it to somebody whose name and reputation was very respected in Coastal Forces. Unfortunately he died, and somehow my book disappeared without trace.

One day, while sketching at my gun, I failed to notice that one of the gunnery officers had come aboard, and was standing right behind me, watching what I was doing, with great interest it seemed. He coughed to attract my attention, and I quickly stood up, and to attention. He introduced himself as Lieutenant Stratton-Long, and asked if he could look at my book more closely, not that I could refuse him, but it was nice of him to ask and not demand. After studying the book for a few minutes he asked if I could design a gun-mounting for twin Oerlikon guns. This was of course well beyond my capability, and I told him so. It appeared that at this particular time such a gun-mounting suitable for Coastal Forces craft had not yet been invented. I think it was the Lieutenant's own idea, so he was naturally disappointed that I could not oblige.

At that time I was merely an able seaman, so I was greatly surprised when Lieutenant Long asked me if I could consider becoming a gunnery instructor. Again I had to say No. I was then very happy and contented aboard 611, its crew were a happy good-humoured bunch, we had three very good officers, so I saw no reason to consider leaving the boat, and wanted to stay. He accepted my refusal with good grace, but asked me to think some more about his suggestion, and if I should change my mind he would be willing to take it further. Diplomatically I told him that I would consider it, but inside me I doubted very much that I would.

Once we had completed everything necessary at Weymouth, we had to leave our berth there and move to the Portland docks. The only obvious reason for doing this was to provision ship; although not so convenient so far as going into Weymouth on night leave; this was compensated by our Captain granting weekend leave.

During my last leave spent at home in Catford, someone at the Plough and Harrow had asked me if I could obtain a 'prick of tobacco' for him. Naturally he did not expect it for nothing, and after telling what the going rate was for this tobacco, I agreed to bring him some on my next leave. Now this is real sailor's tobacco; we had a choice each month of buying tins of either cigarette or pipe tobacco, manufactured cigarettes, or the natural tobacco leaves, and it was the last I had been asked for. You bought a bundle of leaves, dampened them, added a little rum, and rolled them tightly into the shape of a spindle, it was then tightly bound with tarred hemp, and stowed away to mature. The end result was a very strong tobacco, suitable for pipe smokers, real pipe smokers

I hasten to add, or the hard few who liked to chew tobacco. All in all it finished up as powerful stuff, 'Nelson's vintage' one might say. In my locker on board, I had this tobacco already prepared; all I had to do now was to get it to Catford.

The Dockyard gates were guarded by armed sentries, also on duty were Naval police, and HM Customs officers, so getting anything past these gates presented a rather daunting proposition. This was not going to deter me, everyone took chances in those days, and the thought of getting caught, although known to be a possibility, never stopped anyone so far as I knew. At 11.00 a.m. those of us who were going on leave mustered on the upper deck. We were examined to make certain we were correctly dressed, given a mild lecture on how to behave, warned not to disgrace the Royal Navy when on leave, then allowed to proceed. We all walked as casually as we could toward the dockyard gates, I had my tobacco dangling on a length of string, down my right leg, inside my bell-bottom trousers. Providing it did not become necessary for me to run, it would not be obvious, and in this way I nonchalantly strolled past the sentries, past Customs, and the Naval police cheerfully waved us all on our way. Such nice fellows too.

The risks however did not stop at Portland. Often a roving patrol would appear on the train you were travelling on. They were usually in search of deserters, but they had the power of search if necessary. Fortunately this did not happen on the journey, but when we arrived eventually at Waterloo station it was bound to be teeming with police from all three services, plus the railway's own police force, many of whom would be in plain clothes, so everyone had to be alert and watchful all the time.

Luck was on my side. I was stopped by the Naval Patrol, but on production of my official leave pass I was allowed to proceed without any further search or delay. These are the times when you are made aware of your own heart-beat, and the amount of time that it takes to get back to normal.

The next day I took the tobacco to the Plough, where I was paid the princely sum of one pound. The grateful recipient was overjoyed. I never knew what he did with it, but I am fairly certain that he did not intend to smoke it himself. I have a vague recollection that something was said about it being given to his old father-in-law. It was ironical, that although the proud owner of my tobacco, Bob Bishop, was to become much friendlier towards me, he was cautious about his family. I never knew he had daughters, and if I had it was a certainty that he would not have allowed me anywhere near a daughter of his. At that time I was not concerned anyway; his eldest would have been the same age as Sylvia, so I would have considered her to be too young as well. In conversation with Bob, he did mention that his son was also in the Navy and that the last he had heard was that his son was aboard HMS *Hood*, that unlucky battleship that was sunk by a freak shot from either the *Bismarck* or the *Prinz Eugen* in an engagement during 1941. Bob did not know if his son was still on the *Hood* at the time, and the war ended before he knew.

That weekend leave was quickly over, and I returned aboard the 611, happy, revitalised, ready for almost anything.

About this time, RAF pilots were painting weird and wonderful figures and cartoon characters upon the fusilage of their planes; saucy sayings, such as 'Here is a present for you Adolf', 'A headache for Hitler', and countless other inscriptions designed to irritate the Germans were written on the side of the huge bombs they were going to drop upon Germany. This amused me and I decided to do something similar, I did not bother with any inscriptions, but upon the protective shield of my pom-pom I painted the irate figure of Donald Duck on one side, and Popeye the Sailor on the other. Fortunately our officers did not object and the cartoons amused everybody, so I had to paint whatever was requested by the other gunners upon their gun shields.

We were not as lucky as when I was aboard the 320. We did

not have the equivalent of Jeff Goodey, so everyone had to share certain duties, particularly the duty of cooking for the whole crew. It was going to be some time before we would find someone brave enough to take this on; in the meantime we all would have to take our turn at it.

We were supposed to learn how to take over the duties of anyone that might die in action. It was not necessary to become expert at these jobs, but to know enough to be able to act with confidence when needed.

Aboard all boats and ships, 'painting ship' was always a priority. Cox'ns everywhere wanted their vessels to look better than the others, and would beg, borrow, and even steal the necessary paints and equipment to improve their boats. For some reason, I never did a great deal of painting as the crews aboard these new larger boats were enough to allow us gunners to concentrate on our guns, leaving the miscellaneous work to others. This provoked many moans and groans of course, but it never caused serious rifts among us.

That dread I had of submarines was renewed by the sudden appearance in Weymouth of two midget submarines, each one crewed by two men. Knowing how the devious minds at Admiralty worked, and how they enjoyed having fun by drafting men to the most unlikely situations, I felt totally insecure until we put to sea and left Weymouth for good. About that time stories were being circulated about an ordinary seaman who was making a name for himself in the Drafting Office of HMS *Hornet* at Gosport, where the fate and destinies of all ratings in Coastal Forces were decided. It was said that that ordinary seaman never saw an angry wave, much less the enemy; he was promoted to able seaman, leading seaman, and petty officer, without, as far as most of us knew, ever leaving the base. It was a ridiculous fact that so many men were actually afraid to upset him, in case he arranged for them to be drafted somewhere unpleasant. Whether he was able to do this, and actually did, I do not know, but many would swear it was true. Rumours do run wild in the Navy, and as they pass from man to man, so they get exaggerated, just as they do in civilian life, but I would agree that he was someone to keep well away from.

Everything that needed to be done at Weymouth and Portland had now been completed, so off we sailed for Gosport, which was going to be our home base, as part of a flotilla, protecting our convoys as they passed through the English Channel. We would be tied up alongside the base, a prospect we did not relish; we would be too damn near that drafting office for comfort. It was a very apprehensive crew aboard HMMGB 611 when they arrived alongside, but we quickly settled down and mostly even forgot that man existed. One man however was pretty pleased that Gosport would be our home base, our cox'n, Petty Officer Smith; his home was here, so he would be able to spend much more time with his family when we were not out at sea.

Some other boats from our flotilla were already here, and the last two arrived within the next day or so. The 18th MGB flotilla was now ready, able and willing to take on whatever enemy we could find.

Before we even had a chance to take part in an operation of any kind, their Lordships at Admiralty decided that we should have a change in leadership, so they took our Captain away from us. It was probably because of his experience in command of merchant ships really. He was genuinely wasted aboard our small craft, and without any doubt achieved far more for the war effort in whatever ship he went to, most likely a destroyer; and whoever his lucky crew turned out to be, it was we aboard 611 who were the real losers.

The man who took over command of 611 was an entirely different kettle of fish. He was Lieutenant Ian (Spud) Lyle RNVR, and later became a very respected and capable gunboat captain in his own right. He was, according to stories told, nicknamed 'Spud' while training at Naval College, because it was said that he always had a hole in the heels of his socks. This was not hard to believe. It was well known that Naval officers possessed wicked senses of humour, and when at college they spared nobody.

As our Skipper, he proved to be somewhat of a Jekyll and Hyde character. Before 1000 hrs each day he was unbearable, and to be avoided at all cost; we would feel the raw edge of his tongue without warning, and often without reason. It was a lesson we quickly learnt, and when he was due to 'surface' everyone would disappear from the upper deck on some pretext. He would wander around the boat looking for anything that was not as it should be, no matter how small and insignificant; he would then send for the cox'n and instruct him to deal with the culprit. This we did not mind too much, the cox'n would always be fair and reasonable, but if our Captain wanted to deal with the unfortunate man himself, we knew and feared the worst.

After 1000 hrs it was a different world we lived in. The Skipper had downed his first whisky of the day, and he was a different person entirely. He was at all times a brilliant sailor, and could turn our boat around in its own length. This might sound easy, but I can assure you that it is not, and is no mean feat. He was never a man who would mix with us on the lower deck. I believe he genuinely found it difficult even to make conversation with us on the rare occasions that he had to. One imagines that this was due to his upbringing, but after all there were many other Naval officers with even more illustrious backgrounds than his, who could converse with ratings quite easily.

Any fraternisation with the crew was left to the two junior officers, who were as popular as ever, and in view of their Commanding Officer's attitude toward ratings it was to be for everybody's good that they were. Nevertheless, mixing or not, Spud knew each one of us by name, and a great deal about each one; he also knew how best, in his way, to deal with us.

All the time we were able to keep out of his way, and not giving him cause to complain too much, life aboard the 611 was fine. Of course there would always be the usual small disagreements when you had thirty or more men grouped together in a confined space. It must be stressed that our mess-decks, on which we lived, ate and slept, were not to be confused with cabin space on civilian cruise liners, and later, when more men were added to the crew, not every man had his own bunk, but in the harbour the last ones to join the boat would have to sleep on the mess tables and be thankful for that. Most of the friction between members of the crew was of minor importance, and everything regarded as being serious would, when investigated thoroughly, usually turn out to be less serious than thought, often owing to exaggeration or even misinterpretation. In crowded living conditions, small incidents were often blown up out of all proportion, but that is caused by human frailty, which exists inside us all.

Soon after joining the 611, I received a letter from my mother. She had received a letter from the Red Cross in Switzerland, informing her that her son Alan was alive and well; he was now a prisoner-of-war, and held in Germany. This welcome communication was quickly followed by a letter from Alan, but the part of it that impressed everyone the most, was that although it was short and to the point, it was almost word for word, as spoken by that medium at the spiritualist meeting. 'Coincidence?' Many people have said that, and maybe they were right, but whatever it was, it made me think more seriously about mediums in general.

By this time, we had all been together long enough to confide in each other, and talk about the various aspects of our lives, so when I received the information about my brother, the whole crew shared in my pleasure: perhaps even Spud Lyle too.

Owing to Spud's disposition, and of course my own, it obviously was not going to be very difficult for the two of us to disagree. He was used to getting his own way; he was also in the unquestionable position of being able to make sure that he did. As for me, well, at twenty years of age, nobody could mistake me for an angel, and that little bit of Welsh that I inherited from my ancestors made me often obstinate and headstrong, to put it mildly, and no doubt contributed a great deal towards our Skipper's attitude towards me.

As we were moored so close to HMS *Hornet*, we accepted that life when in harbour was not going to be free and easy for us, and we were very close to two other major Naval bases, so our activities could be watched by some very senior ranking officers. Some of them were not kindly disposed towards officers of Coastal Forces, and would seize every opportunity to criticise them, including of course, us. Consequently this meant that our officers kept a very close eye upon what we did, and how we were dressed; sentries when patrolling on the jetty beside their boat had to be alert at all times, and never fail to give the salute entitled to the visiting officer; the wrong one meant trouble for both the sentry and his officers. When we were on the upper deck for any reason at all, we always had to look busy during working hours; it must never be thought that life in the Navy could be enjoyed. This was the attitude that our former Skipper objected to, but which was approved by his successor.

For obvious reasons, our cox'n was the only member of our crew who enjoyed being at Gosport, so when we were allowed ashore we usually crossed by ferry to Portsmouth, where there was plenty of life and noise. It meant that we had to be constantly on our guard against encounters with Naval patrols, but generally the word would be out as to where they would be, and mostly we were able to avoid them, so we enjoyed many night leaves spent in the town.

Strangely, as when aboard the 320, my closest friends were stokers. The best was probably Joe Swift, who hailed from Liverpool. Joe was quiet and steady, two years my senior in age, but

*AB Jones, me, Stoker Joe Swift. Taken just after closing time in Newhaven, which accounts for our various expressions.*

the right man to be by your side in any trouble, not that we looked for any, and never actually encountered much. Liverpool not being exactly convenient, Joe seldom went home for short leaves of any kind, so when I invited him to come home with me to Catford, he jumped at the chance. My mother thought he was delightful; his Scouse accent was a constant delight to her, and won her over completely. Together we visited every possible place of entertainment in south-east London, and he loved every bit of it.

Our officers were cast in the same mould as most Coastal Forces officers were. They had joined for ACTION, and that was what they now lived for. Our Skipper was no exception: if anything, he wanted more than anybody else, so if volunteers were asked for, no matter what, providing it meant us going to sea, then he was right up front.

One one occasion a force twelve gale was blowing in the Channel, a convoy had been caught in it and ships were struggling their way eastwards. Although protected by destroyers and armed merchant ships, it was feared that despite the weather, the Germans would have a go and attack it. We thought the situation ludicrous, and that it would be impossible for any attack to be made; it was even doubtful as to whether we could have negotiated past the harbour entrance safely, the wind was so strong, but our Spud just had to volunteer. Fortunately, although we had to stand-by just in case, we were not allowed to attempt it. However bad the weather might be, 611, because of Spud, was always there, waiting to put to sea for our King and Country. Officially there were rules and regulations stating up to what force gales we could be at sea, and they were less than force twelve, but there were rare occasions when we did, and on these occasions it must be admitted that Spud gave us inspiration. He would be on the bridge the whole time we were at sea, in all weathers, soaked to the skin and enjoying every moment. It was almost as if he had a personal battle against the elements.

In ordinary weather conditions, patrolling the convoy lanes up and down the English Channel on routine procedures was often boring and monotonous. Those days of espionage work seemed to have been most enjoyable; they were not really, but the privileges that went with the work made them seem so. More than likely it was being able to operate from Yarmouth and Felixstowe that made them so very attractive; after all, both these towns were much preferable to being in either Gosport or Portsmouth.

# CHAPTER 12

# Special Operations,
# and one not so special

IT was nothing unusual for our Captain to disappear from our
boat. Often it was just to visit another boat to have a drink with
its Skipper, sometimes it was a visit to the base commander, so on
this occasion when he disappeared none of us wondered where he
was off to, or cared. We would enjoy the peaceful atmosphere
that would exist in his absence, and make the most of it, as we
never knew what his temper would be like when he did return.
This time, however, he was away for twenty-four hours, so we
imagined that he had been called 'further afield' than HMS *Hornet*
this time, and later we learnt that he had been called to London
for a special briefing.

When he returned, he called a special meeting with his two
junior officers. This lasted for almost an hour and then they
returned to their normal duties. The lad who looked after their
cabins and meals was questioned, but he knew nothing, and had
been ordered out of hearing range when the three officers were
in conference.

It was normal for each boat when in harbour, to know if it was
going on patrol that evening, or if it would be on 'stand-by', and
most definitely if it had engine trouble, or something else that
might prevent it from putting to sea.

All boats' crews, when they knew that they were not going to
sea that day, would look forward to enjoying all-night leave, and

this would be given – 'piped' being the Navy term – at 1600 hrs. Those who were going ashore would sneak below well before time, to get themselves ready to leave the boat as quickly as possible; there would be competition for use of the small wash-room facilities, then a change of clothing, no precious time having been wasted. Then, after inspection by the duty officer they would hurry ashore. Precious leave time must never be wasted. If one was going ashore then one must get there as quickly as possible, before someone changed their mind and ordered the boat to sea. It was known to have happened.

This day, though, was going to be different. Leave obviously was not going to be given, the cox'n would have been told in

*'D'-class Motor Gunboat, converted to torpedo boat.*

advance, but I guessed something special was in the wind. I had experienced this sort of thing so often when aboard the 320, and now it was happening again. As usual, some of the lads had sneaked below and started to change their clothing, but there was an air of uneasiness, and then we heard that the cox'n had been called to the Captain's cabin, so all we could do then was to wait. After ten minutes or so, the cox'n joined us on our mess-deck; he pulled a long face and said, 'Sorry lads, no leave tonight, we will be putting to sea.' That was all he could tell us, or rather, that was all that he was allowed to tell us.

Those that had been hoping to go ashore now changed back into working rig, and sadly put away their Number Ones.

The engine-room staff were summoned below, and we heard our engines being tested, then a message came from the Captain, via our cox'n, ordering us to prepare for sea. Groans from us all, although by this time it was no longer a surprise.

At 1700 hrs exactly, we cast off and headed for the open sea. We sailed with the Isle of Wight off our starboard bow. It was now completely dark, no moon, no stars to be seen, and plenty of cloud. We still knew nothing about this trip. Spud Lyle was not as forthcoming as Peter Loasby, and did not believe in sharing information with his crew.

While we were under way, nothing much happened but the usual testing of our guns and signals exchanged with the many passing vessels. Occasionally a destroyer would appear on the horizon, radios would crackle, and the destroyer would disappear, apparently satisfied that we were friendly, and not an E-boat. The outline of our boat was still an unfamiliar one to any man outside of Coastal Forces, so they could not afford to take chances; neither could we.

The presence of the destroyer was soon justified as after a little while the silhouettes of a convoy appeared. Even though we had established ourselves as friendly, that destroyer kept itself between us and the convoy.

At this time we were in mid-Channel, and obviously heading for the French coast. Several attempts had been made to coax information from our telegraphist, Bill Cooper, who also hailed from London, but without success. Bill definitely was not going to risk the wrath of our immediate Lord and Master, Lieutenant 'Spud' Lyle. I have a feeling that he would have approved of my addressing him that way. From an unknown source came the rumour that we were going to 'chart buoys off the French Coast'; it was the same old chestnut again but this time I fervently hoped had nothing to do with German battleships. I did not mind the prospect of an engagement with E-boats, but anything larger could be suicidal. So, sceptical as I was, furtive enquiries revealed that there were no spies on board, so a landing was not anticipated. Charting buoys seemed possible, but I still found it hard to believe, so I was not going to accept the story too easily.

Up to the time we encountered the convoy, we were carrying out normal sea duties, which meant half of the crew on watch, the other half down below, some trying to snatch some sleep, others busy writing home.

We had passed the convoy on our port side, and it was now out of sight. About half an hour later 'action stations' was sounded and everybody took up their appointed positions. A messenger came to us all from the Captain, telling us that we would remain closed up at action stations for several hours. Under no circumstances would he allow anyone to leave his position, and any call of nature would have to be dealt with on the spot. Meanwhile we must be completely noiseless; anybody making the slightest sound would be answerable to the Captain. That threat was enough, almost enough to make us all stop breathing completely.

However I knew from past experiences that the sound of a spanner dropped upon the deck would travel for miles, especially if any U-boats were in the vicinity, and this was likely for two reasons: firstly the presence of that convoy; and secondly that the

Germans had established a base for U-boats on the nearby French coast. There was also a base for E-boats nearby. So it was made very clear, that our Skipper was taking no chances, and our mission, whatever it was, was also very 'hush-hush'. For me this was quite like old times, and if it had been less cold I might even have enjoyed the occasion.

The dark outline of land came into view; it was nearer than calculated, although we did not realise this until after the mission had been completed. We slowly kept a measured distance from the shore, running on our silenced engine. Apparently it was normal for all our boats to have a silenced engine fitted, ready for espionage trips.

Suddenly it happened. Around two in the morning, fog descended around us quickly; it was so dense that visibility was impossible beyond twenty to thirty yards. Even though this fog was much cleaner than a London pea-souper, it was every bit as thick and dense. We literally could not do a thing except drift with the tide.

Silence was still the operative word. Conversation of any kind was forbidden, engines were stopped altogether, so we were now at the mercy of the tide. Radio silence was also enforced as we were so near to the coast that any wireless activity would have given our bearings away immediately. It also seemed to be very cold, getting wetter, and more miserable all the time. To make matters worse, nobody knew how long these periods of fog off this coast would be likely to last. Our navigator had not been told to expect this, and all the time we were drifting without any control over our direction.

Our boat had been pointing westwards when we arrived in sight of the coast. The officers on the bridge would have known if we were still heading in the right direction, but the rest of us closed up at our guns and other positions were completely in the dark. Some of the lads afterwards admitted that all they could think about was that they were a long way from home, dangerously near to the enemy, and enveloped in a white, thick, almost cotton-wool-like substance called 'fog'.

Every so often one of our officers would visit us all to make certain that we were awake and vigilant. They need not have been concerned, because I would have thought that most of the men were like me, scared stiff. Again, it was because of the uncertainty, not knowing what could happen or what was going to happen. These are the conditions that can break a man, not actual action; in action you are too busy fighting back to think about anything else, but this situation was something different, and our Skipper was no better informed than we were. He had his job to do, and we had ours; we were on equal footing whether he liked it or not and it was hoped that we were all going to do our jobs well. All there was, was complete silence, we were drifting towards we knew not where, we were now feeling the strain, we were tired, our imaginations were running riot inside our minds, and we all knew that there was exactly nothing that we could do except hope that our nerves held good.

It seemed like hours later but in fact was only one hour, that the fog lifted as quickly and suddenly as it had fallen, just as if someone up above had lifted a blanket off us. All I can remember was noise, the sound of signals, bells, raised voices, all engines roaring away as we sped with all possible speed westwards. It seemed almost panic-stricken, but really Spud and those with him on the bridge were in full control of the situation. If they had any fear at all it would have been about how the rest of the crew were shaping up.

They need not have worried, everything happened so quickly that nobody had a chance to do anything, except to remain at their positions as previously ordered.

What actually happened was that as the fog lifted, we could see that we were less than a mile from the shore. But, to the horror of everyone who could see north, off our starboard side, one hundred and fifty yards, two hundred at the most, on our seaward side, lay a German E-boat, fortunately facing the opposite direction to us. The E-boat had obviously been caught by the fog just as we had; it also had drifted with the tide, and being a much lighter craft it had moved towards us much faster, completely unaware that we, or any vessel, were nearby. The only thing that did puzzle us when we had time to think about it was, why were they also keeping radio silence? Being so close to France, and one of their own bases, it had not been necessary; they could have been in radio contact all the time, giving their bearings or even asking for their instructions. However it was fortunate for us that they did not.

As the sound of engines roaring shattered the still of the night, both boats sped away at maximum speed in opposite directions, and not a shot was fired. For which all of us aboard 611 will be eternally grateful.

It was also a very good thing that we all had been well trained, and our nerves had stood up to the predicament so well. It does not bear thinking about: if one man had panicked and shots had been exchanged we might never have made it back to England. The E-boat would not have worried us too much, we could have taken care of him, but being so close to shore, the gunfire would have been heard, and in no time there would have been an assortment of boats and aircraft looking for us, with dire results. We gunners had been instructed not to open fire under any circumstances unless ordered to do so by the Captain, and this would only have happened if we had been spotted by the enemy's shore batteries. Then our first target would have been their search-lights, followed by the silencing of any guns. By this time we would hopefully be speeding on our way out of range. All this is pure speculation, it is true, but it came damn near to happening.

When this kind of operation was undertaken, there was always the possibility of the presence of E-boats. In our case it was said to be most unlikely and information obtained about locally based enemy boats had stated that they would be away upon an excursion further to the east of where we were going. How and why this particular E-boat should have been where it was was never found out. Our operation ought to have been carried out in complete safety and secrecy, but now of course any future visit to this area would have to be aborted. When talking over the situation, we reached the conclusion that the E-boat crew were just as surprised as we had been and most likely just as thankful that no shots had been fired, as they would have come off worst; we were so much more heavily armed than they were.

It was not known whether or not we had completed whatever our mission was, or if there was anything else that should have been done, but if there was it was cancelled, and we sped at full speed towards home.

Our Captain was obviously in good spirits. This indicated that things had not gone as terribly wrong as we had thought, and later, through the traditional grapevine, we heard that we had done whatever we were supposed to do, and that the mission was regarded as a success.

Eventually we entered the Solent, then into Portsmouth harbour, and berthed at our usual spot at HMS *Hornet.* The usual procedure then took place; we cleaned ship, cleaned and oiled our guns, and only then, except for the unlucky man detailed to act as sentry, could most of us collapse upon our bunks. That night operation took so much out of us all, that when night-leave was granted later, only our cox'n went ashore, to go to his home; the rest of us could not have cared less. Had the cox'n not been married, I doubt whether he would have left the boat, but then, as a married man he had his obligations.

According to our reckoning, we were due for some real leave, so much moaning by us all forced the cox'n to have a word with our 1st Lieutenant about it. Fortunately Sub-Lieutenant Turner was of the same opinion and agreed to approach the Captain. We were in luck. Spud was still highly delighted with our little adventure, so much so that he made instant representation to the Base Commander, and to our delight leave was going to be granted.

After what we had been through, we were sure that we would get fourteen days of bliss. It actually finished up as four days, and being told that we could not be spared for longer. Somewhere behind this I felt the hand of our Skipper. It was not that he begrudged us a longer leave; I am sure that he was under the impression that we were like himself, keen to get out there and have a go, so leave was of secondary importance. Maybe, because he did not appear to want leave, he did not think that we ought to.

During one of my visits home, I had been told that another of my cousins, Arthur, now a leading seaman and RDF operator, was now aboard one of the Navy's newest and largest battleships, HMS *Anson*, and it so happened that right then she was in Portsmouth dockyard. As Arthur would not have known where I was, or what sort of craft I was serving on, or even if I was still in England, any contact between us two would be entirely up to me.

From a telephone at HMS *Hornet* I contacted the battleship's gangway and spoke to the Duty officer. Once he established there was a genuine family link between the two of us, he arranged for leading seaman Miller to come to the phone. As Arthur picked up the phone, I could hear him ask who it was at my end, and I was the last person he expected to hear. Of course he was delighted to hear my voice, and upon telling me that he was free that evening I invited him aboard the 611 for a meal before going ashore together. With my usual aplomb I told him that he could see how 'real sailors lived'. Ignoring the way it was said, Arthur was pleased to be invited. The only drawback was that I was really part of the duty watch and it was my turn to cook the evening meal. I managed to get someone to stay on board in my place, but my 'stand-in' would not do the cooking, so we settled that I should cook, and then go ashore after.

It was near enough 1800 hrs when Arthur put in an appearance. First he enjoyed a guided tour of our boat, by one of the other lads, as I was busy in the galley. Apart from the tot of rum that I had put aside for him, the tour of our boat was probably the only other part he would enjoy.

A culinary expert I am not; maybe as a seaman I could just about get by, but I could never pretend to be able to cook, I try, I try hard, but to leave me in a ship's galley, and expect me to use my imagination is something else, it is equivalent to the work of the Devil himself.

It so happened that we were short of food on board, and a fresh stock of provisions was not due until the next day. I had not been aware of this when I invited Arthur aboard. I wanted to impress my cousin, and I most certainly did just that. There was very little for me to choose from, so I baked a sort of shepherds pie, mixing corned beef with sardines, to the appearance of hash. It looked reasonable, and I do not doubt that any fish in the harbour would have enjoyed it, because nobody else did. So amid considerable sarcasm, it was all thrown overboard. While the rest of the men on board scavenged around for something to make sandwiches from, I quickly changed into my Number Ones and hurried ashore with Arthur as fast as we could go, in case they changed their minds about standing-in for me. We made straight for the Royal Sailors Home, where we bought a meal, ate it, and then enjoyed a few drinks together.

The evening spent together was an enjoyable one, despite that cooking fiasco of mine; this has never been forgotten by either of us, even now, fifty odd years later.

Closing-time at all the pubs was sounded, so reluctantly we had

to say our goodbyes and parted company. We did not realise at
the time, but we were not to see each other again until after the
war had ended. It was quite possible that after sampling my
cooking Arthur would not have wanted to anyway, unless extract-
ing from me a guarantee not to attempt it again.

The winter of 1942, although not as severe as the previous one,
was still uncomfortably cold. It seemed to start early, and it was
no surprise to find a thick layer of snow covering the boats and
harbour one morning. It did not lie for long. Whether on the
other side of the English Channel they also had snow I do not
know; if they did, then it never stopped their E-boats from putting
to sea, as we were alerted to go out and deal with them.

The noise created by six 'D' class motor gunboats when preparing for sea was terrific, twenty-four powerful Packard engines
roaring away as they were tested, each engine capable of flying an
aircraft. All six boats cast off, making for the harbour entrance,
each manoeuvring with care, to make certain there were no
collisions. Slowly we passed the entrance, giving the customary
salute to the C in C, and proceeded out to sea. To see a flotilla
of motor gunboats together in this way was an impressive sight,
even to those who were now used to it.

There was one boat that was unfortunate enough not to be able
to sail at the same time. Somehow its propellers were fouled by a
heaving-line. This is a length of rope, weighted at one end to
enable it to be thrown ashore for someone to catch, with a
mooring line attached on the other end, enabling it to be secured
to a bollard, making the ship or boat safely tied and secured.

The Captain of this boat was Lieutenant T.W. Boyd RNVR;
he had already won the DSO for bravery, and was a very competent officer. It was said that he came from a family that owned a
fleet of fishing trawlers on the north-east coast, and I can quite
believe it, as he was an extremely tough man, but also very well
liked by everyone. His crew loved him, and would do anything

for him, but he never asked them to do something that he could not do himself. The fact that he was an officer made no difference whatsoever, he would prove that he was capable of doing the worst possible tasks before expecting his men to do the same.

Usually when propellers were fouled this way in harbour, a diver would be sent down to clear it, but this took time; a diver had to be found and the necessary authority obtained to use him. To Tom Boyd this was unnecessary delay; he wanted to be out at sea with the rest of the flotilla. If there was going to be some fun then he wanted to make certain that he missed none of it. Without hesitation, he stripped off his clothes and, clad only in his birthday suit, dived into the murky, oily waters of the harbour, and cleared the propeller himself. His boat was then 'under way' after the minimum delay, and after no doubt a large stiff drink, he was back on his bridge by the time it was passing the harbour entrance.

All speed was made to catch up with the rest of the flotilla and together the six boats made for the area in which the E-boats had been reported. Unfortunately, especially for Lieutenant Boyd and all his efforts, no enemy boats could be found, so after patrolling thoroughly across and around the area for a considerable amount of time, the disappointed D-boats returned to HMS *Hornet*.

During the next ten days or so, we had to endure many similar false alarms, deliberately caused by the Germans in some way no doubt, to create maximum discomfort for us.

The day following our fruitless chase around the English Channel was the day on which our four days' leave should have begun. But instead we were kept on tenterhooks for the next ten days, with E-boat warnings being received almost every day. Sometimes we put to sea looking for them; sometimes we waited for more tangible evidence before we wasted precious fuel by putting to sea unnecessarily. To get us to waste precious fuel was of valuable importance to the enemy, and considerable effort was made to get us to do just that.

Our leave was eventually decided. During the four days our engines would get a thorough overhaul, and various other small things would be attended to; so off on leave we went.

Four days was enough for Joe Swift to get home to Liverpool. It would mean that he could spend two whole days with his family; the other two, of course, would be taken up with travelling. So on this occasion I would spend my time at Catford on my own. At this particular time I was still friendly with Sylvia, so the leave was an enjoyable one, marred only by my sister being ill; this of course added to my mother's worries.

On the day that I was due to return to Gosport, I decided that I wanted to stay home longer, just long enough to be assured that my sister would be all right, but to do this I had to find a way which would not add to the worries already troubling my mother. Despite calling upon several doctors to ask for their co-operation none were willing, so to stay at home a little longer would mean going AWOL, and I did, for two extra days. My sister became a little better, and to my mother's great relief, I returned to 611 of my own free will. It was common knowledge that one was safe if only staying over the leave limit by two days; more than that would risk a call by either the local police or even a Naval Patrol. This I knew would cause my mother to worry ever so much more.

As I neared the 611, I discovered that I had butterflies in my stomach, also a rather sinking feeling. My appearance on board was greeted with hoots of merriment, catcalls and considerable sarcasm and wit. Within minutes the cox'n appeared, and took me before the Duty Officer, who told me to report outside the Captain's cabin, to be punished, the next morning. This was duly carried out, and very uneasily I stood before the Captain; also present were both of the other officers, and the cox'n. The charge was read out, and I was asked why I did it. Giving my sister's illness as an excuse did not help, but I must admit, much to my surprise, Spud was sympathetic. Not enough however to let me off, so I was accordingly punished with seven days stoppage of leave, and rum, the latter being the worst part of the punishment, because most of the next seven days would be spent at sea anyway. The other members of the crew were sympathetic and all gave me a little drop of their own rum to me; in this way I might even have been better off.

## CHAPTER 13

# *Punishment for all, nobody escapes*

AROUND this same period, the weather was too bad for any of our boats to be able to go to sea. I had completed my punishment, but was unable to go ashore because of duty; it would have been about 2030 hrs, I was lying on my bunk reading, while most of the crew were ashore, when suddenly there was a commotion. It seemed from all the noise and footsteps crossing our deck that there was a great deal of activity. At first I took little notice, but the lad who was on sentry duty on the jetty by our boat, asked me to come up on deck. Reluctantly I joined him on the jetty, asking what was wrong, and wondering what on earth he could want of me. 'Stand here, Jack, for a few minutes, and take a good look at our officers', which I did; it was obvious that something was up.

To my amazement, it seemed that every officer in our flotilla had gathered together in a group on the quayside. Every man was dressed in his very best uniform, complete with medals and in some cases, swords, I thought. They were, all of them, well under the influence, of quite a few gins I would imagine. Making considerable noise with their laughter and loud voices, they had a quick discussion, unfortunately out of range of my ears, and then marched off towards the base wardroom. They were then singing quite loudly. It is not known at what time they returned, as it must have been well after midnight, when I for one was fast asleep, and not a bit concerned as to what they had been up to.

The following day was rife with rumours, but nothing made

sense enough to be believed, until a few days later we heard that our flotilla was leaving Gosport. At that time we knew not where we were going; the officers were saying nothing at all, and when they met to discuss whatever was happening, it was done in their cabins, not where they could be overheard.

On the day that we left Gosport it seemed that an imaginary cloud hung over us. Somehow we appeared a sad, sorry and almost forlorn lot. The atmosphere created by the subdued officers also influenced their crews, yet, speaking only from 611's point of view, we knew almost nothing about whatever the problem was. The grapevine had told us one little bit of information: we were sailing to Newhaven, and that was where we were going to be based from then on. This was not something to look forward to. In comparison to Portsmouth it was a miserable place, just a few public houses, not very lively ones mainly, and very little else. Smithy our cox'n was well and truly browned off.

Our arrival at Newhaven was unheralded; certainly there were no flags or welcoming committee. We berthed along the eastern bank of the river, alongside the huge sheds that belonged to the Southern Railway. The docks at Newhaven were for rail traffic only, right up to the outbreak of war. There were a few mine-sweepers based there, and a mixture of other small Coastal Forces craft, but we were obviously the elite.

The first man from our crew to go ashore was our caterer, in search of a source of fresh food supplies. On his return he was able to give us all a quick description of the town and any possible attractions, stressing quite shamelessly that he thought the latter did not exist. We were, he said, roughly two miles from the town. The railway station was more convenient, it was part of the docks, and trains to London and Brighton were frequent and still oper-ating. This at least was good news, because if the town was as dead as reported we would be using the trains a great deal.

There did not appear to be any local dance halls, nor were there any at Seaford, which was the next town, only three or four miles away, so Brighton would be the popular choice to spend our night leave, or London for many, myself included. The northerners in our crews would save their money to spend on longer leaves, which made sense. Joe Swift, however, would be coming to Catford with me, along with another stoker.

There seemed to be one major drawback however. The town was full of Canadian troops. We had nothing against them, and appreciated the fact that they were over here to give a hand against the Germans, but it also meant that there would be an abundance of Military Police, the notorious Redcaps, and they were bound to interfere with our lads, which was not going to go down well at all.

The following day in harbour enabled the various members of crews that were friendly to get together, to mix a little, and then we learnt the details of what had happened at Gosport, and the reason for our departure.

That night when we saw our officers dressed up like 'dogs dinners' in their finery, was apparently a night that was going to be talked about for a very long time, maybe for years to come. For some reason, possibly jealousy upon the part of the officers who formed the base staff at HMS *Hornet*, antagonism erupted between them and the officers of our flotilla. It must have been a few days prior to that fateful evening, the result being that our officers had been banned from using the wardroom at the *Hornet*.

Our officers, quite rightly we all thought, were indignant about it, and determined enough not to take this ban lying down. So, one of the gunboat Skippers, it was never said which one in case he was victimised, called a meeting of all officers in our flotilla, to discuss the implication of this ban, and possible means of retaliation and revenge. A resolution was put to the vote, and the result was unanimous; no officer would have dared to go against the wishes of the rest of them anyway as the stigma behind such an action would stay with the officer concerned for the remainder of his career.

So that evening, their great occasion arrived, and under the influence of 'liquid encouragement' they had marched, singing lustily, to the *Hornet* wardroom. What they originally intended doing remains a mystery, they might even have intended friendly persuasion, but the best laid plans of mice and men often go astray, and that seems exactly what might have happened.

The officers at the base heard ours coming. The noise was probably heard well in advance of their appearance; anyway they realised that trouble was in the offing, and locked themselves in the wardroom bar, refusing to allow entry to the motley throng outside. This was meant as a deterrent, but they had never had to deal with a situation such as this before. Our officers were far from being a docile lot and the sight of the closed wardroom door was like showing the proverbial red rag to a bull, and our officers had their own version of a bull, Lieutenant Tom Boyd DSO, RNVR, a man who was afraid of nothing, and was not prepared to let a closed door come between him and that bar. The few drinks inside him would have only served to make him think that all this was a personal affront to himself.

What happened next has only been related to me. Naturally I could not have been there so I do not know how much was fact or how much was fiction; when situations like this happen, it is normal for it to be exaggerated, if only a little. Whatever did occur was of a serious nature, that much cannot be denied.

The story is that Tom walked to the opposite end of the corridor, turned to face the wardroom door, lowered his head in the same way that a bull would, then ran full tilt at the door. Under his weight and the power he possessed, the door simply smashed to pieces; the rest of our flotilla officers poured into the bar. It was said that a free-for-all followed, one that was up to Hollywood standards. How much was drunk and how much was smashed was never revealed, but it must have been a sight to have seen. We were told that no item of furniture in that bar was left in one piece when the fracas was over.

It was all too serious to pass unnoticed or unreported, so it quickly reached the ears of certain Admirals, who, not really approving of the type of men who were now officers in the Royal Navy, commanding little boats, and often not showing them the respect they felt was due to them, made their displeasure quickly felt. Payment for the damage done to the wardroom and the property therein was expected. No doubt it came to much more than they ever dreamed of, some were not really in a position to afford it, but they paid up along with the rest without complaint.

It would have been emphasised that such behaviour was a disgrace to the Royal Navy and not to be tolerated, and I doubt very much that the Admirals considered it to be down to 'high spirits'. Stoppage of leave to our officers was imposed, just how long is not known but I was of the opinion that it was still in force when I eventually left the 611 the following year. Partly in an attempt to hurt the officers more, it was decided to move the flotilla away from Gosport, away from civilisation in their eyes, to Newhaven; in that way, the likelihood of such an incident occuring again would be prevented.

That was how the 18th Motor Gunboat flotilla came to be based at Newhaven.

The usual anti-E-boat patrols followed. It seemed to us that we were making more patrols than we used to, and it was probably true, that by going to sea more often, it cut down on the cost of entertainment, and the less affluent officers would be given the chance to recoup their losses in this way. It also partly relieved their frustrations; their sea-duties would occupy their minds, and if they encountered the enemy they would be able to take it out on them. It was also noticed that when the need for patrols lessened, somcone dreamed up exercises and manoeuvres; there was certainly no chance of us stagnating in the backwaters of Newhaven.

Fortunately for the crews, it was impossible for us to be at sea all the time. Our boats used a terrific amount of fuel, and this had to be replenished with more from abroad, so with consideration for our merchant seamen on convoys, we had to be as economical as possible. Supplies of fuel were even more precious because it was used for aircraft also.

We reconnnoitred places of entertainment nearest to the base, but Joe Swift and I were not too keen, so when we were ashore on night-leave we put the railway station to good use, and we would catch a train to London, and on to Catford.

We always went to my home first, to see my mother. She became quite fond of Joe, and then when we began to bring Lofty Walker home as well, she took a liking to him too. Now that we were based at Newhaven the three of us could come to Catford quite often, and so brought a little more pleasure into my mother's life. Maybe it was not such a vast amount, but it gave her something to look forward to, and to talk about to the family and neighbours.

At home we would have a wash and brush-up, and then set off for Lewisham, where the liveliest pubs were. We would often call first at the Plough and Harrow in Catford. It was against my nature to neglect visiting Mrs Marriott; she was far too nice a person and I did not intend to offend her in any way. In fact, as a token of my appreciation for the way in which she always made me welcome, and of course for those records she gave me for the 320, I did a self portrait and gave it to her. It remained on the wall of the lounge bar for several years.

After remaining in the Plough for about half an hour, we would make for Lewisham, merely a mile away, where there were two public houses in particular that were lively and always had music of some sort. They were both in the High Street, and approximately only a hundred yards apart; they were the Castle, and the Black Bull.

At most public houses in those times, the saloon bars contained pianos, and only on very rare occasions would it be difficult to find someone to play them. Mostly of course the publican would employ a pianist; this was safer for the piano, of course, as to allow many different people to pound away at it was simply asking for trouble, apart from making it unsuitable for a skilled pianist to play properly. The larger places and the more enterprising would engage small bands and have a stage built in their saloon bars, usually in the corner furthest from the door. They would also organise talent competitions, making certain nights more popular than others.

When we first started visiting Lewisham, it was the Castle that we frequented most. This was only because it was better known to me than the other, as it was where Laurie and I used to drink before we entered the Navy. The beer was good and plentiful; spirits were in short supply but that did not concern us, so we were quite happy with what they had, along with the entertainment.

Being able to enjoy the friendship of both Joe and Lofty on these occasions helped to push any thoughts of girl friends right out of my mind, but it was when they were not with me that the one certain girl would again occupy my thoughts. There would not be any hope of casually bumping into her, not in any of the places that we would visit. In any case I was not in a position to know whether or not she was still unattached, and there was nobody that I could ask.

As the evenings livened up and progressed favourably it would depend upon the contents of our pockets as to whether we stayed in the Castle or moved on to another place. After sounding out other establishments we decided that the Black Bull was our best bet. It was conveniently near, by the time we entered the bar it would be very much noisier, and it was also the popular choice of the girls of the Women's Royal Army Corps, stationed nearby, manning the searchlights and 'ack-ack' guns at a place called the Hilly Fields, which was close by. The Hilly Fields was one of the highest parts of London, which made it an ideal situation for a battery of anti-aircraft guns.

The girls stationed there were a mixed bunch. Most were from Yorkshire. Down-to-earth in their ways as all Yorkshire people are reputed to be, they were good-hearted and determined to enjoy their new found freedom in London. It was 'new found', and it was 'freedom'; most had never been away from their home towns before, and they all found London to be fascinating instead of the wicked city they had always heard about. The only real danger they were subjected to was from the air-raids, but they had grown used to these and never really bothered about them at all; they were there to do a job, and they were going to enjoy every minute when not on duty.

It was not long before the three of us found ourselves in the company of a crowd of the Yorkshire girls. There was not much doubt that they liked the idea of having sailors for company, instead of the soldiers on their site. Our uniforms alone made a pleasant change from the drab humdrum of khaki (their words not mine), and of course, like everybody else, they thought they knew what sailors were like. Naturally we paired off, and I found myself with a pleasant young lady by the name of Olga. I am afraid that her name alone put me off, I could not stand it, so our friendship was really doomed from the beginning. I do not think I could even imagine myself getting affectionate with someone called Olga.

Upon two consecutive occasions when the three of us came on night leave to Catford and finally ended our evenings at the Black Bull, we finished the evenings in the company of these same girls. It was all very friendly, very jolly, and as far as we three were concerned we would have been quite happy to continue the friendships.

It was not to be because on the next visit, and in the same company, we were joined by another girl from their regiment. This girl's name was Pat. She was also a Yorkshire girl, from the same part of the county as many of the others, but Pat was a girl who would stand out in any crowd. Pat had everything in the right places, her Yorkshire accent was soft and encouraging, and her looks would compete successfully with any star from stage or screen. This was obviously why the other girls never really welcomed her into their company. Pat, without any doubt, knew this, and deliberately flirted and teased with any male company.

There was going to be only one outcome to Pat joining the company. At first it would have been simply to annoy the other girls; this was far from being the first time she had done this, and now she was setting her sights upon me. Joe's Scouse accent did not appeal to her, and Lofty was far too young in her opinion; that left me to direct her charm at, and after a few drinks I was, to say the least, vulnerable. All the time, an angry looking Olga was glaring away at us, until she could conceal her anger no more and erupted. She immediately attacked her rival, who was not backward in retaliating. Fortunately the girls were quickly separated, neither being seriously hurt, apart from to their egos. Olga was escorted back to their camp by her closest friends, leaving Pat and two other girls in the company of Joe, Lofty and myself.

The friendship between Pat and me quickly developed. Perhaps it was only infatuation, but I certainly was not aware of it at the time. It was also more than possible that Pat was only playing with my affections; again I did not know it at the time, and if anyone had told me this, I certainly would never have believed it to be true. I could not get up to London enough and there was no doubt that so far as I was concerned, Pat was perfect for me; I was really smitten. Yet, and it was true, I still made comparisons between her and that certain someone else, I could not help it. Using my imagination to its extreme: they had the same figure; both had the same sort of smile that even the Mona Lisa could not compete against; the shape of a girl's legs in those days was important, and I could not fault either of them; but there the comparison ended, for Pat was as fair as the corn in a field, against the luscious colouring of a brunette.

Because there were only four stokers on board our boats, it was not always possible for Joe and Lofty to get ashore at the same time as I did. Before meeting Pat I would have remained on board with them when they were on duty, or maybe visited Newhaven instead of going to Catford on my own, but now it was different, and the attraction was becoming more and more irresistable. So visits to Catford became more frequent than ever. Fortunately it made no difference to the friendship between Joe, Lofty and myself; they understood, and at every opportunity the three of us would come up to Catford just the same, although Joe and Lofty would leave Pat and me to our own resources quite early each evening, arranging to meet and travel back together.

It was not long before I took Pat home to meet my mother. Although she apparently liked Pat, she was suitably cautious and was wise enough to know that the friendship being enjoyed by Pat and me could in some ways be likened to so-called 'ship romances', when two people meet on a cruise, then part at the end of it, and never meet again. She actually tried to warn me, but twenty-year-old young men never listen to their mothers in this respect, and I was no exception. There were times when I could discuss Pat with her, pointing out reasons why I admired her so much; on one occasion when I said how smart she looked in her WRAC uniform, my mother strongly emphasised that many girls who looked smart in a uniform never looked as well in civilian clothes. At the time I never really understood why my mother made that particular comment; it did not seem either justified or relevant. Despite everything, Pat and my mother seemed to get along very well with each other, and upon one occasion when Pat had no option but to stay the night at our home, they shared the same bed. Of course there may have been a very good reason for this, but to protect whom I wonder?

The rendezvous between Pat and myself would continue for several months to come, even after I left the 611, but meanwhile I at least was on cloud nine. Even when Joe and Lofty came along, the combined friendship we enjoyed was an exceptional one for us all, with no regrets at that time.

There was one moment around this period when I was on leave, walking toward the main shopping centre of Catford, during the early evening. I met another friend of mine from the pre-war days; he had joined the RAF as a 'boy airman', meaning that he had not been old enough to join as an ordinary recruit, but was so keen that he would not wait until he came of age. Ted and I had been very good friends right up until he enlisted. Being close friends I knew his family quite well, and liked them all very much indeed, so much so that even today I tend to regard them as a typical example of what a happy family should be like.

Ted was about to rejoin his squadron, and was just ending his leave, so there was no opportunity to enjoy his company again, but he was able to give me some news that I needed. It was not quite what I would have wanted, I have to admit that, despite what was going on between Pat and myself. Because of his brother, Ted was very well acquainted with that certain someone I just could not forget, so it was nothing unusual for me to ask if he had any news about her. Without hesitation he told me that she was well and happy, she had joined the Womens Royal Air Force, had fallen in love with a pilot, and married him. Slightly taken aback, all I could think of was to tell him that I wished her well and hoped that she would be happy, then, feeling a little disappointed, we said our farewells and went on our respective ways. As I walked away from Ted, I thought over what I had just been told, and felt sad, but in my heart I knew that I had been expecting to hear something like it; so to myself I said once again, 'I hope that you will be very happy, and have chosen well.'

If I had thought that, knowing now that this girl was married, she would no longer occupy my thoughts, I had another think coming, because despite the close liaison I now had with Pat, this someone else would still not be easy to forget. I had known her too long, I had wanted her too long, and if she ever needed my help, then I knew that I would always be there. There were times when I regretted not asking Ted where she was based, but at the same time I realised that it was probably for the best that I did not.

Back at Newhaven, the atmosphere in harbour was monotonous. Sea patrols were carried out regularly and were as boring as they ever were without any action; there was action against E-boats every night towards the eastern end of the Channel and along the east coast in what was now always referred to as 'E-boat alley', but we were missing it. Our patrols were in the same area as when we were operating from Gosport, and because of the proximity to Portsmouth where many destroyers were based, the Germans were not so active in this part of the Channel. This did not make our presence unnecessary; on the contrary, we were there to lessen the risks when the destroyers were elsewhere on duty, and therefore were a vital part of convoy protection around that area.

Most of the skirmishes that took place were with the seventy-footers based at Ramsgate and Felixstowe, and it was quite possible that the Germans did not fancy taking on our more heavily armed D-boats. They only remained to fight when there was not an alternative; usually their superior speed enabled them to make a quick getaway.

There was one patrol that we took part in together with three other boats in our flotilla. We had been patrolling for several hours without so much as a bleep on our radar screen and we were slightly east of Newhaven, about mid-Channel, slowly cruising along. Our officers were craving action of any sort to relieve their own boredom, though we, and most likely the other crews as well, were perfectly content to enjoy the peace and solitude while we could.

Suddenly there was an air of excitement about. Signals were exchanged with the other three boats, all four coming as close to each other as was safely possible, in order that conversation could take place between the Captains. The sound of our engines made it difficult for us to understand clearly what was happening, but within minutes all our engines were revved up and away we sped eastwards.

From my position by my pom-pom I had been able to hear some of the conversation between the boats' officers. According to information given out from the Admiralty there were no other Coastal Forces craft active in our end of the English Channel, the nearest being somewhere in the region of the Wash. Yet, showing plainly upon our radar screens, were a number of small craft coming towards us at speed. It meant only one thing to our officers, and me now that I had heard their conversation: there was a flotilla of E-boats heading our way, they might even have us as their intended victims. With a bit of luck they would keep coming towards us and not be able to avoid conflict. Most likely they would not realise that we were aware of them, and this would give us extra advantage.

All four crews were now at action stations and individual gun crews were instructed where to aim for on the enemy craft. The target for my gun and its crew would be the engine rooms of whichever boats came within our sights, this should put their engines out of action and cripple them. Our other machine-guns were to 'rake the enemy boats' bridges, destroy their officers and whoever happened to be on the bridge at the same time'. With good shooting and a fair amount of luck, their communications would be put out of action. Our six-pounder guns aft would aim for the bows of the enemy boats.

So we were now ready for confrontation with the oncoming enemy boats. There was, perhaps, a little apprehension; it is seldom possible to know this much in advance that your enemy is coming towards you and unaware that you are prepared and waiting. It was bound to create tension among the crews. In most other engagements there was very little warning, and the shooting would have started before one realised it; there was no time for tension then. On this occasion we were anxious to be within range of the enemy and for the fracas to begin.

If any fear existed on board the 611, it never showed. Our Skipper stood there gazing through his binoculars in the direction the enemy was expected to appear; he stood ramrod straight, showing no concern at all. Both of the other officers were also there, along with the cox'n and the man on the wheel. The only thing that mattered now was the enemy, I do not believe that any man aboard us gave any thought to the possibility that we might be sunk, or that some of us could be injured or worse. Perhaps if the entire crew had heard the conversations that I did it might have made a difference, but even so, any qualms that they might have experienced would be long gone now, and hopefully they would be thinking as I and my gun's crew were: 'Come on, let's get it over and done with, and make tracks for home.' God knows we had plenty of time when on espionage trips to conjure up morbid thoughts, that is what time combined with uncertainty does to you, when direct action has to be avoided at all cost.

The sky was very cloudy, but every so often the moon managed to break through the clouds. On one spell of moonlight we could see the dim outlines of the oncoming craft. They appeared to be much smaller in size than we were, and plainly considerably faster; that much we could deduce from the wake they were throwing up. With all actions of this kind, the oncoming boats were challenged by our signalmen with Aldis lamps. There was no reply at all. The boats were now uncomfortably close and the signal to open fire came from our bridge; at the same time I imagine the same signals being given on board our other boats. Pandemonium reigned. Bullets and shells were flying everywhere, sheer bedlam, then all of a sudden voices were screaming loudly for all guns to cease firing. At the same time every possible upper deck light was switched on, and the area was one large blaze of light.

Although radio contact had already been established, and heated conversations were taking place between every boat in that area, we guns' crews were completely mystified as to what was then happening. After what seemed to be an endless amount of time, in fact it could have been no more than fifteen to twenty minutes, along with our other three boats we started our engines again and turned around, heading back the way in which we had come. The other boats, being very badly damaged, took longer to do exactly the same. Our six-pounder crew, who were able to watch the other boats until out of sight, said that we were nearly out of their sight before they made any movement at all.

It would have been impossible for any of us to remain in that area any longer, the firing would have been picked up by the Germans, and they would have taken the opportunity to finish us all off with a Luftwaffe attack.

As we sailed away westwards and the other flotilla would have been making their way east, possibly to Dover, we learnt what had happened.

The information given to us from Admiralty had been correct; there should not have been any Allied craft in our area, not for one hundred and fifty miles at least. The action taken by us had been absolutely correct, there had been no alternative.

The craft we had thought were enemy vessels were actually a flotilla of seventy-footers, mixed torpedo and gunboats from an east coast base. They should not have been within a hundred miles of us, but owing to a navigational error they had sailed completely off course in our direction. They had no idea as to who we were, they never saw us apparently until we were on top of them, I cannot understand this at all, unless by some freak chance the moonlight was not in their favour, I had heard no other explanation given at all. The fact that our challenge to them was not responded to was also strange; that was a disastrous error on the part of someone in that group of boats. The consequences were that some good men were killed unnecessarily, and boats were very badly damaged. We heard afterwards that an offer had been made to tow and escort the other boats to a safe destination, but the offer was refused.

It was bad enough that we damaged our own boats, but when lives are lost it can be very traumatic, so it was a great relief to me personally when I was told that I had not been responsible for any of the deaths that had occurred. I did however, accurately hit the engine-room of the leading boat, smashing one engine and making a shambles of the engine-room interior; the engine-room staff had to be treated for shock, but apart from a few cuts and bruises they were unharmed, I am pleased to say. Nobody wanted to be told whose gun did the damage to the bridge of one boat, killing the men on duty. It was a good thing that this information was witheld, and I am thankful that the bridge had not been targeted by me. Without attempting to be humorous in any way at all, I was beginning to wonder whose side Fate decided I should be on. There was the incident while aboard the 320 with the Lockheed Hudson aircraft, and now this. I could not help wondering what might come next. The cox'n remembered hearing about the aircraft incident, and did his best to convince me that I was not a 'Jonah'; in both these incidents, our boats and our crews remained unscathed, and while I was aboard boats that luck had held.

Once we were back in Newhaven information about what had happened was more plentiful, and signals received from Admiralty completely exonerated us from all blame. We were naturally very pleased and relieved to hear this, but it did nothing to relieve the feeling of remorse that still existed.

It would be true to say that what had happened damaged our morale to a certain extent. It was going to take a little while before we could get it out of our systems and for some maybe this would never happen. It served as a reminder that mistakes as well as accidents can be just as dangerous as conflict with the enemy, however innocently they are caused.

Fortunately, and I must add 'in their wisdom', our officers decided that increased time at sea would be the best medicine for us. If we were kept busy and on our toes it would enable us to forget the incident sooner, and I am sure that they were right. The behaviour of everybody seemed so different at first, and I am sure that we all were determined to act normally, as though it all had not happened, but there was still underneath a kind of caution. It did not show enough to make any difference to the way it affected the running of the boats, but I cannot help thinking that it was lucky for us that we never encountered the enemy during this period of what I can only describe as 'readjustment'.

By this time, as a crew, there would not be any better. We had learnt to know each other's habits and ways; we could accept that those from the north of England, Scotland, Wales, Ireland and from overseas, might do things or say things that would seem strange to those of us from the southern half of the United Kingdom. The fact that some things always led to leg-pulling was merely part of life; indeed quite often this leg-pulling would relieve the tension and stop a small incident from becoming a serious one.

Smithy, our cox'n, had made himself liked by us all. He was experienced enough to know when it was best that he should not hear or see certain things that happened among the crew, and if at any time a referee was required, or judgement needed, he was ready to oblige. When at first we all joined the 611, he delegated many of his duties to his capable second cox'n, leading seaman

Febry, but the latter had left us to take a petty officers course, so much of what he used to do was now shared between the older, more senior, able seamen.

Able seaman Jones was one of the senior men. A former newspaper reporter in civilian life, his home being in Manchester, he had adapted very well to life in the Navy, and could be relied upon to do most things efficiently.

The close friend of 'Jonesy' was able seaman Charlie Nesbitt, a cheerful Cockney, who was the oldest on board. He never lost his sense of humour all the time I knew him. At most places we were based, Charlie would find accommodation to rent, and his wife would take up residence, so that he could be with her as much as possible.

It is not possible for me to go into detail about every member of our crew; in comparison with destroyers and above, our thirty-three was not many, but although we all were on friendly terms many did manage to isolate themselves from the rest. It was not done out of cussedness or to be deliberately unfriendly; for some being aboard 611 was their first taste of sharing their life with others, and this takes a little getting used to.

There was one ordinary seaman who must be mentioned. By pure coincidence his home was also at Catford though we had not known each other before joining 611. For no apparent reason at all he and I never became close friends. It may well have been because of my friendship with Joe and Lofty, the two stokers. I certainly never gave him the cold shoulder; on the contrary, I would have appreciated his company when travelling home on leave but it was not to be.

When we were at sea, my turn for duty would coincide with that of the cox'n. I enjoyed his company when we were together off-watch, and I would benefit from his experiences. The following story might not show him at his best, but it was humorous at the time, and one could say it benefited me. If we had finished our watch and it was o800 hrs in the morning, it would naturally be time for breakfast, and we two would be the first to get below. We would share the same table, and with a twinkle in his eye he would ask if I was hungry. Of course at twenty years of age I was always hungry, just as everyone else would be. By this time our breakfasts would be placed in front of us, the traditional 'fry-up': eggs, bacon, sausages, sometimes tomatoes or fried bread, at times even both. He would then trim the fat off his bacon, and as soon as the other lads made an appearance he would dangle the bacon fat from his nostrils. I must admit it was a sickening sight to see, and it had the desired effect; one look at the cox'n was enough and they would either return to the upper deck quickly or into the heads, shouting loudly as to what we could do with their breakfasts.

It was not a very nice thing to do, but it did not continue for long. Somehow the officers heard about what was going on, and I believe that a quiet word in the cox'n's ears did not go amiss.

When this happened at first, the lads would be very angry, but would not take any action against us. After all, if our cox'n had been a nasty vindictive man, he could have made life much more difficult for the young ordinary seamen. Apart from this one, not very nice, demonstration, Smithy was well liked and respected, and the lads did not hold it against him.

After completing several more patrols, the 611 was once again singled out for something special. This time, because of its very nature, I began to wonder if, and a big if, the reason why we were chosen for special duties was not because we were extra good at them, but simply because we were expendable? We realised that if anything was to happen to us on these special occasions, a lesson would have been learnt, and another boat sent out to do the same work, but because of us the crew would be wiser and of course luckier.

That was again speculation; the real reason I am sure was that our Skipper, like most officers in Coastal Forces, wanted action and the recognition that went with it if successful, and of course if he survived.

So, following the usual procedure, one afternoon the expected night leave was cancelled and as dusk fell, we slowly made our way out of Newhaven, and into the open Channel. At the same time, the other boats in our flotilla put to sea, so that it appeared that we were all taking part in a normal patrol, but an hour or so later we separated from the rest and turned westward.

Once against, no details or information were given to any of us. Spud had taken his usual place upon the bridge, and we expected him to stay there for the duration of the voyage. We had learnt by now the ways of our Captain, and expected nothing from him; nevertheless it was aggravating. In this particular instance, it turned out that it was better for us that we did not know any details; there would have been a chance that knowing could have unnerved someone, with disastrous results, and instead of becoming the success that it did, the lives of us all could have been lost.

One hour later, after leaving the rest of our flotilla, our cox'n came round to talk to us all, and give some instructions from the Captain. We were, he said, to be more vigilant than ever, if that were at all possible, especially the gunners. We would shortly be at action stations and this would last for several hours. He could not be more explicit. The guns' crews formed a valuable part of the lookout operations and on this trip we must not miss a thing; any slackness would be dealt with very firmly by the Captain when we returned to base. He omitted to say 'if we returned to base', but I somehow felt that was what he nearly said.

The more lookouts there were, the more chances we had of survival. The order had now been passed to us all, that we were now at action stations. The cox'n was still making his rounds, visiting everybody; we were, he said with a twinkle in his eyes and a rueful chuckle, about to cross a German minefield. To lend emphasis to his words he pointed to the port side, where about one hundred and fifty yards away, lay a mine. Smithy explained that this one had broken loose from its moorings, and the danger was not so much those that broke away, but the ones we could not see just below the surface of the sea.

Being a wooden constructed craft we had very little to fear from magnetic mines, but the ordinary type, such as the one we had just seen, did constitute a menace. If seen in time, they would be guided past with the aid of a boathook. Smithy had volunteered for this task himself, as he felt that he was the most suitable and competent person to do it; my own opinion was that he was probably right. I most definitely did not want the job, not that I would have been allowed to as I was needed to man my pom-pom.

It was going to take at least an hour to cross this minefield and, if we were lucky, this would mean another hour needed to cross it on the way back; again that little word 'if' was not said.

Time passed very slowly; that hour seemed like twenty-four. There was one dreadful moment when another mine came very near to us, causing some consternation, but the cox'n warded it off with his boathook quite easily, and we continued on our way.

Very soon the coast of France appeared to our port side. I was unable to guess the distance away, possibly ten miles. It was no more than a long, endless black silhouette along the horizon, until it suddenly disappeared and we could not see a thing in front of us; it looked just as if the sea had opened up and swallowed what land there had been. By now we had cleared the minefield, three of our engines had been shut down, and we were running on our silenced one only. Almost soundlessly, the experts would insist, but then they had never been near the enemy coast to hear it as we could, but I believed them, there was no other choice.

The cox'n had now returned to the bridge. Afterwards he told me that he had aged several years while 'mine watching', and was sure his hair was greyer. I pretended to scrutinise his head very carefully, and told him that he was only as grey as he always was, but there was now much less hair. The book that he threw at me missed.

A messenger was sent round to us all again from the bridge; the 'no noise' situation was now imperative and anyone making a noise of any sort could not expect to live after the Captain had dealt with him. We gunners were told that under no circumstances were we to fire our guns unless personally ordered to from the bridge, even if we were under fire. If attacked by enemy ships we would then be given the necessary instructions as what to do. Absolute quiet was going to be vital. We were, we were then told, about to enter the harbour at Le Havre, a French port of major importance, and of course now in the hands of the Germans.

We all felt extremely uncomfortable. This was something more than we had bargained for, it had been reasonable to cruise up and down the French coast as we had done before, but to actually enter this harbour looked like madness. What on earth was the purpose? It was not long before we were to find out.

It was not possible for me to see how our officers were behaving; they obviously had not mutinied, I could see that much. I was told afterwards that our Skipper showed no concern whatsoever, fortified perhaps by an occasional nip from his bottle. However, whatever Spud was like when we were in harbour, nobody could ever accuse him of setting a bad example when at sea; at times like these he was excellent and never showed any signs of fear. This did not mean he was unconcerned, the welfare of his boat meant everything to him; I like to think that sometimes he was even concerned for us.

We seemed to be heading slowly, in a straight line, to the centre of the harbour, so slowly that at times we appeared to have stopped. Then we saw a flash of gunfire from inside the harbour. Within seconds there sounded the scream of a shell passing overhead, and an almighty splash as it hit the sea just aft of our stern.

It was obviously what Spud had been waiting for, as our engines revved and we increased speed, turning to starboard. We were just in time, as another shell landed exactly at the place we had been; the German gunners were 'on target'.

Another shell was fired from another shore position in the harbour. It fell into the sea off our starboard side, well away from us, then another was fired, this time off our port side, but closer, they were straddling us very efficiently. Fortunately Spud was gauging their accuracy very well indeed, or maybe it was one of the other officers? Whoever it was, he was doing a magnificent job of it, and was keeping us alive. Several times shells would arrive in exactly the spot we had just vacated, I wondered how long it would be before the German gunners tumbled to what we were doing, and, what was more frightening, how long before they sent out a flotilla of E-boats to deal with us. It did not bear thinking about at all.

The purpose behind our visit to Le Havre was now established; we were there to chart exactly where the enemy gun emplacements were. There was only one sure way to find out, by giving them a 'sitting duck' to fire at, and that was what we were. Truthfully it can be said that this night was one of the most uncomfortable any of us would ever experience.

It was a pleasure to note that our boat had now turned around and was facing out to sea again. Our mission apparently was now accomplished, so we headed at speed towards England, and home, well, Newhaven at least. We had not looked upon Newhaven so favourably before, but now we just hoped that we were going to make it.

Homeward bound, we were feeling just a little relieved. We had survived the shelling by the Germans, and had marked their gun positions on a chart, but before we would be able to celebrate there was that minefield to negotiate again. Once more it would mean cutting our speed as much as possible, and this time we would not be as fresh as we were, therefore the possibility of a mistake happening was greater. It was to Spud's credit that, although the same message about vigilance was given to us all, he did not add any threats to it. He must have been very tired himself, maybe that helped him to understand how we were feeling. But there was also the risk that he could be very irritable too.

As we drew nearer to the minefield, so the sky became cloudier and travelling conditions more hazardous because of the darkness. We knew then that it would be more difficult to spot the mines.

There was one consolation: the cloudy conditions made an attack by enemy aircraft unlikely, and if any E-boats had been sent after us they would have to negotiate the same minefield as us. Although the Germans would want us destroyed, they might not want to risk their own boats. All this was really clutching at straws, because if the situation was reversed we knew that a minefield would not stop men like our Skipper from chasing the enemy, and without any doubt, they had men who were just as courageous.

At this time, our thoughts were about the possibility of boats being sent after us from Le Havre. Most of us never gave a thought to the existence of an E-boat base further along the coast, and boats from this base would be in the position of being able to intercept us without having to go anywhere near the minefield.

The existence of this enemy base had not been overlooked by our officers. We learnt later that information had been given to us before we left Newhaven, that the enemy boats would be lured away from this area to enable us to get safely home, and some kind of diversion had already been planned.

If there were still boats moored at the base, it would be likely that they would be undergoing repairs; if any were seaworthy they would not be too keen to engage in conflict with us, unless they were vastly superior in numbers. If we managed to cross the minefield with the minimum of delay, depending upon the time any E-boats had left harbour, it was also possible that even with their superior speed they would find it difficult to catch up with us.

A few breaks were appearing now in the sky. We were not so happy about these; it made the possibility of enemy aircraft more likely. We did in fact hear the drone of aircraft, somewhere ahead of our position, but when nothing came towards us we could breathe a sigh of relief.

We had now reached the minefield. Our cox'n had taken up a position near to our bows, armed again with his boathook. Another man stood alongside him to help spot the mines. We had now slowed right down, so much that we were almost drifting. Apparently no chances were going to be taken because of our tiredness; even so the risks on this return crossing would be greater as there was no way of knowing whether more mines had broken loose from their moorings.

We must have taken longer than an hour to cross the minefield on this return journey, but we managed it successfully, and from my position at my gun, I cannot recall having seen the cox'n use his boathook once.

After that there was only the slight danger of coming across an odd loose mine, and there was always this risk wherever we sailed in the English Channel or the North Sea, and the mines were not always German; many of our own would also break away from their moorings. The order for full speed ahead was given and we raced for home, tired, but elated that we had successfully completed another mission.

We entered Newhaven harbour, which looked a dreary place at all times. Nobody took any notice of us as we berthed; I thought that they probably never missed us when we left them, and now they might well be thinking we were simply late getting back from patrol.

Immediately we were berthed, everyone set to cleaning. We

gunners had to strip, dry and oil our weapons, the stokers were busy down in their engine-room, and the rest were clearing and cleaning the upper deck in general. Everything had to be 'ship-shape and Bristol fashion' before we would be allowed to turn into our bunks for some well earned sleep.

Night leave was granted as from 1600 hrs, and although the prospect of seeing Pat was foremost in my mind, like everyone else I was too tired. Anyway I was not 'watch ashore' that night, so it would have meant asking for someone to do my duty for me, and there would be tomorrow, when all three of us would be able to take the train to Catford and elsewhere.

To be classed as 'Duty watch on board' did not always mean that there was anything special to do, unless it was your turn for sentry duty. Otherwise time was your own, usually spent by sleeping, or catching up with letters to family and friends, some times a game of cards would be set in motion, and at the larger bases there was the added attraction of tombola.

Next day it was work as usual. The cox'n would find all sorts of fiddling little jobs for us to do, cox'ns were very adept at this, and when you had a Skipper like ours it was important and very necessary for him to see his crew fully occupied. Actually he was not seen at all that day, he did not make an appearance until late the following day, so it was possible that he had been somewhere to make his report about our trip.

Night leave was granted. Joe Swift did not feel like coming to Catford with me, so it was just myself and Lofty. When I was getting myself ready to go ashore, a sickly feeling came over me; I suddenly realised that I was practically broke. Joe could not lend me any money as he was short too, and Lofty needed what he had to spend, I very nearly changed my mind and stayed aboard, but I badly wanted to see Pat. The cost of the railway fare was not a problem, that was already organised, but I still needed spending money. So for the first time since joining the Navy, I broke a 'golden rule' that had been made on the advice of an uncle, which was always to keep a little money hidden away in reserve for emergencies. Never be tempted to use it just to enjoy a drink, there will always be an occasion when that reserve will be useful. It might be needed to buy something, or to get you out of trouble of some kind. It was only £3 10s. that I had hidden amongst my kit and this was not an emergency, but the temptation was too strong. After all, it was my money and I want to be with Pat again for a few hours, so the decision was made, and Lofty and I caught an early train to London and then on to Catford.

We made the usual visit to my home, then went on to Lewisham. This time we gave the Castle a miss, and sat in the Black Bull waiting for Pat to appear. During the time we had known these girls from the ack-ack site, we had never asked for its postal address, so that we could contact the girls by letter if necessary. I suppose we were so confident that they would always meet us at the pub, that it never entered our heads that there would be times when they could not leave the camp, or wanted to change meeting places. This was now about to happen, although we did not know it.

It was after 9.00 p.m. that Lofty and I realised that we were not going to see the girls that night. The temptation to go along to their camp was strong, but resisted in case it caused any trouble for the girls. We questioned a few Wracs that were there, but we learnt nothing. Either they did not know the girls we asked about, or they were being cagey; either way it meant that we were not going to have the pleasure of their company this evening, so we decided to cut short our night in Lewisham, and eventually re-turned to Newhaven.

# CHAPTER 14

# *I make a decision,*
# *will it be right or wrong?*

CONDITIONS aboard our boats in winter were not too bad, provided that the interiors were dry and, what was more important, that we had a change of dry clothing when it was needed. Unfortunately this was not always possible, and after a particularly rough night at sea it was nothing unusual to go below and find the mess-deck awash with sea water and all the bedding and men's kits soaked. The lockers used to store our clothes etc. were at floor level and were not designed to be waterproof, so it was easy for any water to seep through.

Then there was the pungent smell of sea-sickness that would cling to everything, and always there would be blocked toilets. It all helped to make life pretty unbearable at times. Then when it came to meal times it would be discovered that there was not enough crockery to go round, most of it would have been broken while at sea. This would result in a dash along to the other boats to borrow crockery from them until we could replenish; usually there was no trouble and we would be able to borrow, but once in a while there would be difficulties if the other boats were also short of gear.

Somehow those on duty would manage to collect enough crockery from somewhere, so that we could have our meals. The officers were more fortunate; whoever had the task of looking after their quarters would see that all of their gear was stowed away carefully, and he would be in serious trouble if he forgot.

Many a time after one of these rough sessions at sea, it would not be possible to have a cooked meal, and the only thing available would be soup. In those circumstances a cup of soup would taste better than a four-course meal at the Savoy Hotel in London. A meal at the Savoy was not a luxury that we could afford in those days, but believe me, the comparison is apt.

It has already been mentioned that our Skipper enjoyed going to sea in rough conditions, and it had to be a very strong gale to stop him, or perhaps someone of higher authority. It was therefore accepted that we were used to stormy seas, because of our Skipper, but some of our crew would never be able to get used to the rough seas, and Peter Loasby's prediction about me would not work with everyone.

The weather was bitterly cold. It seemed as though I was always falling foul of the Skipper, and he made certain that I was not going to forget the occasions. When aboard the 320 I managed to keep out of that particular officer's way, but that was because at that time he was not a member of our crew. The difference here on board the 611 was that Spud was, and that made it almost impossible to keep out of his way if he made up his mind to catch you out.

Right now I felt that a decision must be reached. We had been out in very rough seas; my spare clothes were all soaked, along with everybody else's; I was wet and very miserable, the cold made it all seem worse; to top it all, I had again fallen foul of 'his lordship', and I was still smarting from the effects of his tongue.

I thought back to Weymouth, and the words of the Gunnery Officer, when he suggested that I became an instructor, I was sure that he was sincere at the time, but would he be still? There was only one way to find out, and that was to put in a request to see Spud and ask permission to take the course. There was the additional worry as to whether Spud would grant his permission, so I would have to word my request with the utmost delicacy. So the decision was made. My request was given to the cox'n, who in turn handed it to the 1st Lieutenant to deal with, who arranged for me to go before the Captain.

There were butterflies in my stomach the next morning as I stood before the Captain. The stony look on his face was far from encouraging. It was 1030 hrs so he had knocked his first drink of the day back; you could always detect the symptoms if you knew what to look for.

When asked for my reason behind the request, I carefully explained what had happened at Weymouth before he had joined us. Now I wanted to take the course in order to better myself, and receive a higher wage. He could not argue with this; it was, as he admitted, logical, and therefore he was prepared to submit my request supported by his recommendation, to the Gunnery school. He did not think that it would be refused, but suggested that I did not build my hopes too high. To my great surprise, he even wished me every success, and what was even more surprising was that after that, all the time I was still part of his crew, his attitude seemed to mellow towards me. Even so I still did not take any chances with him, and still kept out of his way as much as possible.

Despite the weather, the wet and the cold, there was an element of truth in the reason I gave for wanting to take the course. Right from when I first joined the Navy with Laurie, it was almost my ambition to be able to go home on leave sporting many gold badges on my arms. This was not actually for personal ego, or even for the extra money that went with badges; it was to impress a certain somebody, and I had it in my mind that perhaps, if I were able to impress her, there might be a chance to further the relationship.

Of course after meeting Ted when on leave as I did, and the

information he gave me, that reason was now irrelevant, but it
was still important to me. I still wanted to impress her, but it was
going to have to wait until 1945 before the chance came. I do not
know in all honesty if she was impressed, even a little bit, then,
probably not.

Sub-Lieutenant Lewis called me to one side a few days later and
informed me that my request had gone to Whale Island. It was
going to take time, these things could not be hurried, but he was
confident that it would be accepted, and eventually I would be
on my way. Harry Lewis was a good sort, in many ways rather
like Bob Goodfellow aboard the 320, not in build it is true, but
in temperament and nature, and I always liked him. I do recall
asking him if Spud was glad to see the back of me. He never
answered in so many words, but gave a grin; I realised that it would
have been foolish for him to have replied anyway. Later, I was to
learn that the opposite was true, and that Spud would have preferred it if I had remained as part of his crew. To my way of
thinking he should have treated me differently, then I might never
have requested to leave.

By this time, Newhaven had become a very active Coastal
Forces base. Apart from our flotilla of D-class gunboats, there were
now B-class motor launches, seventy-foot torpedo and gunboats,
harbour defence craft, and extra minesweepers further down-
stream. The few public houses in the town were benefiting tre-
mendously; they were now appreciating the Navy being present.
This fact was noticed by the Canadian troops based there with
increasing annoyance, as until we had arrived there they had
virtually reigned supreme in the town. Although they were paid
considerably more than our troops, they now had competition
with the local girls. It was now a vastly different situation for them,
and regrettably their tempers were very short-fused.

At first our 'Jolly Jacks' lived up to their name and reputation.
They intended to enjoy life to the full and they wanted to live

each day as it came. After all, unlike the troops who were there probably for quite some time, our lads were going out to sea and never quite certain that they would return.

The possibility of trouble between the Canadian troops and ourselves had been contemplated by our officers, and no doubt the Canadian officers as well, so when a warning was given out to us all, it did not come unexpectedly. We were warned not to tangle with the troops ashore, as our lads only wanted to enjoy themselves. They did heed the warnings, but unfortunately it was to be all one-sided; the peace and quiet of Newhaven was about to come to an end.

The Ship Hotel near the centre of the town was by far the most popular place there, music loudly blaring away non-stop during opening hours, and of course it was always full to the brim with Canadian troops. Mostly our lads kept away from there, but at times some would patronise the place, keeping a low profile. One evening was enough to ignite the fuse. Two lads from one of the boats in harbour decided that they wanted to drink in the Ship Hotel, so in they went, found a quiet corner and proceeded to enjoy the evening's entertainment.

The two sailors were not of an aggressive nature, and most certainly were not the type to pick fights; they enjoyed each other's company and had never been in trouble before. Little did they know that some of the Canadian soldiers had been working themselves into a state of resentment ever since they had walked in, and now they were about to explode.

What happened next is only hearsay. The two sailors did not remember exactly what started it all, but according to the story told, one soldier accused them of stealing his drink, and before any attempt was made to deny it, several soldiers attacked the two sailors, and promptly beat them up, quite badly.

It is not clear how the two lads made their way back to the base, but their condition horrified their shipmates so much that revenge was the only thing in their minds. It was too late then to do anything about it, and it was agreed that the best solution would be to spread the gory details around all the boats in the harbour, and ask as many as possible to accompany them to the Ship Hotel that night.

No pressure was needed to get volunteers. Shipmates of the two injured men planned their action for the next evening. Their caterer had gone ashore that morning on the pretext of purchasing fresh food, and obtained descriptions of two Canadians who appeared to have been the ringleaders. It was decided that there would not be a mass onslaught, but that they would gradually filter into the Ship Hotel in small groups, remaining peaceful until near to closing time. In the meantime the two soldiers in question would be identified and watched. Nothing was going to be done to arouse their suspicions, but once the time arrived to act, then it would be every man for himself. In all there were somewhere in the region of a hundred men who said that they would be at the pub that evening.

The weather was on their side. It was far too rough even for our Skipper to volunteer for anything, and this is exactly what the lads wanted. When 1600 hrs came, there was not the usual mass exodus ashore, only a few who went in time to visit the local cinema, promising to be at the pub as soon as the main film was over. During the next couple of hours the boats' crews that were allowed ashore left the base in varying numbers, with reasonable intervals of time in between, so that nothing would appear suspicious to any officer who just might be watching.

Feelings were running high, many had saved their rum ration so that it could be drunk just before going ashore. This of course helped to fuel their anger and indignation, and the suggestion that the Canadians must be taught a lesson invoked no opposition.

It so happened that the two soldiers in question were absent that evening, the reason was never established. The two bars were now packed solid with servicemen and the landlord was overjoyed. His till was ringing continuously, like church bells after a wedding, but this was going to be much more macabre; hopefully the tills would not sound a death knell. As the time went by, so the men became less sober, and more touchy; some were becoming aggressive and they could not be held back for much longer. Then something sparked it all off, it was believed to have been a dispute over change from buying a drink. However, insignificant it was, it was enough and as the two men they wanted were not there, the landlord had to bear the brunt of everyone's anger.

In the eyes of the sailors, the obvious answer now was to teach the landlord a lesson together with any Canadians that were still there. As soon as the fight started the landlord could see that he could do nothing, and retreated to his cellar as fast as he could, taking his staff with him. Unfortunately for them, there was no telephone there, so he was unable to phone for help. The fight grew more intense. Not all the men who had promised to be there came, but there were more than enough, maybe fifty sailors. A count of the Canadians was never made, and it was never mentioned in the official complaint that was made afterwards by their officers.

The inside of the pub was now a shambles. The Navy lads felt they had avenged themselves. It was a disappointment that the two real culprits had been missing, but a lesson had been taught and they hoped that some had learnt from it.

There was no further reason to remain in the pub, so they all gathered outside, singing and cheering as loudly as possible. If any Military Police were about they kept a low profile on this occasion; the ordinary police were also noticeable by their absence, and who could blame them?

There was only one thing left to do and that was return to base, so, still singing and cheering, the happy mass marched towards the base. Here again, the story is somewhat vague, but it seems that a bus appeared. It had to slow down, then stop, because it was unable to pass in safety. In no time the driver was hauled out of his cab, and a sailor, presumably a stoker, climbed into the driver's seat. There was no mention of a conductor or civilian passengers but most of the other cheering men climbed aboard, and the bus was driven slowly to the base.

Bad though this incident turned out to be, things might not have been reported, if someone had not stopped a Naval dispatch rider and separated him from his motorbike. This was the most stupid thing to happen, as the unfortunate rider had no choice but to make a report, and this was going to bring trouble to everybody involved.

There is an old saying that 'the Devil always looks after his own'. In my case I prefer to think that I have a guardian angel watching over me, because on the evening this all happened, I was duty watch on board, and was actually carrying out sentry duties when the lads arrived back to base.

From where I was at the time, on the upper deck of 611, I could hear the noise of the returning sailors when they were still a mile or so away. Then the bus came into sight, but I thought nothing of it, except perhaps that it was moving rather slowly. Why there should be so much noise was another thing I was unable to understand. Of course I knew what was meant to be happening that night, and assumed that it was all over and done with an hour or so ago. How wrong I was. The bus was parked outside the main gates. Luckily it could not be driven inside the base or I am certain it would have ended in the river, or worse, aboard a boat: that would have been disastrous. In my time I have known men who would have done exactly that, almost unbelievable I know, but true.

Now that they were all in the vicinity of their own boats, it had a sobering influence upon them. They quietened down considerably and filtered aboard their own boats. Many of them had carried away from the hotel whatever they could carry, table, chairs, drinking glasses, whatever was movable. Now they realised that none of it would be of any use aboard their boats and there was only one solution. It was all thrown into the river, where it slowly drifted out to sea; luckily the tide happened to be flowing in that direction.

What happened to the dispatch rider I never knew. He must have retrieved his bike and proceeded on his way, but without any doubt at all, the man had to report the incident for his own sake, and to cover any damage to his bike. There also had to be a report of some kind from me, so as diplomatically as possible I merely mentioned that at a certain hour a great deal of noise was coming from outside the base, but I was unable to see who was making it. My sentry duty finished at midnight, 2400 hrs; it was all quiet by then, as if nothing out of the ordinary had happened.

Nothing was said during the following day, and at dusk we put to sea as a flotilla, the weather having quietened somewhat. Some-one expressed his hope that last night's fracas had passed unnoticed. I did not believe this for one moment, and thought it pretty certain that we would hear the worst soon after returning to harbour.

We patrolled all night, but with no excitement of any kind. If our officers had heard about what happened, they were not saying anything, and our wisest policy was not to ask questions.

The next morning we returned to base, cleaned and tidied up, then carried on as normal. Everything was as it should be. There were no signs of a visit from the Military Police, or the civilian police. The crews of the other boats were obviously nervous, but this was to be expected. One man did come along to our boat, to ask me what I had reported. When I told him about my report he was relieved, and expressed the hope that nothing further would happen.

No such luck. After the Senior Officer of our flotilla had made his report regarding our night patrol, he was informed about what had happened on the evening before last, and obviously instructed to find the culprits and punish them accordingly.

Upon his return to his own boat, messengers were sent to all the other boats' Captains, requesting their immediate presence. The officers concerned wasted no time. What was actually said was never disclosed, but the wheels had been set in motion, and many unhappy faces were waiting to know what was going to be said and done. They did not have long to wait. A signal was sent to every boat under Coastal Forces command. At 1000 hrs the next day, all officers and crews were to muster on the jetty, alongside their own boats, when further instruction would be given. No member of any crew was to be allowed to leave the base, and the purchase of provisions must be left until the parade was dismissed.

The next morning, all crews were assembled on the jetty as ordered. Despite continual requests for 'quiet', whispered conversations were going on all the time. Nothing more had been said as to what the gathering was all about, and some were even confident that it had nothing to do with the fracas; others were betting on what form the punishment would take.

Two officers appeared. They ordered the various cox'ns to march their crews to given positions, bringing everyone close enough to be able to hear everything that was to be said. After ten minutes of shuffling around, everyone was in place, and sheepishly waiting for whatever was coming next.

The Senior Officer appeared. Along with the other Captains, he climbed onto the small platform that had been hurriedly placed in front of us all. Although faces were serious, none looked as though Armageddon was due, in fact I believe hopes were raised by some of the men, but once the Senior Officer had begun to speak, they knew better. He said that a signal had been received from the C-in-C, Portsmouth, detailing what had happened to their dispatch rider and the stolen bus. Instructions had been given that no stone be left unturned until the guilty men were found and punished, according to King's Rules and Regulations. Full responsibility was accorded to the officers at Newhaven to see that this was carried out and nothing like it ever to happen again.

The air was now electrified. We were wondering exactly how much the officers knew, and what punishment was going to be handed out. These and many other questions raced through the minds of every man there. The Commander then went on briefly to relate what had happened according to his information – it was fairly accurate – and then asked for anyone concerned to step forward. This was repeated again without success. It was then said that as he knew who the men were, he would ask once more for them to step forward, or he would have no alternative but to punish everybody irrespective of who they were or where they were at the time of the incident. We waited while the officers held a quick discussion to decide what next to do.

Order being called for, the Commander then addressed us all again. He proceeded to give what can only be described as a 'good dressing down'. The good name of the Royal Navy had been disgraced and it must never be allowed to happen again. Then he read the signal he had received from the C-in-C, Portsmouth. He went on to explain why we were now based at Newhaven. He regretted that we were being punished for something the officers had done while at Gosport, and acknowledged that Newhaven was not exactly the most convivial port for us to be based at, but there was nothing that he could do about that, we all had to make the best of the situation. He then told us how much, or how little, he knew about the confrontation with the Canadians at the local hotel. Although he and his officers understood, and were to a certain extent sympathetic, it must never be allowed to happen again. The landlord of the hotel concerned was not going to take it further, on the understanding that in future the town would be patrolled by the Navy as well as the 'Redcaps'; this had been agreed, and our Captains were going to organise a rota system affecting all boats' crews. Indirectly we had been responsible for creating extra work for ourselves and for increased discipline.

As it was not possible to punish any individuals, and in his own personal opinion it would not be fair to punish everyone as heavily as Rules and Regulations decreed, and because the incident would never have happened had they not been banished to Newhaven, he would only impose a leave ban, taking place as from then and to remain in force for seven days. His next words were heartily cheered by us all: 'There would not be a stoppage of the rum issue.'

Once the order was given for the parade to fall out, many of the men who had taken a major part in what had happened gathered together to discuss the result. When it was realised that I had been the sentry on duty that night, they all wanted to know what I had put in my report. When they heard that my report had been short on information, and no names had been mentioned, their gratitude showed plainly on their faces, along with many invitations for me to go aboard their boats for a drop of their rum.

An official apology was sent to the Town Council, to the Commanding Officer of the Canadian regiment, and to the landlord of the Ship Hotel. The Canadians also suffered a ban on leave, for how long I do not recall; in consequence, the takings at all the public houses locally dropped considerably. It was interesting to note, however, that there was no animosity shown towards the Navy by the local tradesmen, and once the bans were no longer in force, the Canadian troops and the Navy men mixed quite happily, with only the odd disturbance now and again.

The Military Police were increased in numbers, and nightly patrols by men off our boats were enforced. Occasionally sailors were disciplined by the Redcaps, but mostly any problems with our lads were left to our own patrol to deal with, and our lads on

patrol never attempted to restrain any soldiers creating a disturbance; it was considered diplomatic not to do so.

In all we had been let off very lightly. The stoppage of leave
would cause very little inconvenience as the seven days would
probably coincide with an increase in sea-time.

# CHAPTER 15

# Retribution, and the determination to win

THE week passed as anticipated. We were out on patrol most of the time. The weather although far from being good, was bearable for most; the usual lads were feeling a little queasy but they were beginning to take their sickness for granted. Now they knew from the sympathy shown by the most experienced among us that in time there was every hope that they too would cease to be sick, and that encouraged them. The cox'n no longer tormented them with his breakfast caper, so they began to eat more, which helped their stomachs to cope with the action and roll of the sea.

The incident with the Canadians was really a 'one off', we all knew that it should never have happened, but it did. It was rumoured that the two soldiers who started the trouble were severely punished and transferred elsewhere. Contrary to the image generally given to sailors, fighting ashore is not a normal occurrence, and the demonstrations such as had happened in Newhaven very rare. But when someone is picked on unfairly, whether or not the trouble is of their own making, it is another matter.

Night leave was granted again, and Joe Swift, Lofty and I were making our way to London once more. My two companions were quite happy to accompany me home, and afterwards on to Lewisham and our Wrac friends. It was strange that neither Joe nor Lofty became seriously involved with these girls. We all enjoyed each other's company but, except for Pat and myself, nothing went any further.

I was becoming more infatuated with Pat as the days went by. Since the conversation that I had had with my friend Ted, I was more or less convinced that any hope of a closer friendship with the girl I had known for so long was now completely out of the question. I also knew that she was not the type to treat her new status as a married woman lightly; there would be no hope at all where I was concerned. Despite this mode of thinking, and what was happening between Pat and myself, I still felt that there was a hole in my life that could never be filled. If I could have shaken this feeling off, I would have been much better.

When I was with Pat, she appeared all honey and sweetness, but there was never any explanation as to why she had never come to meet us a couple of weeks or so ago, I never attempted to press the question at all, I was happy to let it go, but Lofty, in all innocence did ask. He never received an answer, but a frosty silence existed between Pat and him for the rest of the evening.

Life was not too bad at all, in fact it had become quite enjoyable; the tension that had existed between the Captain and myself had all but disappeared. I would not go so far as to say he was friendly towards me, I am content just to say that things were definitely easier.

There was friction aboard between members of the crews, as was inevitable, but never, during all the years that I was to spend in Coastal Forces, did I know of actual fighting on board. This was unimaginable; we all relied upon each other far too much.

The quality of our food has already been mentioned, spoilt only by the likes of myself. It was not a laughing matter, because of food rationing. Nobody approved of wastage, but some of us were never meant to be able to cook. Some of us however probably could have done so with a little help or training, and something else that is valuable to a would-be cook: encouragement; there is always far too little of this valuable commodity, yet it costs nothing to give.

We always grumbled about our pay, or the lack of it. No British serviceman could admit to being paid well, and we were definitely worth far more than we received. It was also commonly thought that the Yanks were overpaid (later to be added to this were the words 'over-sexed, and over here'), and definitely not worth it. But it was not all antagonism between our two nationalities; there were times when friendship became the custom of the day. There were the rare occasions when a couple of American soldiers would find their way through the dockyard gates and wander aboard one of our boats. When this happened, and the newcomers were friendly, they would be made welcome and a tot of our rum would seal the friendship, which would result in an invitation to their base or camp. Then their hospitality would put ours to shame. Before we left the camp we would be given several cartons each of their cigarettes; they always seemed to be able to obtain an endless amount to give away. That was something never to appeal to me; no foreign cigarettes came up to ours in my estimation, and I would rather go without than force myself to smoke any others.

Life was not all harmony. There were times when we did not see eye to eye, mostly after an unpleasant spell at sea when nerves were taut, and over some insignificant thing tempers would go, and reason with it. These are the times when suspicion creeps into someone's disposition, and it is often difficult to eradicate once the seed is sown. In those days, the term 'circumstantial evidence' was not often used – possibly not understood either – but it existed, and easily became blown out of all proportion. Happily those occasions were rare on board Coastal Forces craft.

It was also proof of a cox'n's worth, to be able to put a stop to any incident, no matter how large or small. In most instances he would diplomatically keep out of arguments among his crew as to take sides would cause resentment from one side and from the man's shipmates, but it was difficult at times to remain neutral and to resist reporting someone to the Captain.

It was now 1943, we had had lousy weather during the last months of the previous year, but even though only January, the weather was considerably milder. This meant more patrols for our boats, and more attacks on our convoys from both aircraft and E-boats. There was one thing in our favour. We heard rumours that the work carried out by Coastal Forces boats was being officially recognised. The Minister for War, Lord Beaverbrook, actually came to Newhaven to speak to us. We all paraded on the jetty one day; he came, walked along our ranks, spoke to a man here and there, had lunch with the officers and went on his way. He probably felt better for his visit but we never thought so. It was a complete waste of time, to get dressed in our best uniforms for a 'brief encounter', so brief that by the next day we had forgotten all about it.

It was also becoming common knowledge that the enemy boats were not so keen to meet up with us and our presence alone would be enough to deter an attack on a convoy. Unfortunately this was not the case with enemy aircraft, although we were by no means sitting ducks. All aircraft that spotted us would attack without hesitation, especially if for some reason a boat was seen to be alone; that was when we were most vulnerable, and usually we came off the worst. If there was more than one boat, an attacking aircraft could come off second best. It was simple for the plane to attack a boat on its own, attacking from all angles to find its weakest point, but it is a different kettle of fish when there is more than one throwing up shells at them from more than one direction at the same time. So often, after perhaps a few stray shots to tease, an enemy plane would not stay for more as we could put up a dangerous anti-aircraft barrage with the assortment of weapons we had.

Incidents such as those were when the enemy pilots were normal lads like ours, but there were many exceptions, where their pilots were far from being rational or sane, as the next incident will reveal. It is one of such terrible consequences that it will be remembered for ever. It has become a historical fact and its existence as such will shame the German Nazis for ever.

Looking back to the beginning of my life in the Navy, one thing that most people tend to overlook, but which has struck me on many occasions, was the state of my health. Before entering the Service I regularly suffered from the common cold, at least every year, sometimes even twice in one year; they were mostly head colds, but on rare occasions they would affect my chest. The colds would usually last for approximately ten days, so what had changed? What had happened? I can only remember having one cold since joining, and that was while I was aboard the 320. Despite getting soaked through to the skin many times; despite walking miles in the pouring rain to get back aboard the boat after enjoying a night out on the town; despite sleeping in cold draughty huts; despite all this and more, I only ever had that one cold, and not even a 'sniff' since.

In fact the only time I had to attend a sick-bay, was at Whale Island when I developed a poisoned foot; any other visits were to receive inoculations.

Once I reached the age of twenty years I could understand it. The daily rum ration, real Navy rum, would kill almost any germs, and upon that one occasion on board the *Lucky Lady* when I caught cold, my shipmates made me turn into my bunk early that evening and made me drink half a pint of hot milk, into which they put a complete tot of rum, then an extra blanket on top of me, and off to sleep I went. As I slept, I sweated, and I sweated, and I sweated. I can only guess that I lost a fair bit of weight during that night, but what was more important was that when I woke next morning, the cold had completely disappeared,

and I was fit for anything that came along, a full breakfast to begin
with.

Apart from its medicinal properties, in which I am a firm
believer, I still believe in it today, there is another advantage, one
that I am sure the Admiralty are very aware of. After a man has
drank his daily tot of rum, he is ready and capable of eating
anything, no matter how badly it has been cooked, whether it is
hot or cold, no matter, one's appetite can make short work of
devouring it.

The modern Navy does not issue a daily tot of rum. It is a pity
in many ways, but the reason is understandable. In the modern
'high tech' Navy a man on duty under the influence could be a
danger to his ship and his shipmates, and when in charge of some
of the modern equipment in the world today, a man must have
all his faculties on top line. They do not have the cold, draughty
places to sleep in that we had, so the risk of catching cold would
be almost eliminated, and as for the food, well, it would be difficult
to find better, and although we lived well aboard our small boats,
it does not compare with how well they eat today. Their food
now is cooked by highly trained and competent chefs; please note
– chefs, not cooks, because that is exactly what they are today,
chefs who when they leave the Navy are able to take charge of
the kitchens of the world's best hotels.

Well, healthwise I had very little to complain about in those
days; the actual life we led contributed a great deal towards it I
am sure. One could almost say that the wind and seaspray would
also help to blow any germ away, as well as any 'cobwebs'.

There was one other important factor. When a man either
volunteered for Coastal Forces, or was drafted into them, he had
to undergo a very stiff medical examination and if there was
anything not quite right, then he would be rejected. I was always
given to understand that we were subjected to the same rigorous
testing that RAF pilots had, because of the tremendous vibration

experienced on the decks of boats at sea. When travelling at high speed, these vibrations affected the nerves of the body, sometimes very badly.

Until 1944 or thereabouts, an age limit was imposed upon Coastal Forces men. You had to be under thirty and once you reached that age your Skipper ought to apply for someone to relieve you. This did not always happen as many times a man would be allowed to remain because of his skill and ability.

We were enjoying extremely good weather for the time of the year which was making life much more pleasant for us all. In fact, I had practically forgotten that I had requested to leave the boat to take the instructor's course. Although I managed to avoid our Captain's attention most of the time, he was still behaving quite well to us all, and I honestly felt that I would not object to being part of his crew for the remainder of the war. Impossible, really, as even if Spud wished it, there would be others that would do their best to move me on, as I am sure happened with many others.

The day was a Wednesday, the date was January 20th 1943. We had been on our usual patrol the night before, everything had been cleaned, or oiled, or stowed away safely, rum had been issued, and we had eaten a good dinner. I do not think anybody on board had a single complaint. There would be night leave granted as usual, as from 1600 hrs, but not for me, perhaps that was my only grouse! Because it was such a nice day and I was not sleepy, I did not feel like writing any letters, so I sat on an ammunition locker on the upper deck, reflecting on what life might have in store and if there would be any surprises for me. Probably all kinds of things passed through my mind on that occasion but little did I know the true extent of one surprise that was in store.

A 'make-and-mend', the Navy's term for time off work, had been granted for that afternoon, and the Captain had given permission for those who were entitled to shore leave, to be able, if they wished, to start their leave immediately after dinner, lucky fellows. Lofty and Joe were occupied in the engine-room still; they had stopped for their dinner, but something made it necessary for them to work on it right away. Our Captain was either ashore, or possibly with other Skippers, conferring, or making their report on the previous night's activities, over a glass or two I am sure. Our other two officers were presumably still enjoying their dinner.

At this particular moment I was about to stand and walk over to the port side guard rails, alongside the bridge. Purely by chance, with only yards between the two of us, stood ordinary seaman George Hamblett, who acted as my No. 2 in my guns crew, to assist the operation of my pom-pom on the fo'c'sle. It was probably some time between 1230 and 1300 hrs.

Inland from us, somewhere over the South Downs, in the region of the town of Lewes and beyond, we could hear the wail of air-raid sirens. In only seconds all the sirens in our vicinity had joined them. George and I immediately ran for our gun, and made it ready for action. At that time we two were the only men on the upper deck of any boat in harbour, and definitely the only two closed up at our gun and ready to use it in the action that followed.

As I looked up into the sky towards the Downs I wondered what was coming, or even if anything would. Sure enough, there it was; an aircraft was approaching us fast. Right then it could not be identified as it was flying towards us which made identification more difficult. Any doubts George and I had were quickly dispelled. The safety catches on our guns had already been released and the first shell was in the breech; we were operational, and ready, when we heard the rattle of machine guns. The plane had opened fire at us, or at the base; it was a Focke-Wulf fighter bomber, and was flying only a few hundred yards above us, slightly to our starboard side, above the west bank of the river. We had what I can only describe as a perfect target. Opening fire as he had meant that we did not require permission to do likewise though under normal circumstances and with an officer present this would have been necessary. George and I opened fire at the enemy plane. George was wonderful; although at that time he had not undergone a gunnery course and had only been instructed by myself, our combined aim was perfect. 'Spot on', we saw our shells simply pour into that aircraft, and almost immediately flames and smoke were gushing from the plane's fusilage.

The Focke-Wulf continued on its way towards the harbour entrance and the sea, but in the seconds it took to reach the harbour mouth, at least one trawler had manned its guns and opened fire. It was said later that they had also hit their target.

The enemy plane continued to fly out to sea but so far as George and I were concerned there was no way in which that plane could possibly complete its journey across to France, and even more im-possible for it to reach its original place of taking off. The trawlers were in a better position to watch the plane's flight than we were, but even so, they could not see the end of it; it was reported to have gone down into the sea, and we are certain that it did.

At the time that George and I were hitting our target, the crews of the other boats had arrived on their decks. Some were now manning their guns, but there was no target for them to fire at. All guns crews had to remain closed-up at their positions until the all-clear sirens were sounded; this was normal practice anyway, as for all that we knew, there could have been more enemy planes as well as the one we had shot at and hit. Fortunately none came, and after some time had passed, the all-clear sounded and we stood down. It has to be said, George and I felt good. As our shots hit that plane, a loud cheer went up from all the other lads who were on deck. At first it did not seem real, the ease with which we hit that plane was almost unbelievable, but hit it we certainly did.

Naturally the event was the topic for discussion nearly all that afternoon. In the end we reached the conclusion that the pilot of the Focke-Wulf was probably mental, he must have been to have flown so low over what were obviously armed Naval vessels. It was also an insane move on his part to have opened fire on us as early as he did, thus giving us good warning of his intentions. It is just possible, like so many pilots of that time, that he had flown far too many 'sorties' withut a break; he may also have thought that he really did belong to 'the master race', as Hitler would have them believe and as such nothing could stop him. Sorry chum, but we did. And we cannot tell a lie, we were not sorry at all.

Our Captain quickly returned aboard, and after receiving all details and relevant information, he sent a signal to the Admiralty requesting credit for what we had done. This was standard procedure; although he personally had not taken part in the incident, we were his crew, manning the guns on his boat, so he should also have received credit for what we did.

Unfortunately this was not to be. Admiralty, in their so-called wisdom, decreed that as none of us had actually witnessed the entry of the plane into the sea, we could not officially claim it as our success. Unofficially it was agreed that the enemy plane had not succeeded in making it across to France, and that it had gone down into the sea; after it had been hit by us its flight became lower and lower until it finally hit the water.

We were very disappointed at the decision made by Admiralty, but there was nothing further that could be done about it. We thought their decision was very unfair. Had we been at sea then we might well have seen it crash, but we were not, we were in harbour, moored alongside; there was no way in which we could have possibly seen what happened to that plane once it had cleared the harbour entrance. Because of its speed, despite being hit, it was over the entrance to the harbour and out to sea in minutes, but it was obvious to all that watched, with the amount of smoke and flames belching from it, it could not possibly get far. We were given to understand that the usual search by rescue craft was made for the pilot, but nothing was found. My personal opinion was that nobody bothered to search thoroughly once they knew what the pilot had done.

Several hours later we were informed that this same plane, our Focke-Wulf, had earlier attacked a school in London, apparently machine-gunning the children at play in the grounds; he also dropped a bomb upon the school, killing many children. This of course was extremely sad news, but it served to make George and myself even more jubilant over what we had done. When comparing the pilot's actions in machine-gunning and the way he did it, with how he acted when he saw us, we had no doubts that it was the work of that same plane.

*Sandhurst Road School, minutes after being bombed and machine-gunned on January 20th, 1943 (photo courtesy of the* Kentish Mercury *newspapers).*

For some time after all the fuss had died down, the feeling of excitement and satisfaction remained with George and myself. In a way we were still tense with excitement, and time dragged slowly until it was time to turn into our bunks.

Two days later, I learnt from home that the London school that had been bombed was in fact Sandhurst Road School, Catford, south-east London, the school to which I went as a child, until the age of eleven years. The school was only approximately four hundred yards or so from my home in Sandhurst Road itself. (I actually lived in that same house for forty-six years.) My mother had been at home when the bombing occurred; our home was at the bottom of the hill which constituted half of the road while the school was situated at the top of the hill, just over the brow.

At first when I heard, it just did not seem possible, but the information was checked, and found to be correct. No other school had been bombed and machine-gunned, and after we had shot the German plane we were told quite definitely, that the same plane had bombed a London school.

We were even told about the route the plane had taken after the cowardly act. He had flown towards Sydenham and Forest Hill, two districts forming part of the borough of Lewisham, to the west of Catford, then on towards Croydon, past East Grinstead and on to Newhaven, intending no doubt to escape across the Channel, and back to base. Seeing our base and the boats there must have seemed like a bonus to the pilot and, not thinking straight, he obviously abandoned caution and consequently suffered for it. Fate then took a hand.

As he had already dropped his load of bombs, he had none to drop on us. Bombing us would have done him far more good than his idiotic machine-gunning ever would, and would certainly have been more acceptable than the vicious, foul act of attacking defenceless little children.

That pilot was mentally unstable, or his adrenalin was running so high that he was unable to think straight. Whatever the reason was, he thoroughly deserved what happened to him, and I, along with many others, am so pleased about it.

The revelation that the school concerned was actually the school I had attended as a child, made it all a remarkable coincidence, but in wars, these strange things happen, though I never ever thought that one would happen involving me. George Hamblett was absolutely thrilled at the news, and will still talk about it today. He actually visited my wife and me when we were living at nearby Chatham, about eighteen years ago, one Sunday afternoon, when we were able to exchange a few reminiscences.

Had we known about my connection with the school at the time of our shooting the plane, it would possibly have made a difference with the Admiralty attitude. The newspapers alone would have revelled in the story and it would have made first-class propaganda for us, but this was something that was pure chance, and there had been no possible chance of the two incidents being linked at that time.

The following weekend I arrived home on leave, and found that Catford was still seething with anger over what had happened. There was no doubt that had Londoners been able to get hold of that pilot, he would have been lynched on the spot, and most people would have not only agreed with it but also helped. It was one of the foulest acts carried out during the war.

There were many stories circulating about what happened, some of miraculous escapes, and some of misery and unhappiness. Among the latter one story was about the death of little Pauline Carpenter, aged four years, one child that I knew. Pauline's mother grew up in the next house to us at Sandhurst Road and her uncles and aunts were all regarded as close friends of my family.

The story was put around that the pilot did not know that it was a school that he had bombed, and mistook it for either a factory or a barracks. This was complete nonsense, and I dispute it vehemently. I have been given first-hand proof that he was flying low enough to have been able to have seen the children playing, and would have recognised them as such. Some women not far from the school could actually see the pilot in his cockpit and they waved to him before they realised that he was German. What is more, Sandhurst Road School was situated at the top of a hill, one of the highest parts of south-east London, it would have been instantly recognisable.

This Focke-Wulf had been flying low over residential property for several miles before attacking the school. A lady at Grove Park, three miles away as the crow flies, could actually see the pilot in his cockpit, and feared for the safety of a nearby hospital, but he passed over the hospital, probably not knowing what it was. No, that pilot was evil, and I am very proud to have helped put him in a watery grave,and I am sure that for many, even that was too good an end for him.

After the attack on the school, German propaganda sources reported that the attack made on that occasion resulted in their bombs being dropped successfully upon their designated targets, but what those targets were was difficult to identify. The man who it is thought sent the aircraft over that day, was Oberst Josef Priller, who was the Kommodore in command of the Nazi squadrons that included the plane that bombed the school. It was said that the pilot who was responsible for that terrible deed was a Hauptman Schuman, but if he took part in later attacks  upon Allied positions and was finally killed sometime in March, then he could not have been the 'mad' pilot, whom many of us are confident that we shot down after attacking us at Newhaven.

Another eye witness at that time reported seeing the German plane clearly from a factory only a mile away as the crow flies; the lady in question could see the plane as it flew low and towards the school from a south-easterly direction.

# CHAPTER 16

# To be an instructor, or not to be?
# That is the question

THE excitement of the 'evil' German pilot being shot down existed for just two days in reality; after that it was back to normal for us all. Convoys were passing through the English Channel more frequently now, so all craft engaged in convoy protection were kept very busy. That included us, we were out on patrol almost every other night, and if needed in between too. Various operating tactics were tried, but mostly the attacking E-boats were driven off before any damage could be done by them in our area. The overall success was a triumph, but our officers were almost desperate for direct conflict. It was no fun to them to have to chase enemy craft with little hope of catching them. The crews did not exactly regard the convoy work and fruitless chase as fun, but the frustration felt by the officers was understood. Although the final aim for both officers and men was the same, victory for us and defeat for our enemy, the crews did look at things differently.

For us all it had now become our 'way of life'. We worked hard and played hard, we lived under difficult circumstances, and we carried out orders given to us without question, very often in complete ignorance as to why, where or from; that was what we were paid to do. There was another way of looking at life aboard the motor gunboats and torpedo boats, we could be likened to the knights of old, riding out to do battle with the enemies of their country. We rode out, not on our horses but on the decks of our boats, to do battle for the same reasons, and if we had not been so superior in our armament, battles would have been on a 'one to one' basis. Of course we would also have been engaged in much more conflict had the odds against in number of E-boats been considerably greater.

There was also that other comparison that all Coastal Forces men were justifiably proud of, much of our fighting was like the cowboys and Indians warfare. 'Wait until you see the whites of their eyes before you open fire': that may or may not have been true in the days of real cowboy and Indian wars, but it was certainly true in Coastal Forces warfare.

On most of our night leaves, Joe, Lofty and I went up to Catford, eventually finishing in the company of the girls at the Black Bull. All seemed well between Pat and myself, and the memories of another were beginning to fade, yet, infatuated though I was, the subject of marriage was not then in my mind. It was not that the friendship with Pat was not of sufficient importance, it was, but right then there still existed a great deal of danger, and it would have been bad enough for my mother if anything happened to me, and I seriously did not want anyone else hurt too.

There was just once when the subject of marriage came into our conversation. On one particular evening Pat was feeling very low, really fed-up; my own interpretation was that the other girls in her unit were making life hard for her. They could not be blamed, in my opinion, Pat did get their backs up on many occasions. I had been told this by some of the other girls when Pat was not around. During our conversation in the local park, she sounded very depressed; she wanted to leave the WRAC and the only sure way would be to have a baby. We discussed the pros and cons, the whys and wherefores, and the 'ifs and buts', but to my old-fashioned way of thinking this could only be the product of marriage.

Although we discussed this at length, no decision was to be reached. Perhaps that guardian angel had been looking after me again? We parted that evening as usual, and no more was said on the subject at all.

A few days later, back on board the 611, a surprise came out of the blue. I had by now completely forgotten my request to take the gunnery course. I had been enjoying life aboard, my social life ashore was a very happy one, and there had been quite a lot of excitement recently, so there was no wonder that the matter had gone out of my mind.

Now my request had become reality. It had been approved and processed; the signal had been received by the Captain, and in a couple of days I was going to be on my way. I was not sure now that I wanted to go; after all, I had made the request at a time when I was not very happy, and also one of my reasons was to 'show off' in front of one particular girl. Now that she was married the point was not quite so valid and I had to face the possibility that I might never see her again. There would be one person made happy, that I knew, my mother, but Pat? I had never really considered her thoughts on the matter, and this should have made me think more seriously about our friendship.

Word had gone round all the boats, and invitations to go aboard various boats for rum came in fast and furious. The day of leaving arrived. I had no choice, the cox'n assured me that there was no way that I could back out now that the wheels had been set in motion. It was HMS *Excellent* for me. Everyone generally supposed it to be the result of the Focke-Wulf business; this was possible, but my gunnery record was good and my experience would greatly help if I managed to pass the course. The point that everyone made was how quickly after the incident the orders to proceed to Whale Island came; it even looked to be a consolation prize, in lieu of Admiralty refusing to give their official recognition. Although I knew that Admiralty did not give a damn about men like me. I could not help thinking that it was a possibility, and it seemed that most of the men at Newhaven were of the same opinion.

This was going to be my third visit to the school. This did not worry me, despite cries from the others that they were glad it was not they that would be going. I knew, however, that this visit was going to be the hardest one of all. When taking part in courses as a junior rating, there was always a faint chance of mercy being shown towards you, very rarely, it was true, but even the toughest of instructors had a soft spot somewhere, in many cases not even known by the man concerned.

My kitbag and hammock were packed and lying on the upper deck of 611, ready for my going. I was due to catch a train from Newhaven station at 1400 hrs. The time then was 1045 a.m., so I had plenty of time, especially as the lads were going to carry my kitbag and hammock to the station for me (if only that had been all!)

After drinking my rum, the cox'n gave me an extra one, and as I sat eating my dinner the rest of the crew came over and offered their rum for me to sip, which I did of course. Had this been all, no doubt the situation would have remained reasonable, but it did not. Crews on several other boats insisted that they cheered me on my way, in the usual way, so foolishly I went aboard. Not one boat, not two boats, not . . ? I do not really know how many boats I visited. Aboard each the ritual would begin with a complete tot from the cox'n of the boat, then sippers from practically everyone that drew his rum ration. Finally it was oblivion, it cannot be described by me in any other words.

According to the story told to me some time later, when I passed out, and I was never told which boat I was aboard at the time, they informed my shipmates aboard 611, then between them all, they carried me and my kit to the railway station, where they intended to put me aboard the train bound for Portsmouth. This would have happened, except for a very sensible and level-headed station master, who refused to allow it to happen. Quite rightly no doubt, thinking of his own position should a fatal accident happen, and in the state that I was in this was quite definitely more than just a possibility. There was only one choice left to the men looking after me, and that was to take me back aboard the 611, where I could sleep it off.

The lads successfully smuggled me on board and into my old bunk, sleeping soundly, watched I would imagine by the man who was my relief, and who had arrived on board while I was making the rounds. He must have wondered what on earth he had come to. The afternoon passed without the cox'n or officers knowing anything was wrong. The officers had actually said their good wishes during the morning before the rum issue; they had known what was going to happen aboard 611, but were ignorant of the other invitations.

All would have been well except that orders came for 611 to put to sea. Frantic discussions went on, with only one solution: the cox'n had to be told about me. After inspecting me, he knew that he had no choice but to report me to the Captain, and 'heaven only could know what his reaction was going to be'.

It was not reported what the Captain's reaction was when told, or what his mood was, but it certainly did not bode well for me. It was apparently decided that 611 would put to sea as usual, but with one extra crew member, me. I think that there might well have been the distinct possibility that Spud would consider disposing of me while at sea. It must have been his good nature that won.

Together with another gunboat, the 611 put to sea, with an unconscious man below who should have been well on his way to Whale Island. It was probably an hour or so later, when I realised that someone was shaking me hard and roughly, determined to return me to consciousness. Only then did I know where

I was, and the realisation hit me like a ton of bricks. My first reaction was who could I pray to? What should I pray about? What would my fate be if I ever did reach Whale Island? and what chance was there now of me ever taking that course? Then the shaking stopped, and a quite kindly voice was asking if I was fit again. Upon receipt of my reply to the effect that not only was I not fit, but I was not even sure about being alive, I was informed sympathetically that the Captain wanted to see me on the bridge, at once. With the sound of a hundred guns booming inside my head, I managed a quick sluice under the tap before climbing up the gangway to the bridge.

Also on the bridge at the time was Sub-Lieutenant Lewis, who seemed uncertain whether to smile or scowl at me, and managed an expression somewhere in between; the cox'n who was able to sneak me a wink of encouragement; an able seaman on the steering wheel who was trying hard to appear uninterested, though all the time his ears were directed towards me; and the Captain, who was steadily gazing out towards the horizon. He never moved a muscle, he never turned to look at me at all; his only words were to instruct me to go to what used to be my gun, see what was wrong because my relief could not fire it, carry out whatever repairs were needed, and then return to him on the bridge.

The shock of not receiving the full extent of Spud's wrath must have brought me back into the land of the living, and almost gratefully I staggered on to the fo'c'sle, to inspect the pom-pom and hopefully discover why it would not fire. I felt as though my whole life depended upon it.

Afterwards, when thinking about it, I came to the conclusion that very likely my life did depend upon being successful. Spud would not have considered returning to base because of the pom-pom being out of action, and to have carried on to sea, with the prospect of engaging the enemy without what was probably his most important gun, could have turned out to be fatal. Fortunately fate was with me, or perhaps my luck had returned? Whatever it was, it was in my favour. There was nothing wrong with the pom-pom at all, all that had happened was there was no shell in the breech, naturally it would not fire. It was only nervousness on the part of my relief that was the cause; it might even have been because he could be watched by the Captain from his position on the bridge. George Hamblet could probably have rectified his mistake, but the new man was George's senior and therefore it was his reponsibility.

Once I had explained what the problem was, and loaded the gun, with the Skipper's permission we fired a few rounds to demonstrate the gun was now ready, I then returned to the bridge as ordered, and waited until the Captain was ready for me.

Deliberately I was ignored as I stood waiting on the bridge for the Captain to speak. It was clear that I was not going to get off lightly, and so I wondered, as I stood there, just what my punishment was going to be. It must have been all of ten minutes before he spoke. At first he simply asked what had been wrong with the pom-pom; I explained as best as I could without 'dropping my relief in it'. It might have been my imagination, but for a brief moment I thought I saw a smile appear, but it vanished so quickly, that it could well have been my imagination. I was then told to return below, and when we returned to harbour I would be dealt with properly. Back down below I went. After a while the cox'n came down; we discussed what had happened, and he gave his opinion as to what form my punishment might take. He was not very optimistic, taking into consideration how there had been constant friction between the Captain and myself. In the meantime, he informed me, I was not going to be allowed to remain a 'passenger', I would have to take my turn of duty along with the rest of the crew, which of course I did, and was glad to be able to do so.

The night's patrol passed without incident, and next morning we returned to harbour. I was then informed that I would have to appear before the Captain at 11.30 hrs, and to be waiting by the bridge ten minutes or so before.

As soon as we berthed at our usual place, the Skipper left the boat, presumably to make his report regarding the night's patrol, at the same time no doubt, to discuss my predicament, and what he had decided. He returned aboard about 1045 hrs, and disappeared into his cabin alone, until it was time to deal with me.

The cox'n escorted me on to the bridge, where our other two officers were waiting, unsmiling and trying to look grim. The Captain appeared, and my ordeal began. As it turned out it was not as bad as I expected. The charge was read out, and I was asked to explain. I was then told that I had disgraced myself, a fact that had been brought home to me already. The Captain then explained that he could not possibly allow to me go scot free, he also thought that it would be easier for me if he did the actual punishing. He said that he was tempted to send the details on to Whale Island for them to make a decision on what to do, but having given the matter thought, he realised that to do this would probably mean the cancellation of the instructor's course for me, which, in his own opinion, would be a waste of my talents. This gave me a pleasant surprise. This was not what I had expected from Spud at all; he was proving to be human after all. The change that I had noticed some time ago had not disappeared, and although the dressing down that he gave to me made me feel rather small, I realised that in actual fact I was going to get off pretty lightly. The official punishment awarded was fourteen days No. 11's: this meant stoppage of pay, stoppage of rum, and either extra work or rifle drill.

The punishment awarded, and recorded on my papers, I then left the bridge and went to join everyone down below on the mess-deck. After a great deal of leg pulling, plus a few sips of their rum, I sat down to dinner with them for the last time. I was going to be put on the train at the same time as before, 1400 hrs.

The lads helped me again with my kit, and waited until the train was about to leave before they left me. As I was about to board the train, out came the station master. He apologised for his actions the other day, and said that it was done in the interests of my safety as much as anything else, and hoped that there were no hard feelings on my part. I assured him that there were not, I even thanked him, then boarded the train, and I was off to Whale Island. The worry now was what would be said to me when I arrived; not many men had been foolish enough to join HMS *Excellent* already under punishment, so it was natural that I should expect the worst.

Alone, sitting in the railway carriage, heading towards God only knew what, makes a man reflect over his past, and you know then what you should or should not have done. Regrets certainly, by the bagful, but you know that it is too late and it is now a question of making the best of the situation. Somehow, going to Whale Island under these circumstances is rather like facing a firing squad.

It was not that the journey was a long one, but it was tiresome, and very, very slow. I tried to sleep, but sleep would not come. There was all the time that awful nagging feeling going on inside my head. The uncertainty of it all was far worst than the punishment awarded to me; it was a wonder that I was not out of my mind by the time I arrived at Portsmouth, but then, perhaps I was? I was not fit to judge.

The train pulled into Portsmouth, and after finding the Naval Patrol, who found transport for me to the Island, I was now on the last leg of my journey. Very soon I sheepishly stood before the Officer-of-the-Watch to report my arrival. The duty officer inspected me brusquely, and remarked that I had been expected to arrive the previous day, so where had I been? Without going into too much detail I gave a brief explanation which assured him that I had not been on an unlawful visit to my home. I was then directed to the Regulating Office where they allocated me to a mess, told me what to do about an evening meal, and ordered me to report to the Training Commander at 0800 hrs the next morning. Before I left the office, a petty officer informed me rather abruptly that signals had been exchanged with Newhaven, so I could expect trouble when I saw the Commander in the morning. That little 'pep talk' I could have done without.

At 0800 hrs I stood outside the Training Commander's office. I waited, and I waited, and I waited. Officers and ratings were going and coming all the time I stood there; each time I asked when someone would see me I was fobbed off with excuses, until 0900 hrs when everyone stood to attention. The Training Commander appeared and entered his office. Obviously he had not been there during the time I had waited, and later I discovered that I should not have been told to report at 0800 hrs, as the Commander is never there until an hour later. Well, we all make mistakes, as I already knew.

By the time I was called to enter the Training Office, I felt that I had already been hung, drawn and quartered; there was no way in which I would be able to defend myself, even if the opportunity arose. It was 0915 hrs before the Commander summoned me into his office, and several minutes before he spoke.

The papers he was reading were without any doubt mine; enclosed with them was a hand-written letter of some length. I could not see what was written on it, how much was good, and how much was bad, mostly the latter I imagined. The handwriting, although legible, was not recognisable by me; I had seen some of Spud's handwriting before, but at the distance I was at then I could not be sure as to whether it was Spud's or not.

Whatever it contained, it was not going to do me any good. The Commander looked up at me, his features completely immobile, and commented sternly that they were not used to men joining the school while under punishment, and that he was not sure that I was the right material to take an instructor's course.

When he asked if I agreed it was more of an order to agree with what he said. He then related the history of HMS *Excellent*, and what I could expect, and what form the rest of my punishment was going to take. The course would begin the very next morning, so I had arrived just in time; another day's delay and I would have been rejected. The Commander then dismissed me, with instructions to make certain he was not given cause to have me in front of him again, and in future I was to make certain I did not disgrace the good name of the school.

Hurriedly I left that office, and returned to the quarters in which I was to live for the next three months. Here I discovered three other ratings who were taking the same course. I had seen them the night before, but had no opportunity even to say 'hello'. After acquainting them with a few details about myself, I received in return from one some sympathy, the other two were not concerned either way.

The rest of that day was spent trying to make friends with the other three who were taking the course. It was not easy at first, perhaps because of wariness on their part, when they learnt that I was under punishment, or maybe this would be the attitude they would adopt once they became instructors. I was never going to know this.

The day to begin the course arrived. As well as the three I had met, there were eight petty officers taking the course. From the glances in my direction I assumed that someone had already acquainted them with my situation. That did not worry me unduly, but I knew then that if there was any job that had to be done that they would not want to do, then it was going to be 'Joe Soap' who would be told to do it. Once the course was well under way, conditions for me improved a little; two of the petty officers became quite friendly, so with help from those two, and one of the other three, life for me was actually showing promise.

There were no real difficulties regarding the course. We simply had to refresh ourselves regarding the various guns used in Coastal Forces craft and their maintenance, plus alterations and modifications. We were taught the correct way to convey the information to others, and various other aspects to the skill of teaching. The part that I probably enjoyed most, was called 'Field training': another name for rifle drill and marching around the parade ground, but this time there was the added enjoyment, at least to me, of being in charge and giving the orders on the parade ground. Fortunately my voice was particularly suitable for this, and our instructor informed me that my voice could be plainly understood from any part of the parade. This was not so for all the others; some had to be bullied into shouting louder and even then could not always be understood.

It has to be admitted, in all fairness, that my indiscretions were not held against me while undergoing the course. I realised that I was being carefully watched, but I was not going to make any mistakes now that I had made it this far. When, after a few days, the atmosphere became warmer, I was offered sips of rum at dinner time. It was really true that I was not bothered about the lack of rum, and I only accepted the offers out of courtesy and sociability; after all, having been used to drinking neat rum aboard the boats, drinking grog was not very attractive anyway.

The most difficult part so far as I personally was concerned, was the studying of an evening. I just could not settle to it, this was something I had not bargained for, I never could study out of hours even when still at school; in those days I would do any homework allocated between lessons, and would even prefer to remain in the classroom to do it before going home so that I had my evening completely free. It was exactly the same situation all over again. Instead of homework, there was this need for studying. The others managed it fine, they would simply settle on their beds and get down to it, whereas I would make an attempt, but give up, so had to rely upon a quick browse through my notes before a particular lesson. Fortunately this always proved sufficient to get me through.

The gunnery notebook that I had begun at the time of my first visit to HMS *Excellent* had now become an item of interest to everyone, and I was really proud of it. It was possible that the gunnery officer at Weymouth might have mentioned it to the school officers, as it was not unusual to find suddenly that one would be looking at it over my shoulder, and would then pick it up to examine it closer.

The end of my fourteen days punishment arrived, much to my relief. I would now be entitled to leave, and be able to enjoy visits to local dances etc. It meant, however, that any trips ashore would have to be on my own. The petty officers I knew would not contemplate being seen ashore with someone junior to them, and the other three were too taken up with studying, that came before any enjoyment.

Weekend leave was something different. There was no hesitation about taking that, and it seemed a lifetime since I had been home. Being at Newhaven had spoilt me, as it probably did others; it had been too easy to get home from there. I had not been able to write to Pat, so that might well have caused complications in that direction. Weekend leave would provide the solution, I hoped.

The weekend leave was going to be a 'long one', which meant that it began at 1200 hrs on the Friday, and ended at 1200 hrs upon the Monday. When I fell in on that Friday morning to proceed on leave, I really felt that I had earned it this time. Waiting just outside the school main gates were local buses ready to take us to the main-line railway stations, which they did with the minimum delay.

There was nothing special about the journey home. The train was subjected to the usual delays when sirens were sounded, taking roughly double the usual time to reach London. Once across the platforms and on to the train bound for Catford, it was not so bad; these trains operated shorter quicker journeys, the drivers were much more used to air-raids than their colleagues on the longer routes, so often they did not stop or even slow down when a raid was taking place. So, in no time at all, I arrived at Catford, and was able to catch a bus to take me the last mile or so.

The arrival home was of course greeted with considerable warmth and enthusiasm from my mother. She showed disappointment that it was only for the weekend, but when she realised that being at the school would mean other weekend leaves while I was there, she did not mind so much, and of course, at the end of the course it was hoped that we would get longer leave granted.

Without delay that evening I set out for Lewisham, and the Black Bull, no stops or visits on the way; I had only one thing in mind, I wanted to see Pat again. By this time it was around nine p.m. when I entered the pub. I suddenly realised that this was the very first time that I had been here on my own. I felt strangely lonely, there was nobody I knew there: a few Wracs, some soldiers who might have been on leave, or simply from the nearby 'ack-ack site', the rest were civilians it seemed. After buying myself a drink, I stood at the bar, considering what my best move would be. Somehow I had to get a message to Pat, to let her know that I was home on leave.

After a while, and still not knowing what to do, a group of Wracs entered, and I was able to recognise one, so over I went to speak to her. She recognised me instantly, and I thought that she appeared a little embarrassed. She told me that Pat would not be coming there, as she was on duty, but when she returned to camp she would see that Pat was told that I was asking for her.

The evening was almost over. I considered leaving to visit somewhere else, but decided not to as it was getting near to closing time. As I stood there listening to the band playing, I was aware that the group of girls that had come in were talking about me, and I wondered why. Deciding that perhaps it would be to my benefit if I joined their company, I offered to buy them a drink. This was immediately refused, but they showed no sign of wanting me to leave their company, so I remained with them, talking about things in general, and how they liked being based in London. No other kind of question was asked, I did not intend to be accused of prying. Somehow, not unnaturally I suppose, Pat became the subject of conversation, and I was warned in as friendly terms as possible, that it would be better if I did not take Pat too seriously. They were all in agreement with this, but were not being 'catty'; they could see though that I had not taken their warning well, so one asked if I knew that Pat had been seeing a Canadian soldier. This rang a bell. I did not know, but for some reason my instinct linked the Canadian to the last visit I had made with Joe and Lofty, when Pat was missing. I asked the girls if they remembered that particular day; they could not, but one mentioned that it was around that time that Pat had started to see this soldier. My heart sank. Inwardly I knew the worst, but I was not going to give up easily, and still wanted to see Pat if the girls would pass on my message, which they did, and I looked forward to the following evening not quite as enthusiastically as I normally would have done.

The Saturday passed quite normally, visiting relatives, but there were none of my old friends home on leave. My mind was too preoccupied with what would happen that evening when I saw Pat, if I saw Pat, all sorts of doubts were creeping into my mind. My mother could see that something was bothering me, but wisely asked no questions. Although she had said that she had liked Pat when I took her home, she would not have wanted to share me with her, and that was what it basically amounted to, this friend-ship.

That evening, dressed in my No 1's, I made for Lewisham again, but this time I stopped at the Plough and Harrow at Catford, for a 'livener'. Seeing the old faces that I knew made me feel better, and I left to walk the rest of the way to the Black Bull at Lewisham. It was not far to walk, about three-quarters of a mile in all, and I entered the saloon bar to begin my wait for Pat to show up. As time passed, I began to wonder whether she was going to appear.

It was well after 9.00 p.m. when she walked into the bar; as usual she looked a 'million dollars', without a care in the world. When she walked over to me it seemed that nothing had changed, and my worries had been for nothing. The remainder of the evening proved no different from before; she acted as if she really cared, and that we had the rest of our lives to share together.

We arranged to meet again the following night, same place and same time. I would have liked to have been with her during the day, but her duties would not allow this, it had to be an evening date, and the way in which she told me this was so convincing, nobody I thought, could be so sweet if she was 'two-timing'. I had a lot to learn about girls yet.

Sunday morning at home meant a visit from an uncle. He was of the age where he had been too young for the previous Great War, and now he was too old for this one. It was stupid really, he was far fitter than the majority of younger men serving in the Forces, and far more capable. Sid, however, had joined the London Auxilliary Fire Service, so he was not wasted. He was also a first-class footballer, and had been auditioned for Charlton Athletic, but refused to turn professional as in those days an injury could lose your ability to work as well as play, and there were no high salaries or security as there is today. His ability as a player did not go unrecognised; the London Fire Brigade had their own football team, and he was quickly enlisted into that, his efforts greatly assisting his team to win the Championship.

He had a unique sense of humour, which unfortunately was marred by a leaning toward communism. This resulted in many arguments but these were not allowed to become too heated. This

Sunday was no exception, and was as enjoyable as always. When he left it was time for me to visit my friends at the Plough and Harrow just for an hour, then home for dinner.

The afternoon passed slowly. I walked up the road to look at the damaged school, it was so hard to believe, and so sad.

Opening times for public houses on Sundays were at seven o'clock in the evenings, and I had two hours to waste before meeting Pat. I walked to Catford, had a drink and played records in the Plough, and made my way slowly to Lewisham.

It was still too early for Pat, but all I could do was to wait, no music to cheer me up, as the band appeared later on a Sunday evening. Apparently it was hardly worth their while appearing upon a Sunday for little more than an hour, but they did, and were always greatly appreciated.

9.00 p.m. arrived, but no sign of Pat; at 9.15 a group of Wracs arrived. One came over to me, handed me a letter, said that she was sorry, and rejoined her friends. With a sinking feeling I opened it and read the contents. It was from Pat of course, and was meant to be an apology but it did not read that way. She was sorry to let me down, and made a feeble excuse that she could not leave camp, and thought it better if we parted, so this was saying goodbye. I could feel the eyes of the group of girls upon me. I felt as though my face was beetroot red, and as I passed the girls on my way out, I heard one say to the rest, 'I expected her to do this to him,' and so I left to find somewhere else to drown my sorrows.

Not having anything to delay me, I made my way home, much earlier than my mother expected. She would not object to that of course, and the look upon my face would also be enough for her to imagine what had happened. Mothers are good at that.

The next morning found me awake very early. There was never much for me to do in readiness for a return journey either to ship or boat, nothing now to tempt me into doing something I would live to regret. As soon as convenient I said my goodbyes, making a promise to come home again as soon as possible, and I was on my way. As the train passed through Lewisham I could see the streets below. I never expected to see anyone that I knew, and so I was not disappointed.

# The Matelot's Prayer

Our Father which art at Admiralty
Hallowed be Thy name
Thy ships becalmed,
Thy will be done
As in Queen's Rules and Regulations
And maybe in Heaven afterwards
Give us this day our tot
Instead of 3d. per day in lieu
Lead us not in the ways of temperance
Forgive us our drunkenness
For in that condition
We will serve you blindly
Our ships are our kingdoms
A tot our power and Glory
May it be reinstated or at least
Remembered with the greatest affection
For ever, and ever, and aye.
Amen

JWD

CHAPTER 17

# *Win some, lose some,*
# *what is to come?*

THE one thing I would not do, was to return to my boat, barracks, or even Whale Island, early, so I joined the throng that were enjoying a last drink in the pub near to the school, and then walked the last few hundred yards back through the main gates.

Upon entering the mess, I found most of the others were already back, some, the more conscientious, were even studying. In a way they were to be admired, but I did not envy them.

One of my three classmates came over to me; it was soon obvious to him that things were not quite right, and he asked me why. At first I was not prepared to say what was wrong, but he persuaded me to open up, and I did. He could see that I had taken it harder than was realised, so he talked to me in such honest, genuinely sympathetic terms, that I soon told him the whole story. He was several years older, and also a married man, he understood exactly how I felt, then he gave it to me good and hard. He never actually called Pat any names, but it was plain what he thought, and very soon I realised that what he was saying made sense, and I began to feel better about it, or you could say 'less hurt'. The talk from that shipmate did me a great deal of good; I hope that he knew it, and also knew how much I appreciated his good deed, for that was what it was.

The instructors' course was proceeding well. All those taking part were happy enough, and nobody appeared to have any problems; our instructors were not suffering from indigestion, an obvious sign that the course was running smoothly.

Each evening, if not on duty, I would go ashore, even if I had very little money. Just walking around this part of Portsmouth helped. There were the odd times when I wished that I was able to study like the others. I did try, but it was no good, not for me, personally I considered that I had enough to 'digest' during lessons. I needed my leisure time to 'unwind', and once I was able to do that I felt better, and it did me good.

There was one occasion when ashore, that I was waiting by a bus stop on the main London road, with no particular destination in mind. I was merely going into town.

Standing there, oblivious to the world, I felt a tap upon my shoulder, and a feminine voice said, 'Hello, fancy meeting you here!' I turned around to see a girl in Wren's uniform, actually smiling at me. 'Good Lord,' I thought, 'my luck is about to change,' then I recognised her; her name was Rene, and when I last saw her it was at Catford, two or three years previously. There was never anything between us, and at that time she had her eyes on someone else who lived near to me, but Rene was always a very attractive girl, and I always had a soft spot for her, in fact given half a chance I would willingly have allowed something to develop. We exchanged the usual pleasantries until the bus arrived when we said goodbye. I boarded the bus and Rene carried on with her walk, presumably to her quarters nearby.

Her friendly smile remained with me for years after, and there were many times when I could have kicked myself for not having had the sense to ask her for a date at that meeting. She probably would not have agreed, she may even had been already engaged, even married; I would not have asked such personal questions at that time. Some time after the war had ended I did see her, we smiled and said hello, nothing more as we were both in the company of friends, in different groups. I was with my wife, and she may well have been with her husband.

As I sat inside the bus, I thought about Rene, and realised that I had never even asked her what she did in the Wrens, apart from looking pretty of course; there were so many jobs that the Wrens were capable of doing in these times. I did wish that I had asked, it would have enabled me to ask her to go out with me on another day, but it was too late now.

As the bus continued on its way towards the town centre, I suddenly remembered that something similar had happened when I was here on the short refresher course. I was sitting inside a bus, much as I was doing now, and sitting on the seat opposite me was a very familiar looking man. I had no doubts to his identity; his name was Coleman, and for my last three years at school he had been my art master at the Catford Central School for Boys. He had had in those days great hopes for me, but it was not to be, the prospect of entering the art world would have been too boring, I thought. Leaning across to speak to him, we also exchanged good wishes and he remembered who I was quite easily. I never asked him why he was so far from Catford; he would have been far too old to have been in the services. I can only imagine that he was occupied with some kind of war-work, map or chart drawing perhaps: that was a possibility because of his artistic ability. When my destination arrived, we also said our goodbyes, and I left him on the bus. It can be a very small world at times.

Since I left the 320, I had not been to many dances. My two closest shipmates aboard 611 were not interested in dancing, and Pat had never wanted to go dancing either. Infatuated as I was, I was content with just being with her, so no dancing never bothered me then.

Now I decided that a visit to a local dance hall was just what I needed. It might just be possible that I could meet Rene. It was not that I was feeling romantic, but the prospect of being with someone that I knew, someone that was attractive too, appealed to me; there would have been much that we could have talked about; who knows but it might have been beneficial to both of us? So that was partly why I intended to find the nearest hall where there would be a suitable dance in progress.

It was not too difficult, although I must admit when I first entered that hall that I was not impressed with what I could see. I suppose in some ways I was a snob, there is a little of this in everyone, and it always comes to the fore at some time. Believe me when I say that I had no false illusions about myself. Although reasonably educated – the school that the art master had been at was a very good one, with an excellent reputation – my upbringing was a poor one, financially, though my mother herself had done wonders with her efforts to raise me. No, the dance hall was full, and I could not see one girl to whom I was attracted; oh! how I was regretting that I did not date Rene! There was no point in not going into the hall now that I had paid my entrance fee. Fortunately it was licensed, so I bought myself a drink and proceeded to 'watch the talent', such as it was.

There did not appear to be many girls from the services, and those that were there already had partners, so the prospect of enjoying myself looked remote. I was then contemplating leaving the dance and returning back aboard but before making for the exit I took a slow walk around the hall, without any real expectations or even intentions, but merely to pass some time. I was even thinking to myself that this was one place I would not bother about visiting again. I was not very happy at the thought. This hall was situated in a part of Portsmouth that was not rowdy, which meant that there would not be many visits by Naval Patrols, and there was less risk of being involved in fights of any kind. In my mind it was better to steer clear of the Portsmouth pubs for that reason alone. One thought that was always uppermost in my mind then, was that on all accounts I had to 'keep my nose clean'.

The dance floor was empty as I made my way around it. I had almost completed the full circuit when the band struck up a waltz. My glass was now empty so I put it down, and looked around the hall again in the hope of finding a partner who did not look too bad. Then I saw her, standing by the wall, all alone, almost as if she did not want to be seen by anyone. She was slim, sylph-like, dark hair, small elfish features, smartly dressed in Wren's uniform. She appealed to me, as she did look very, very nice indeed, and I so much wanted to dance with somebody like her. She was obviously alone, and I wondered why. I had no ulterior motive towards her, so I approached her and asked her for a dance. Now I knew why she was alone; she told me that she could not dance, and that she only came there to pass away the time, there was nobody that she knew there, and she had not been in the Wrens very long. While we were talking I do not remember even a wisp of a smile, she was so serious, so much so that my heart went out for her. I wanted to cheer her up, and I wanted to see her smile. That, I felt, was very important.

When she apologised for not being able to dance, I insisted that it did not matter, anyone can dance I said, please, let us try. After giving it a little thought she smiled a little and agreed to try; we managed to get around the floor slowly, until the music came to a stop, when we returned to where she had been standing. Time was now late, and the dance would end soon anyway. She had told me her name was Doreen, and now she had to return to the Wrens' quarters where she was living. At first my offer to escort her was rejected, but I persuaded her that it would be safer for her if she allowed me to walk with her, so she agreed.

As we walked she opened up to tell me more about herself. She with another girl operated a small boat, affectionately called a skimming dish. Their main work consisted of taking mail out to the Naval ships in harbour and lying outside in the Solent; they also delivered messages and signals of importance to the ships, and the various Naval establishments. To carry out these duties, in all weathers, was quite an achievement for girls so young and my admiration toward her was genuine. My feelings at that time were for friendship. I liked what I saw, I liked what I heard about her, so I wanted if at all possible to see her again. When I asked her if we could meet again, she again gave me what I could only describe as her Mona Lisa smile, and after a few seconds thought she said yes, she would like that. We then arranged to meet upon her next off-duty night, which I am pleased to say we did.

Where the Wrens' quarters were was not far from Whale Island. We talked a great deal during that walk, I found listening to her both enjoyable and easy, and now that she had agreed to meet me again, it was simply a question of where and when. Apparently her duties prevented her from stating a particular day or time right then, but if it were possible for me to visit the jetty at the island during the morning break, known in the Navy as 'stand-easy', either she or another Wren would tell me where and when – and if.

At first a little doubt crept into my mind. Was this another 'push off'? Had she been simply 'sweet talking' me in order to get rid of me without a scene? No, I did not think so, and I liked her enough to willingly take the risk.

Next morning when the bugle sounded 'stand-easy', I made my way to the jetty. Luckily our classroom was only a few yards away, so it was no problem to get there. I arrived just in time. Two Wrens were about to leave in their dish. They heard me shouting and realised who I was, and gave me the message that Doreen could see me the following evening if I wanted, outside the Wrens' quarters, and at a stated time. This was all fine to me. I was overjoyed, and began to look forward to meeting her.

The one classmate with whom I was friendly, and to whom I had poured out my tale of woe when Pat had severed our friend-ship, had seen me make my trip to the jetty. He asked me what was going on, so I told him, explaining that no romance was intended, or even thought about. He laughed and simply gave me a friendly warning not to put myself in a position again where I could be hurt; he would not look forward to listening to it all again. An attempt was made to reassure him, but I do not know if I succeeded.

The course was going well for me. My mind was at ease with everything. I knew that I was no longer being watched as I had been when I first joined the school, and now I could look forward to enjoying the company of a very nice girl. It was proving to be quite an enjoyable world I was now in. I had completely recovered from the parting with Pat, and had no regrets at all; there still remained a possibility that I might see Rene again, but as this was very uncertain it was not going to be a problem. Anyway should I be lucky enough to see Rene again there would not be any reason not to spend time together; after all, my friendship with Doreen need not supersede everything.

On that evening when Doreen and I met again, we decided not to visit another dance; although she was willing to learn she was not very keen, and I did not want to press the issue. We decided then to visit the local cinema, where the film showing featured Judy Garland and Mickey Rooney. It was very enoyable, and under its influence perhaps, the two of us began to share feelings that had never been intended. We all know that the back rows of a cinema are not just there to watch a film, it may have been that we both needed affection as well as company; whatever it was, being together that evening, in that cinema, brought us closely together.

In the film Judy Garland sang the words of a song called 'Our Love Affair'. It was, and still is to this day, a beautiful song and as we walked back to the Wrens' quarters, we decided that this would be 'our song', and we should now see each other more often, which we did.

This girl, this young Wren, was not like any other girl that I had known. She was totally honest in everything she said or did, she was undemanding, and understanding, so much so that at times she made me feel inadequate; there were times when I feared that I was experiencing again that feeling of inferiority that I had known before joining the Navy. It was not quite like that though, because had it been so, I might never have passed the instructors' course; because it just is not possible for an instructor to feel, or be, inferior.

Thinking seriously, I wanted Doreen to meet my mother. The next weekend I was due for leave; unfortunately Doreen was not able to get weekend leave, but she was prepared to come to London on the Saturday evening, and stay overnight, returning to Portsmouth the following morning. It would be something of a rush visit, but that was what she wanted, so I agreed, and we made the arrangements to meet where everyone was said to meet, under the clock at Waterloo Station.

That meeting place sounded so 'corny', yet it really is the most sensible place to choose, and despite its popularity there are never too many there to prevent people meeting successfully; the only thing missing for us would be a flower in my buttonhole, but then without a top coat, where would you expect to find a buttonhole on a sailor's uniform?

My mother had been told about Doreen, and roughly the time to expect us to arrive home. The only thing left was for me to make my way to Waterloo and the meeting place. I left reasonably early, to make certain she did not have to wait there on her own. It would be safe for her, of that I was sure, there were far too many people about for there to be any danger; nevertheless, I still did not like the idea of her waiting there on her own, so I arrived under the clock, nice and early.

I never actually stood under the clock until our time of meeting arrived, but from where I stood I had a clear view of the area all the time. The time arranged came, a train from Portsmouth was just in and I watched the barrier gates, expecting Doreen to come through them at any second, but no, the last person from the train came through the gates and it was not her. I felt sure that she had been delayed, but would be on the next one, so I checked the timetable, and went into the buffet to pass some of the time away.

Approximately an hour later another train from Portsmouth arrived: same procedure, same result, not a sign of Doreen. Seeds of doubt began to grow, alternately with concern. It would be hard to define at that point which were the strongest. There really was no choice but to wait for the next train, and then I even wondered if there was a chance of her arriving on a train from another destination, it was possible, so now I had to wait under that clock all the time, and try to watch people arrive from all platforms. This I did, and not very happily. I knew that even if I knew the telephone number of the Wrens' quarters, which I did not, there would not be any good achieved. If she had changed her mind she would not want to speak to me, and if she was still on her way, which now seemed unlikely, a 'phone call would be a waste of time.

Rather miserably I decided to wait for just one more Portsmouth train, then nobody could accuse me of not making allowances. I knew that not many men would have waited this long, and it did seem a little ridiculous to have wasted all this time, just standing here at Waterloo Station, under that damn clock. I was now beginning to hate the sight of that clock.

The Portsmouth train arrived. It emptied. The last person came through the gates, and that was that, I had been stood up. So I made my way home, to explain to my mother as best as I could. Although she sympathised with me, she did try to make excuses; she said that from all that I had told her about Doreen, she did not sound like a girl who would deliberately do that sort of thing to anyone, and when I returned to Portsmouth I would know why. With regret I must admit that I was far too angry to accept what my mother had said. The weekend was spoilt and the only thing left was for me to drown my sorrows. This I managed quite well, not at Lewisham, but mostly in the Plough and Harrow.

Monday morning arrived, and I was on my way back to the Island. Feeling as I still did, there was no way that I was going to seek out Doreen and ask for an explanation. At the same time I was not going to tell anyone what had happened; I could imagine the derisive laughter if I did, and I certainly could not put up with that.

Everybody seemed to be fresh, and anxious to resume the course. Now that we were into the second half nothing appeared difficult; the end was in sight, which was encouraging for us. As hard as I tried, it was not possible to forget that weekend, but stubborn to the end, I was determined not to make any enquiries, and made no attempt to go ashore at all.

Then it happened. I cannot be certain why I was walking along a particular part of the Island, or even why this Wren happened to be there at the same time. Except for Doreen and Rene, I could not tell one Wren from another, and had not taken any notice of what any of Doreen's friends looked like, but they evidently had given me the once-over; possibly, in Doreen's interests, they had even vetted me, to decide if I was suitable. I wonder what made them miss certain points?

As I was about to pass the girl, she asked me to stop for a moment to talk. She knew all about that weekend, they all had talked about me and how they thought I had taken it, but they could not understand why I had not been in touch with Doreen since; knowing all about Doreen's side of it, quite understandably it was me that was at fault in their eyes. In future I will always accept with the best of good grace that things are never as simple as they seem, or that there are always two sides to every story, and

Doreen's side, when I knew about it, was one that seemed almost unbelievable.

When we arranged our date, I knew that she would be on duty aboard her skimming dish right until the last moment before going ashore to catch the train to London, and she was. The last run she had made was to take a signal out to a ship at anchor. The water even inside the harbour was a little rough and possibly because of this, Doreen fell overboard into the water, and could easily have drowned if her friend had not been there to help. Quickly they took her back to their quarters, where they thought that after a hot bath and something to eat she would go to bed, which of course she should have. But no, Doreen was made of sterner stuff. She had a date to keep; even though in her heart she knew that her train journey would be a waste of time and that I could not possibly have been waiting still, she still caught the first available train to Waterloo.

The other Wrens at the quarters were furious with her. I expect they told her that 'no man is worth all that trouble', and I would agree with them, but would also remind them that it cuts both ways. Not always, but sometimes, and in this particular instance I agree that I probably was not worth it.

Doreen arrived at our meeting place three hours late. Little did she know but I would not have left very long before her arrival; but at times like this, to miss someone by only minutes is no advantage over missing someone by hours.

Of course when I was being told all this, I felt as guilty as hell, and more than a little ashamed of myself. My instincts about Doreen had been that she was one in a million, and now it was being brought home to me how right I had been. She certainly deserved someone better than me. Now I had to make it up to her somehow.

The Wren could see how embarrassed I was, and after hearing my story she was able to understand how awkward a situation it really had been. She said that she would explain to Doreen, and was there a message that she could give from me? This was an opportunity I was very grateful for, and after establishing which evening she would next be free, I asked for Doreen to meet me again, and I am pleased to say that she did.

Sheepishly and feeling embarrassed I arrived at our usual meeting place. I was not even sure of what I was going to say to her, but I need not have worried. After a few minutes Doreen appeared, we exchanged greetings, and quickly the situation resolved itself, and we were back to normal.

The instructors' course was nearly over, the next week we had examinations, so most of our group were swotting like mad. Even I made an attempt to study during the evenings I spent on board and the temptation to spend every possible minute with Doreen was resisted. She understood, and it was to our advantage as we appreciated each other better when we did meet.

Examination time arrived. The silence of the classrooms was dreadful, it almost made you frightened to draw breath in case it upset anyone. Nobody attempted to joke, and the possibility of failing or passing was not part of the conversation, that was definitely taboo.

This was the hardest part, not the examinations themselves, but the atmosphere surrounding us. No prisoner waiting to hear the judge pass sentence could feel any worse. In fact our situation was worse in a way, yet we would go through even worse afterwards, when waiting for the results. Despite the confidence I had shown when drilling on the parade ground, when my turn came to take charge of the group, I had a few butterflies in my stomach. It should have been nothing to worry about really, I was more than capable of carrying out this particular part well. Obviously I did, and I believe I achieved quite high marks.

It was now all over, we would learn our results and fate on the following Monday. I was duty watch over the weekend, so it meant that not only could I not go ashore at all, but I could not see Doreen either. This I regarded as the worst part but, as always, she understood and grumbled far less than I did about it.

Monday morning, we were all assembled in a classroom, every man showing signs of nervousness. Some were putting on an air of bravado, and denied that they were worried, but it showed, even with the oldest and most experienced. No matter how hard one tries, a little twitch of facial muscles, finger movements, shifting of feet, and many more little symptoms give it all away.

The Training Commander entered with his retinue, a list was handed to him, and he began to state the results. We had all passed, he condescended to bestow a little praise, but was careful not to overdo it. We were not going to be allowed to leave the island with 'big heads', no matter how pleased we were. We had completed the course and were now qualified as 'QR1's (SV)'. The letters stood for 'Small Vessels'; this was so that we could not be confused with those who completed the longer course, which covered the larger and more powerful guns on board the larger ships.

At first I could not understand why the letters (SV) were chosen. Why not (CF) as for Coastal Forces? Nobody could or would offer an explanation, but later that year I was to find out for myself: at times we would be expected to instruct other sections of the Navy, i.e. men who manned the Commandos' landing craft, men who manned the guns aboard merchant ships, and I also had the unenviable task on one occasion to have to instruct trawler men. Now the letters made sense, but why on earth could this not be explained to us? Their Lordships certainly work in weird and wonderful ways, well, weird anyway.

Our results were then duly posted on the notice-board for all to see. Our next place to visit was the clothing store, where we would be able to purchase our new badges. This done, we hurriedly sewed them on to our uniforms. When I had completed my sewing, I felt as proud as the proverbial peacock, as I expect the others did.

As I sat upon the edge of my bed, wondering what to do next, a voice came over the loud-speakers, stating my name and that I was to report to the Training Commander's office without delay. The others in my group, who were present then, instantly 'took the mickey'; they insisted that my passing had been a mistake and it had just been found out, and many other discouraging comments, but I had to comply with the order anyway, so off I went quickly, to the Training Office.

With some trepidation I entered the office, and waited to be told to enter the inner sanctum. When I did, I was surprised to find only one officer present, the Lieutenant who had been in charge of the division that the four of us who were not petty officers had been in. The Navy described him as our Divisional Officer. In a way I was pleased that it was not the Training Commander, but I was still puzzled as to why I had been sent for. His first words were to congratulate me upon passing the course. Then he lectured me for a while about not letting the school down in the future; of course I said that I would not, and meant it too. Then the subject of my age was mentioned, and the lack of a good conduct badge. At first, he said, it was thought the absence of one meant that I had had one taken away, because of what had happened when leaving 611. Then, when reading my documents, it was realised how young I was, and now that I had passed out as an instructor I might well be the youngest gunnery instructor in the Navy, ever. This was not a cause for concern, but the absence of the GC badge was; it could provoke senior ratings, and this must not be allowed to happen. It was suggested that I wear one along with the other badges, it would only be necessary to wear it unofficially for a few months; there would naturally be no pay attached to it until I officially came of age. That was all it was,

I was not in any trouble for once, in fact it was quite the opposite, and I felt very pleased about it all.

The next day a notice appeared outside the Training Office, informing everyone in our group that we were to muster outside the Drafting Office the next morning at 0800 hrs, when we would leave the Island and be transported to Weymouth, where we would undergo the final month of our training. We had known this would happen; although we had qualified as QR1's (SV) at Whale Island, and that qualification could not easily be taken away from us, we had to complete this last month of training before we would be allowed to fulful our duties elsewhere.

That evening I went along to Doreen's quarters and asked to see her. We had not arranged to meet that evening, but because of the impending draft, this meeting was vital to me. We did a great deal of talking that evening; we had both known this was going to happen so, although sad, it had been inevitable. I imagined that it would not be long before I could obtain leave of some sort, we would correspond as frequently as we could, and if I could give her enough warning about leave, then she would come to London again. This time there would not be any upsets, Doreen was determined about this, and I had no doubts about her meaning every word. Now all that had been said, we had something to look forward to while we were apart.

A Naval bus was waiting next morning to take us to the train, and in no time we were on our way to HMS *Bee* at Weymouth.

It was another of those long, awkward, boring journeys, mile after mile of flat uninteresting countryside. In reality this was not true, it is beautiful country all the way, but we did not appreciate it because our minds were full of other things, which for me included Doreen and a possible leave.

We arrived at Weymouth, and were immediately billeted inside the territory that had been commandeered by the Navy for the use of the Gunnery School. It had nothing attractive about it at

all. I did not fancy living in this place, and talking about it to one
of the petty officers from our group, he suggested that I obtained
permission to live ashore in private accommodation. If granted
then the Navy would pay for it, food as well, although we would
have to have our mid-day meals in the base, which also meant
that we could draw our daily rum ration. The necessary request
was made to the Gunnery Officer, and granted without any questions or problems. I went ashore that evening, along to the Globe
Hotel, and asked Mrs Dawkins if they would allow me to stay
there. Luckily for me they agreed, and I moved in with my kit
the next day.

No time was wasted once we had completed the usual joining
routine, it was down to work with a vengeance. There was one
noticeable difference between this establishment and Whale Island:
there was no awesome reputation to fear, and the attitude of the
officers was also different. They were on the whole friendlier
towards us; this made us feel more comfortable, and we could look
forward to an enjoyable future while we were there. There were
lessons for us to learn, but we also took charge of classes; these
were made up from the Coastal Forces craft moored alongside the
pier.

There was one particular lesson I would never forget. We were
taught to shoot with a revolver, in what they called the 'Shanghai
method'. When firing the revolver, the person concerned must
stand in such a way that only his side was toward whoever he was
going to fire at; the idea was to present your opponent with as
small a target as possible, and this made sense to me. I see on films
today, scenes of men with weapons, all standing facing their
opponents squarely, presenting a very full target to be aimed at,
and I am sure it is wrong. We had to draw our revolvers very
quickly and fire immediately at the target. Although the ability to
hit the target was the most vital part, complete accuracy was not
important; it was considered that once you opened fire at someone,

the fear of being hit would be strong enough to make his aim uncertain. These lessons were taught upon the flat roof of the pier pavilion itself.

We also went to sea on target practice, aboard whatever boats were in harbour. On one occasion I was detailed to go aboard the *Grey Shark*. In command at the time was the legendary Peter Scott, Lieutenant Commander RNVR, who was the Senior Officer in command of the 1st Flotilla of steam gunboats, SGBs as they were usually known. The *Grey Shark*, SGB 6, was normally captained by another officer, and Peter Scott had his own boat, the *Grey Goose*, which at the time was undergoing a refit somewhere, so Peter Scott was using this boat as his own temporarily.

These SGBs were built of steel, as opposed to the all-wood construction of other Coastal Forces craft and they carried more powerful armament than their nearest rivals, the 'D' Class motor gunboats. They were also 150 feet in length and resembled miniature destroyers. My own impression was that they were not able to manoeuvre as well as the 'D's'; they were supposed to be faster, but I have my doubts regarding this. Their firepower however was devastating for their size, though this advantage was lost if other craft were able to out-manoeuvre them.

Only nine were ever built, two of which were destroyed by an enemy air attack upon the yards where they were being built, so they never even saw the sea. I thought this was sad. When these boats were first built and commissioned, they were known only as numbers, i.e. SGB 6, SGB 9 etc., but after considerable pleading to Admiralty by Peter Scott, it was decided that they could bear names. Because of Peter Scott's well-known interest in wild-life, they were given the following names: his own boat was named *Grey Goose* and the others were *Grey Shark*, *Grey Fox*, *Grey Wolf*, *Grey Seal* and *Grey Owl*; only two were named after bird-life. It is not known what happened to the seventh SGB; mysteriously it seemed to disappear.

One weekend leave was granted during that month of training, and I went home. Unfortunately it was not possible for Doreen to get leave at that weekend, so it was going to take longer for us to be together again. It was possible then to tell my mother exactly what had happened when Doreen failed to arrive at Waterloo; in return I received a mild rebuke from her for my doubts, and I promised not to act that way again where Doreen was concerned. The weekend leave, although a long one, passed all too quickly, and I was soon back at Weymouth resuming duties.

Towards the end of the month, Weymouth Town Council decided to hold a 'Spitfire Week'. This was a fund-raising event, when it was hoped to squeeze enough money out of everybody in and around the town to pay for a Spitfire to be built. It would end with a Grand Parade of all the services, including the Home Guard, Fire Brigade, the Police, Air-raid Wardens, and many other people involved in providing the week's entertainment. The Royal Navy was to lead the parade, as was our right as the Senior Service.

On the last afternoon of the week, the parade proudly mustered at the east end of the town, on the front, close to the clock tower, and to the music supplied by a band we marched off towards the Civic Buildings, where the Mayor and other dignitaries were due to take the salute.

One of our Gunnery officers marched in front of our platoon, which was made up entirely of base staff and all the instructors, and I was in the front row, right-hand marker, marching proudly along. Unfortunately the route had been changed unbeknown to us, so we were marching along the original route quite happily, until it was realised that we, the Royal Navy, were completely on our own; the rest of the parade had turned off at the new place stated, and were proceeding quite well without us. The officer in command of us never turned a hair; we marched on, along the original route given, then unexpectedly we reached a road junction, and to our amazement, the rest of the parade joined us at the correct moment, behind us, and we all reached the saluting base as though nothing had happened. The Mayor took the salute and everyone was happy. It was possible that most of the watching crowds lining the route never knew of our *faux-pas*; no doubt the Mayor and his dignitaries were eventually told, but when they were waiting for the parade to reach them, they knew nothing about it at all.

Once Spitfire Week was over, and I believe it had been a successful week's effort, we all settled down once more to the daily routine. Nobody ever referred to what had happened when I made a fool of myself at Newhaven. I am certain that the Gunnery Officers at the school would have been told about it, but if so, then they were decent enough to give me another chance to prove to everyone that what happened was a one-off.

It seemed that almost every day more boats would arrive for their guns' crews to receive extra training. The length of time they stayed depended upon what guns they had on board, and how many. Most of the gunnery ratings were quite happy to endure this extra training, but there were always the 'stroppy' ones that knew it all, or at least thought they did.

The last week of the month's training for us at Weymouth arrived. We had not been told what would happen when it was completed; of course there was plenty of speculation and we were certain that we all would not remain part of the Gunnery School here. At this particular time I do not think that any of our twelve instructors wanted to; some were hoping to be based nearer to their homes, while others fantasised about going to romantic places, South Africa maybe, even the USA. It was all pure guess-work until the end of that week, and it was almost here.

Several of our group put in applications for leave to be granted. Just as I was thinking about doing the same, we were told that six of us would be going on draft the next day to HMS *Hornet*, at

Gosport, and we should apply for leave when we arrived there, it could not be granted from Weymouth.

The next day five petty officers and myself were on our way, bound for the *Hornet*; the other six were taken on as staff instructors at HMS *Bee*, and I believe they remained there until the whole Gunnery School was shifted to another part of the UK, namely Holyhead.

When the six of us arrived at Gosport, we were settled in messes, and four of us had to report first thing next morning to the drafting office. Now, for the very first time I was to see this notorious rating who was reputed to completely control our destinies. I knew that there would not be any wisdom in falling foul of this fellow, so I kept my mouth shut in case. Two of the other three were adamant that they were not going to be 'shunted around by this upstart', but when we all reported to the office I do not recall any raised objections, unless it happened without my knowledge.

The man everybody dreaded seemed to be working conscientiously at the rear of the drafting office. I do not think that he even looked up from his desk when we entered the office. To our surprise, we were informed that we were going on leave, ten days, as from noon that day, and we were to report back to the drafting office immediately we returned from leave. That was all. The other three were asking all kinds of questions as to what was going to happen to them when they returned from leave, all to no avail; we were not going to be told anything, which, after all, was to be expected. Somehow I knew it was all a waste of their time, and to be truthful I could not have cared less. Whatever was going to happen, it would be up to me to take care of myself. I realised none of these three would give a damn what happened to me, so my main interest now was to go on leave, contact Doreen, and enjoy the leave as much as possible.

There were still two hours or so before rum issue and our

dinner, so I sat down and wrote to Doreen, informing her about the leave, asking if she would come to London. Could she also obtain a long leave pass, and state clearly if and when she would arrive at Waterloo. This time I did not refer to the clock, and wherever I stood waiting was of no consequence; the important thing was that we were going to be together. As I would soon be London bound myself, any reply from her would have to be addressed home. I think this was the first time I had given Doreen my home address, it had not been necessary before. I had never asked her for her home address; although I knew that it was then at Acton, I had never pressed her for more details.

The letter was posted at the mail office in the barracks. I had my dinner, collected what gear I would be taking home with me, and was lucky enough to be allowed to board a lorry bound for the main Portsmouth railway station. Then on to the waiting London train, and I was away on my first ten days leave for a long time.

Everything was straightforward, no problems in transit at all. I changed trains at Waterloo, and very soon I had arrived at Catford Bridge railway station. It was not long before a bus arrived, which took me the last mile home.

The look upon my mother's face when she opened the door to me was wonderful. I had not been able to warn her about coming on leave, it had all happened so quickly. In those days very few people possessed telephones, so a telephone call had also been impossible. She had a premonition about the reason behind the sudden leave, but kept it to herself, in case it would worry me. That it worried her apparently did not matter so far as she was concerned.

There was a very popular saying that, in Victorian times, and later, during the twenties, would be framed and hung above beds or fireplaces. Always prominently displayed, simple and to the point, the words were 'Home is where the Heart is'; it was something I sincerely believed to be true.

My home at Sandhurst Road, Catford, approximately four hundred yards from where the children had been killed while at school, was where I had lived for the twenty-odd years of age I was at the time. It looked nothing special: a typical working-class terraced house, in a typically working-class area, no frills, nothing fancy, nothing to boast about, only the bare rudiments of comfort, but it was home to me, and I would keep returning to it for many years to come. My mother, having been widowed for nearly nineteen years, had been denied a state pension of any kind during her widowhood, but had achieved a near miracle in being able to supplement the pittance she received from what was then known as the 'Relief'. Against odds she had managed to rent the house and support me when a child. The 'Relief' was then a very poor apology for what is now known as 'Social Security', and bears little resemblance to it at all. In those days even a radio was a forbidden luxury to have while 'on the Relief'. My mother supplemented her frugal means by knitting, sewing and crocheting for friends. When war broke out and women were needed to return to work, she was able to resume her original trade as a bookbinder, earning, for the first time in many years, a complete wage. This of course dispensed with the assistance from the 'Relief', and the petty restrictions they imposed upon people. At least the 'Relief' meant that we did not starve, as we might have done without it.

Despite everything, this was still my home, and where I hoped to bring Doreen if she was able to come to London on leave.

That first evening at home was spent quietly, the only enter-tainment being the radio, but in those days it was luxury, and a joy to everyone. At first I was reluctant to mention that Doreen might possibly be visiting us. I was more than a little superstitious about anything like that, but when someone is watching you very carefully, anticipating news of some kind, I had to tell her what was in the offing. It did not take long for her to drag the full story out of me, and it was also obvious where her sympathies lay. It took me quite a while to convince her that I really had waited a very long time at Waterloo station that night, and although embarrassed it would have been impossible to have waited indefinitely. Why did I get the feeling that the guilt was mine? I ought to have been able to convince my own mother, especially when I was not really at fault.

The afternoon post brought the letter I had been waiting for. My letter must have been delivered to her quarters on the same day of posting, and Doreen's letter in reply written that same evening. The contents of her letter, although very welcome, did not contain news that she was coming to Catford on long leave, even just a couple of days would have been nice, no, she would only be able to manage to stay overnight. She expressed disappointment, but there was nothing she could do about it, so we would have to make the most of what we had. The letter then contained information as to where we would meet, and when. At least I had something now to look forward to. I did not think it fair and in a way resented it, but I had seen enough of life now to know that it is not always fair.

Naturally the first thing to be done was to tell my mother. She was pleased, and made no attempt to hide it. I had to promise that I would bring Doreen straight home, and not stop at every pub on the way; she need not have worried as there was no chance of that at all.

The next morning I set off in good time and caught the train to Waterloo, where I waited anxiously for the Portsmouth train to arrive. There was no question of waiting under the clock, and no need. I was there at the barrier as the train drew into the station. As always, it was packed with service men and women, very few Wrens though, and soon I was able to see her, having been seated towards the rear of the train. It is strange how one particular thing remains in one's mind for years after. I can remember her walk as she came towards me. It was almost leisurely and unhurried; her step was confident, as though she was very sure of herself as in many ways she was, yet underneath she was still a very shy and reserved person.

We greeted each other as might be expected, not over demonstrative, but just enough to convince each other. We saw no reason to hurry, but in no time at all we were seated on the train taking us to Catford.

Our arrival at home did not appear to have been noticed by the neighbours, I was not sure whether I was disappointed or not. It was not that I needed or wanted the seal of approval from anyone, but it does something for your ego when someone stops to compliment you about who you were seen with. My mother made up for it, however; she was obviously quite taken with Doreen, as I was to discover a day or so later.

The fact that Doreen could only stay for one night was, to say the least, disconcerting. There was not much that I could think of for us to do except an after dinner bus ride into the clean green countryside of Kent, so that was what we did.

We caught a bus that showed its destination as being Keston, a delightful little place just outside Bromley. When we arrived at Bromley Common we got off the bus, chose a quiet turning with the delightful name of 'Rookery Lane', and walked along it until we found a nice peaceful spot where we could be alone. We just sat and talked, it was enough just being together, nothing else was needed. After a while we walked back towards the Common, bought ourselves a drink in the Crown, and then made for home.

The next morning came too soon. We took no chances regarding Doreen's train. Doreen was concerned about missing it, and of course there was always the possibility of air-raids delaying her journey back to Portsmouth. The Navy did not accept excuses for being late back to ship, not even air-raids.

Her train was standing at the platform. Although it was already crowded we had no difficulty in finding Doreen a seat. We said our goodbyes, looking forward to when we would be together again. Little did we know what would be waiting for me upon my return to Gosport.

Once Doreen's train was out of sight, I made my way to the railway buffet for a quick drink before making my way home. I needed cheering up, as spending the one day only with Doreen had made me appreciate her more. It really was true that she was different to any other girl I had known. There was a sincerity about her that was unmistakably hers only. The uniform made her 'one of a crowd', but it stopped there, and only if she approved did that 'something extra' become obvious.

A little saddened, and perhaps also a little hurt, I made my way back to Catford, and home in time for dinner. After enquiring if Doreen had caught the train in time, and asking what time I thought she would arrive at Portsmouth, my mother asked no more questions. She was prepared for me to give any explanations in my own good time, which I did later that evening.

It was after I had been out. I had a quick drink, all on my own, at the Plough and Harrow. The usual regulars were there, but I was not feeling very sociable and preferred my own company. After a while, I had had enough of being on my own, and made my way home, prepared to have an early night. Despite my mother's presence, the house seemed empty. It was really inexplicable, Doreen had only been there for what amounted to a few hours, yet her absence was felt. Perhaps since my spiritual experiences I was able to pick up vibrations – that is the expression used, I believe – but maybe it was just my imagination? I really thought at the time that Doreen and I had a future together, and why not? Everything appeared favourable. I knew that my mother had hopes in that direction now, and I need not ask if she approved. It was written all over her face, and in her voice when we discussed it all later. Sadly, yet perhaps for the best, it was not to be, but the final decision was a long way off at that time, and neither of us were aware of the way things would finally end.

There were nine or ten of us living in Sandhurst Road at that time who were in the Navy, yet mostly when I was on leave none of the others were. If Fate had a hand in things she certainly never arranged our leaves to coincide. At the same time, there were at least double that figure of other servicemen who lived on the road, men that I had known all my life, yet the one man whom I did make a friend of during that leave was a newcomer to the road, a young soldier. His name was Len Hutchins and he lived in the house on the corner of the road.

We became friends purely by chance. He was talking to his next-door neighbour, and as I was about to pass them I heard a voice say, 'Why don't you ask Jack?' I stopped to say hello and was then engaged in the conversation. I am unable to remember now what was asked, but during the remainder of that leave Len and I were inseparable companions. As happened to so many servicemen and women, it was years before we were to see each other again. He came through the war safely, came out of the Army, then decided to make a new life for himself. He enlisted in the Royal Canadian Mounted Police and found a new life for himself in Canada, where I believe he still is today.

During that leave there were plenty of relatives to visit, my sister being the most important, especially as it meant her home cooked cakes would be available. They were so delicious I was always unable to resist them. There was also my first niece to make a fuss of. The state of the war at that time was still uncertain; age limits for men had been raised so my sister's husband, Alf, had now been called up and was now in the Army, making my visits more necessary.

There had been more news from my brother. Although conditions in any prison camp were never good, Alan never complained. He had met one of our cousins who had been taken prisoner sometime before Alan; strangely, they had never met before then, but when it was discovered they were related, I believe they were allowed to remain together during their confinement. Alan had always been lucky at gambling; it was never a mania with him, he was not addicted, but simply enjoyed games of cards where he could pit his wits against others, especially if money was at stake. Invariably he would win, and when after the war ended, he came home, I think it safe to say that he never arrived home broke. Good luck to him, he deserved more, as all prisoners of war did.

Every time I came home on leave, and walked past that alley on my way home, despite the knowledge that the certain someone was now married, and most probably living away from Catford, I still glanced along that alley in the hope of seeing her. Fate again made sure that it would never happen, and I never did. It was probably thirty years later that I discovered that the chances of seeing her along that alley were practically non-existent, as her family were no longer living in that area, and had actually been bombed out of their home. However, I did not know this at that time, and I carried on looking, and hoping to see her for many years to come. Fate can so often be unkind.

Suddenly, after enjoying seven days of my leave, a telegram arrived from Admiralty, curtailing it. I was instructed to report back to HMS *Hornet* immediately; there was no choice, because of my promotion I could not take any chances, I had to go back on time. I was suspicious, to say the least, and throughout my journey back to Gosport my imagination was working overtime, not making sense, and becoming more and more confusing as the miles rolled by.

Returning to the *Hornet* was never an attractive prospect; even though there were literally hundreds of men in Coastal Forces, there was not one here that I knew, or who apparently knew me. To me this seemed ridiculous: boats' crews were constantly changing, yet there was not a soul here that I knew. But a few months later, a thousand miles away, I would meet many old shipmates, I would meet old shipmates of my brother, I would meet my cousin Danny again, and even see one of my next-door neighbours under punishment at a small Army unit close to the Algerian *Kasbah*. Yet here, at Gosport, there was nobody friendly at all.

None of that really mattered. The following morning, on reporting to the Drafting Office, I learnt the reason for my recall from leave. It was almost, as they say in the Navy, 'a pierhead jump', because the very next day I was being drafted abroad, and they would not say a word.

The remainder of that day was spent in medical check-ups, inoculations, overseas kit, and writing letters home to my mother and to Doreen. An attempt was made to get ashore so that I could say farewell in person, but there was no chance at all, they probably thought that to give leave of any description to me, about to be sent on foreign draft, would be inviting me to desert. In many instances they were most likely right, so I really could not blame them, and it was something I had to put up with.

Immediately my letters were written they were taken to the mail office. The one to my mother was posted right away, but before I could post the one to Doreen I recognised one of the Wrens who operated one of the skimming dishes with her, so I was able to ask her to deliver my letter personally, with a full explanation along with it.

The next morning at 0800 hrs I reported, along with my kit, outside the Drafting Office, where already a crowd had gathered, all of us going on draft together. There were also the three Petty Officers who had passed out as instructors along with me; this time they chose to acknowledge me and be friendly, which I was grateful for.

After a roll call had been made, everybody present and correct, we were ushered aboard a waiting coach and taken to the Portsmouth railway station, and aboard the waiting train. The route taken was via Reading, Crewe and eventually to Liverpool; a lorry took us then to what was Liverpool's most famous dock, the Gladstone Dock. Berthed here was HMS *Dido*, one of our most up-to-date cruisers of the day. We were taken aboard. With the exception of petty officers, there were thirty ratings in our party and we shared a large mess-deck with a party of the same number, all submariners, all of us on passage abroad.

It was rumoured that we were bound for the Mediterranean, it is amazing how information gets leaked. So far as I was concerned it was still uncertain, but I was impatient to know. I am sure that the petty officers knew, but they were given sealed orders and were forbidden to open them until a certain point in our voyage was reached.

The *Dido* sailed from Liverpool the following morning. What did surprise me was that leave was granted to us, until midnight only. I did go ashore, more out of curiosity than anything else; I had only ever heard about Liverpool, and I wanted to see a little of it before I left England for God only knew where. It was a wet night, steadily raining, and around the docks at night, with no lighting of course because of blackout restrictions, everything looked as miserable as can be. It did not take me long to find a pub, but like everything outside it, it was a miserable and depressing place; two drinks and I was pleased to get back aboard the *Dido*.

There was one other little thing. I could not understand the Scouse dialect when I was in that pub; it was like listening to a foreign language, and one that I did not recognise. My old shipmate Joe Swift never spoke like the fellows I met in that place.

The *Dido* sailed early next morning before dawn and most of

*As a gunnery instructor in Algiers, 1943, at the edge of the Kasbah.*

the ratings making up the two parties lined the guard-rails to watch the sight of Liverpool's outline fading in the distance. It was true that I felt a lump form in my throat. I had never left dear old England before, and what was worse, I did not know when I would return, if ever.

The *Dido* sailed out into the Atlantic Ocean, westwards in the direction of America. Three days out the ship altered course and headed for the Bay of Biscay. We were given various little pieces of information, but this last part caused some consternation among many who had not been overseas before. After all, it was common knowledge how men suffered on board ships sailing through the Bay, especially if the weather happened to be bad. In our case, although to experienced sailors the weather at that time was not too bad, it was far from good, and the rough seas were already causing havoc with the crew of the *Dido*, many of whom were youngsters only recently out of training.

As we approached the Bay, the *Dido*'s officers evidently anticipated problems, with their new crew and seasickness, and the possiblity of running into enemy action. Submarines were known to be in the vicinity, and air attacks were quite common. Because of these facts, we were all, submariners and Coastal Forces ratings, put on standby, as there were doubts that their guns could not be manned in an emegency.

An enemy aircraft did approach the *Dido*, but thought better of it and departed quickly. Nothing else occurred of any consequence, and we came through the Bay safely, except for the poor lads that were seasick. It was not known whether any of the submariners suffered, but I do not think any of the Coastal Forces ratings on passage suffered at all.

We arrived at Gibraltar, but nobody was allowed ashore. In fact the *Dido* only stayed a few hours in Gibraltar, then we were on our way again, sailing into the Mediterranean Sea.

The three petty officers must have had instructions to open their orders about then, because a few hours later I was told where I would be going. The orders when opened detailed one instructor to each of four places, all North African ports: Oran, Bone, Mers-el-Kebir and Algiers. They knew that Algiers would be full of 'top brass' so it could be uncomfortable for whoever was based there; in the port of Algiers there would be many ships, large and small, the American Fleet used the port, and the Free French, so it was expected that an instructor based there would be well occupied. Living accommodation would be in a barracks, HMS *Hannibal*, so our three petty officers did not fancy Algiers for one of themselves. The obvious answer was, of course, me, so I was detailed to be the base AVGI for Coastal Forces in Algiers. The three then came to amicable arrangements about their own destinations, and after landing at Algiers I never saw or heard from any of them again.

By a twist of fate, Algiers turned out to be the best of the four bases. The other three closed down after a few months, but I never heard where the instructors finished up. Altogether I was to spend twelve very happy months at Algiers, and became very attached to the place, making many friends, with many Royal Navy men, some of the French people living there, a few Arabs, and even some Americans.

Correspondence was exchanged regularly with Doreen, and we both looked forward to the future, when we could be together again, but it was early days, a great deal was going to happen to me, but that could only be told in another story, perhaps!

# In Appreciation

THE fact that I was in Coastal Forces partly by accident, makes me no less proud. Those two letters after the 'non-substantive rating' of AA3 (LC) literally saved me from being sent to 'big ships'. I quite honestly do not know how I would have existed aboard those ships, possibly well, but I would have been only a number, not a person as we were aboard Coastal Forces craft.

We were likened to the Submarine service, in so much as we were not subjected to *bona-fide* Royal Navy discipline, and our dependence upon each other was vital at all times for the safety of our shipmates and the continuing existence of the boat we served upon. Although dependence upon each other existed aboard all ships, the smaller the vessel so the confidence in each man was of greater importance.

Unlike the larger ships who rarely came face to face with the enemy, and unlike submarines, when our boats attacked they immediately became targets themselves, with no place to hide, but if honest, we all admitted that we would rather be on top of the sea while fighting, than below it.

Unlimited praise must be professed for the engine-room crews and telegraphists in particular, not forgetting radar operators. Like submariners they could not see what was going on during an engagement and their lives were dependent upon the men on the upper deck, officers and seamen alike, and they were always subjected to extreme discomfort.

All the successes of Coastal Forces, even the doubtful pleasure of living aboard the boats, could only be achieved by the skill and hard work of the men and women who designed or built our boats. How well they did their job is evident by the number of boats that are still intact and even afloat today, over fifty years on. So to them I say, 'Thank you, you did a grand job.'

> They responded to the call again
> No matter where or when
> Their Country needed them to fight
> In wooden ships with iron men.

JWD